GROUPS IN SCHOOLS

PREPARING, LEADING, AND RESPONDING

Anne M. Geroski
University of Vermont

Kurt L. Kraus
Shippensburg University

PEARSON

Boston   Columbus   Indianapolis   New York   San Francisco   Upper Saddle River
Amsterdam   Cape Town   Dubai   London   Madrid   Milan   Munich   Paris   Montreal   Toronto
Delhi   Mexico City   São Paulo   Sydney   Hong Kong   Seoul   Singapore   Taipei   Tokyo

Vice President and Editor-in-Chief: Jeffery W. Johnston
Acquisitions Editor: Meredith D. Fossel
Editorial Assistant: Nancy Holstein
Vice President, Director of Marketing and Sales Strategies: Emily Williams Knight
Vice President, Director of Marketing : Quinn Perkson
Project Manager: Susan Hannahs
Production Editor: Mary Irvin
Senior Managing Editor: Pamela D. Bennett
Cover Designer: Bruce Kenselaar
Cover Art: SuperStock
Full-Service Project Management: Mohinder Singh, Aptara®, Inc.
Composition: Aptara®, Inc.
Text and Cover Printer/Binder: Bind-Rite Graphics, Inc.
Text Font: Palatino

Credits and acknowledgments borrowed from other sources and reproduced, with permission, in this textbook appear on appropriate page within text.

Every effort has been made to provide accurate and current Internet information in this book. However, the Internet and information posted on it are constantly changing, so it is inevitable that some of the Internet addresses listed in this textbook will change.

Library of Congress Cataloging-in-Publication Data
Geroski, Anne M.
  Groups in schools : preparing, leading, and responding / Anne M. Geroski, Kurt L. Kraus.
    p. cm.
  Includes bibliographical references and index.
  ISBN-13: 978-0-13-239022-4 (alk. paper)
  ISBN-10: 0-13-239022-1 (alk. paper)
1.   Educational counseling. 2.   Group guidance in education.   I. Kraus, Kurt L. II. Title.
LB1027.5.G4438 2010
371.4'047—dc22

                                                                        2009021794

10 9 8 7 6 5 4 3 2 1
ISBN 10:   0-13-239022-1
ISBN 13: 978-0-13-239022-4

This book is dedicated to those who have inspired our learning curve in group work, and this list is long!

First, we want to acknowledge our deepest appreciations for two counselor educators who mentored us in group work: Dr. Diana Hulse-Killacky and Dr. Peg Carroll. These talented counselor educators and group leaders have left indelible marks in our knowledge and passion for group work and we, in turn, hope to pass on their legacies to our students and practitioners in the field through this book. We also want to thank the students at Carroll Elementary School in Bernalillo, New Mexico and the students from kindergarten–12th grade in Dover-Foxcroft, Maine with whom we worked—thanks to all of you for helping to inspire our passion for groups and for making us work hard and become better group leaders. Thanks, too, to our current students at the University of Vermont and Shippensburg University of Pennsylvania, and those with whom they work in their internship placements—we learn as you learn.

Finally, we dedicate this book to our spouses and our children—our collective family group—who have witnessed the development of this book through long conversations during family gatherings over the years and who have supported us in the writing process: Sally Kraus and Kevin Rodgers, and Jocelyn, Emily, Monica, Ian, Curtis, and Griffin.

PREFACE

For many years, we have observed school counselors who have demonstrated amazing command of group facilitation and leadership skill, as well as those school counselors who have struggled with leading groups with youth in schools. The reasons for this breadth and scope across a continuum have been areas of research for us; but that is not the purpose of this book. Our reason for writing this textbook is to share with graduate students and practicing school counselors alike, clear, concise, well-exampled, directions for leading large and small groups—psychoeducational as well as counseling groups—in school settings. We have written this text with the ultimate goal of helping school counselors adapt, expand, and strengthen their personal and professional command of group leadership skills.

This text builds on students' and practitioners' generalist preparation to lead groups. There are numerous quality textbooks—many of which we reference throughout our text—that more than adequately hold potential to convey a strong theoretical foundation on groups in general. The same can be said for texts espousing the "processes" involved in a wide variety of group work. What we believe is sorely lacking in the existent textbook literature is a book that teaches how school counselors operationalize group work theory and practice with school-aged children and adolescents in schools. We realize that many counselor education programs often have only one course devoted to developing group skills—the content span of such a course is overwhelming! In graduate school, future school counselors often learn to lead groups alongside their community and mental health-counseling colleagues. They sometimes express concern that this training approach too frequently overlooks the specific needs of school counselors. This textbook, we believe, can not only bridge the chasm between practice settings, but also strengthen school counselors' knowledge and skills unique to working with children and adolescents in schools.

When we were in the early nurturing stages of the idea for this book, we debated what school counselors needed to become competent and confident group leaders. So we searched through our own experiences as school counselors leading groups in schools, our extensive training as group leaders, our earlier training as classroom teachers, and a multitude of texts and articles on the subject. We also reflected on the experiences of our graduate students as they have worked alongside school counselors running groups in their internship placements. In the end, we believe this book accomplishes our goal of providing relevant, practical, and user-friendly information for guiding the work of school counselors to conduct classroom and counseling groups in schools.

As you can see from our table of contents, this book doesn't claim to answer every question, fill every void, or address every challenge associated with groups in schools. What this book does is give readers numerous windows through which they can view the wide range of applicable rationales for group work, the preparation and skill sets required for confidence and success in leading groups, the selection or welcome of members for a wide scope of different types of groups, and the "nuts and bolts" of group structure and form—enough so that you will be able to build your own groups. We offer abundant examples aimed at taking away some of the unknowns we believe inhibit many school counselors from leading successful groups in their schools. We doubt any one book could "do it all" for the obvious reason that group work is simply too complex, varied, and demanding. We are confident, however, that this book will transport student and professional school counselors to a place of preparedness, enthusiasm, confidence, and skill. In this text, we strive to offer a gentle yet straightforward direction, while not leaving too much to chance. There is a perfectly good reason to model gentle directiveness through the learning process; we are convinced that future school counselors will realize a similar directiveness awaits them as they utilize group work in their world of school counseling.

There are several additional issues that seem important to mention here: Writing this book caused the two of us to recognize our own professional similarities and differences. In numerous ways—and on many occasions—we debated and usually compromised on how to use this text to instruct, and thereby to bring about the greatest chance for meaningful learning on the part of our readers. This wasn't always easy. During the review of an early draft of the manuscript, one of the reviewers suggested we find "one voice,"—claiming that we needed to pick one or the other "style and voice" and stick with it throughout. We would add that this reader seemed to prefer the more scholarly and more academic voice (we are to this day unsure whether it was Anne's or Kurt's voice!). This feedback helped us see that we were more partial to a somewhat colloquial and conversational tone that, perhaps, strays from the usual textbook style that most of us are accustomed to. We also have tried to meld our voices to avoid confusion. But two of us wrote this book and we are not one. We don't teach the same ways. We don't sound the same in the classroom. In fact, we don't lead groups identically either. We look as different as you would expect. Many times, when we were stuck on how to convey an important point or deliver an important concept—one of us would ask the other, "How would you say this in the classroom?" "How would you teach this?" The other would listen intently, and then say, "That's really good—I like that, I've never thought of saying it that way." We learned more by being open to each other's voices. So, with this in mind, we urge you, the reader, to find room for both of our styles in this book in the same way that we encourage you to take in the information provided in this text to develop your own style of working with youth in groups in schools.

By following our inclination to be conversational, we have attempted to simplify and reduce the professional jargon as much as possible, making room for clear understandings and practical information for carrying out the complex practice demands of leading classroom and counseling groups in schools. That is the intent of our writing style and the focus of this text. We expect that you will find the information in this book useful; we hope that our style of writing makes it accessible.

It was our good fortune that Melissa Hathaway, a practicing school counselor and a regular speaker in one of Anne's courses at the University of Vermont, introduced us to a powerful visual, nearly tactile, metaphor that brought to life for us the intersection of contemporary education and the honoring of cultural diversity in schools. This metaphor comes from Emily Style's chapter titled Curriculum as Windows & Mirrors, in Nelson and Wilson's (1988, pp. 149–56) edited book, *Seeding the Process of Multicultural Education*. We have woven Style's compelling concept of *window and mirrors* throughout this book. Why? We have been impassioned throughout our careers by the urgent imperative for school counselors to "become multiculturally aware" and to always ensure that cultural diversity is embraced, extolled, and wisely accommodated into the work of school counselors We cannot envision a realm where diversity is more vivid than in schools—where children arrive daily with the joys and weights of difference. Culture—be it race, faith, ethnicity, class, ability, sexual orientation, values, or other phenomena that reside under this one broad roof, be it celebrated or ignored—is inescapably present in schools in general, and, of course, in the groups that happen every day in those schools. *Windows and mirrors* is a beautiful and instructive refrain throughout our textbook urging continual awareness to diversity—moreover, it clearly explains "how to" position group members in such ways that opens them to the power, wonder, and complexity of living with others in a diverse world. We see this metaphor as a life-force coursing through *Groups in Schools: Preparing, Leading, and Responding.*

School counseling as a profession is rapidly evolving. Our observations, currently from the peripheral position of our universities, are subject to two distinct phenomena: Academics like us are often directing changes brought to light by emerging research, and we are also always responding to changes that are brought to bear by the profession— we are adapting and responding to pressures and currents in the real world of schools. Our posture in this text is one of straddling the illusory wall that separates both. Admittedly, we represent only a small geography of experience in our current settings— nevertheless this text reflects our experiences in a variety of settings, and it is responsive to the directives set forth by the *ASCA National Model* (ASCA, 2005) established by the American School Counseling Association over the past decade. When we were practicing school counselors, neither of us had a national model to help chart our professional course—we envy the new school counselor who has many more substantial models from which to choose. By conscientiously selecting the model as well as the method that fit most effectively with the needs within your unique context, we predict you have the very best chances of program success. Ultimately, it will be your sound application of best practices—preferably empirically supported practices—that will afford each and every student in your school the opportunity to maximize his or her potential for healthy growth and development in every aspect of life.

We believe that the preface of this text must also forecast what you as readers, students and counselors alike, will encounter as you explore and study our book. To that end, allow us to walk through the three parts, eight chapters, and the Appendices with you. Each of the four chapters in Part 1 addresses a critical component of group planning for small counseling and classroom group work in schools. In Chapter 1, *Getting Started*, we begin by offering the metaphor of windows and mirrors (Style, 1998), to frame this and subsequent discussions on the importance of addressing diversity issues in planning and managing groups in schools. Developmental and ethical issues and how to talk about the group to school personnel are also addressed in Chapter 1. In Chapter 2, *Developing and Writing Group Plans*, our focus is on how to think about and write group goals and objectives that will guide the group in the desired direction. In this discussion, we advocate for strategic intervention planning—planning interventions that match student needs with desired outcomes (Trusty & Brown, 2005). In Chapter 3, *Planning for Implementation*, our focus centers on planning the group process so it will be facilitative of the group's intended goals and objectives. In Chapter 4, *Designing Assessments*, assessment measures and plans for assessing intended learning outcomes are discussed. In Part 2, *Leading*, all of the chapters are about leading groups with intentionality. This term emphasizes the "purposefulness" with which we advocate all groups in schools be led. In Chapter 5, we begin with a discussion of leader philosophical positioning and then move on to discuss many specific group work issues that are related to school counselors in group leadership positions. In Chapter 6, we move on to discuss specific group management strategies. And, in Part 3, *Responding*, we offer varied response strategies for intervening when behaviors become problematic in the group. In Chapter 7, we begin by picking up the thread of our earlier discussion on leadership positioning and discipline philosophy with a brief exploration of what is meant by "a problem" in the group. Next, we offer a number of strategies that can be implemented in the group in response to problems in order to regain better individual and group functioning. We refer to these as *in-group interventions.* Chapter 8 continues with response strategies that require action between group sessions or that require intervention with a group member out of the presence of other group members. These we refer to as *out-of-group interventions.*

The book comes to an end with a brief epilogue, which we hope further encourages you, the readers, to enthusiastically begin or strengthen the groups you lead in schools. The Appendices, which are the last element of the book, are comprised of example classroom and counseling group plans, a table of group worker skills terminology and definitions, and, finally, standards of practice and ethics. The *Ethical Standards for School Counselors* (ASGW, 2004), Association of Specialists in Group Work (ASGW) *Best Practice Guidelines* (2007), and the Association of Specialists in Group Work (ASGW) *Diversity Standards* (2007) are in Appendices E and F for easy reference. In the appendices, as well as in the index, you will find resources to extend your understanding and development as a group leader.

Finally, we are very pleased that this textbook accomplishes what we intended for it to do. We concede that our book may well leave "some stones unturned" but those we leave to be turned by others. It is our heartfelt hope that students and practicing school counselors who read this textbook grow into confident leaders of groups in schools.

ACKNOWLEDGMENTS

Many people have helped us produce this book—too many, really, to name here. A special thanks to UVM Counseling Program Graduate Assistants, Justin Tauscher and Luke Lewis, who assisted with tracking case studies and references on this and earlier versions of this manuscript; and to school counselor, Melissa Hathaway, who introduced us to the Windows and Mirrors concept that originally came from author, Emily Style. Thanks, too, to UVM Counseling Program alumnae Kara Mercer, Nicole Lewis, Kristen Dickerson, and Lindsey Kearns, for lending their work for adaptation to the sample group plans in the appendices. Thanks also goes to Virginia B. Allen, Idaho State University; Fred Bemak, George Mason University; Laurie A. Carlson, Colorado State University; Laura G. Hensley, Louisiana State University; Bette Katsekas, University of Southern Maine; Jasmine E. Khan, Baylor University; H. George McMahan, Georgia State University; Glenda Reynolds, Auburn University, Montgomery; and Toni R. Tollerud, Northern Illinois University, who offered critical and helpful feedback on many drafts of this manuscript. A warm and special thank you goes to Kevin Davis of Merrill/Pearson for having confidence in us from the start and, especially to Meredith Fossel of Merrill/Pearson for her lovely manner, gentle support, professionalism, and assertive guidance from the start to the end of this project. Thanks, too, to Kelly Tavares, for her careful attention to detail in the copyediting process. And to all others who have been behind the scenes supporters of this project, we thank you very much.

Anne Geroski, Ed.D., is Associate Professor and Counseling Program Coordinator at the University of Vermont. Her professional work has included working as a school and mental health counselor in a variety of settings in the U.S. and overseas. She lives with her partner, Kevin, and their three children, Monica, Curtis, and Griffin, in Burlington, Vermont.

Kurt L. Kraus, Ed.D., NCC, ACS, LPC, is a Professor in the Department of Counseling and College Student Personnel at Shippensburg University of Pennsylvania. Kurt's professional career includes school counseling, mental health counseling, and counselor education. His interests include child and adolescent counseling, group work, and the implications of human development on counseling. At publication, Kurt is the Chair of the Board of Directors of the *National Board for Certified Counselors, Inc.* Kurt lives in Carlisle Pennsylvania with his wife Sally. Happily, Jocelyn and Luke, Emily, and Ian all live nearby.

BRIEF CONTENTS

CONTENTS

CHAPTER 1

Getting Started

THE IMPORTANCE OF PLANNING

Effective group work in schools is much more than simply providing students with a group, an activity, and an opportunity to talk. Students benefit as members of classroom and counseling groups when leaders are deliberate in planning and preparing these groups so that they are facilitative of the kinds of outcomes desired. The overarching goal of Part 1 is to optimize the potential for student growth and learning in small counseling or classroom groups by providing group leaders instruction on how to plan and prepare for the groups they lead. There is no substitution and no acceptable alternative to effective planning. Although we realize how authoritarian this statement reads, we simply cannot emphasize the importance of planning enough. In truth, this entire text is a map to the process through which school counselors can navigate groups of all sorts in the schools where they practice.

DIVERSITY ISSUES: THE WINDOWS AND MIRRORS METAPHOR

School counselors grapple with how to help their schools encourage individuals to maintain their ethnic, cultural, and personal identities and how to create cohesive and respectful communities across these differences. They also search for ways to best support students to learn about self and others while in relationship with others. These are challenges that schools face in becoming multiculturally competent. At its heart, multicultural education is a philosophy about education that honors freedom, justice, equity, and human dignity, and it is a practice that honors these principles in school classrooms, halls, and playgrounds (Grant, 1998). When we speak of "diversity issues" in education, in counseling, and in group work, we are referring to many things: a curriculum that offers contributions from multiple perspectives; an environment that confronts racism, injustice, and hate; and an instruction that teaches and scaffolds decision-making, social action, empowerment, and critical-thinking skills.

Holcomb-McCoy (2004) outlined nine areas of competence for school counselors so they can best serve a diverse student population. These competencies identify the necessary awareness, knowledge, and skills school counselors need in order to work with a diverse student body in schools. Holcomb-McCoy's work compels school counselors to understand the diverse ways in which clients seek help; the context of and fallout from racism in our school communities; and the importance of using racial identity theory in counseling, supporting, and working with youth in schools. The Holcomb-McCoy competencies also compel school counselors to respect the variety of parenting styles and family network or kinship relationships that may exist within their school communities and to work to nurture family-school-community partnerships across differences. Finally, these competencies highlight the important role of school counselors acting as advocates and agents of change. Holcomb-McCoy's competencies are supported by the work of others in the field (see the *Advocacy Competencies for Professional Counselors* [Trusty & Brown, 2005]; *ACA Advocacy Standards* [Lewis, Arnold, House, & Torporek, n.d.]; *ASGW Principles for Diversity-Competent Group Workers* [ASGW, 1998]; and the *ASCA National Model* [ASCA, 2005]), which constitute a call to professional counselors to serve in the roles of counselor, educator, and advocate with regard to diversity issues. In all of the following chapters, we aim to help group leaders in schools become more intentional in realizing these multiple roles in their group work.

Style (1998) uses the metaphor of *windows and mirrors* to describe the ways in which classrooms can be structured to help students understand self and others. In her words:

> . . . education needs to enable the student to look through window frames in order to see the realities of others and into mirrors in order to see her/his own reality reflected. Knowledge of both types of framing is basic to a balanced education which is committed to affirming the essential dialectic between the self and the world (p. 150).

We use this metaphor to frame our discussion with regard to diversity issues in each of the three parts of this text.

For us, *windows* must be more than the once vogue "multicultural potluck supper" or "Tourist-Multicultural" (Derman-Sparks, 1993, p. 6) approach to diversity education. It requires us to help students see and respect multiple life styles (a window to see through to the life of others) and multiple perspectives. Implicit to this is that we must help youth grasp the importance of seeing context in individuals' lived experiences, as well as understand how context influences individuals' perspectives and positions. When helping students see the lives of others, the shade must not be closed to the very real effects of racism, classism, sexism, and heterosexism, as well as the power that comes from privilege.

For Style (1998), holding up *mirrors* refers to helping students see oneself represented in the community and collective knowledge of the group. That includes having students see their contributions validated by others and their experiences valued by others, and exposing students to all of the possibilities of what they can do and who they can be.

In summary, *windows and mirrors* refers to the intentional work of the group leader to help students see and respect multiple perspectives; to scaffold students' abilities to understand and confront racism and injustice; to intentionally teach students to make thoughtful decisions and become critical thinkers; and to model, encourage, and support multiple possibilities for all students. Creating these kinds of experiences for students through group work requires careful attention to planning, intentional leading in the group, and thoughtful responses to problems in the group.

WHO IS IN THE GROUP AND WHY

Deciding who should be in the school group is the first step in group planning. Here we begin with a discussion about the unique membership issues in classroom and counseling groups. We will then move into a discussion on some convergent issues that are common to both group types.

Classroom Group Membership

Classroom group work is typically designed to meet the curricular component of comprehensive developmental school counseling programs (Stone & Dahir, 2006) or the curricular dictates of a particular school (Schmidt, 2007; Sink, 2005). Classroom groups are intended for *all* students in the class, and they may focus on cognitive, behavioral, or affective growth and development. Some examples of these types of groups are: a one-time classroom group on dealing effectively with test-related stress and anxiety, a three-session classroom group on identifying and naming feelings, and a series of classroom sessions preceding and following the death of a fifth-grade classmate. Although this latter topic may at first appear to be more appropriate to a small counseling group rather than a classroom, the purpose of this particular group was to be informative and really needed to include all of the children in the class, since they were all affected by the death. It is important to mention here that classroom group work may also be designed in response to circumstantial issues in a particular school and in some cases, classroom group work may parallel or be followed by small group interventions. So, in this latter example, children who desired—or those whose teachers' or parents' thought they would benefit from additional support after the death of their peer—were also given the opportunity to participate in a counseling group, as this was also a part of this school's protocol in responding to this level of crisis.

It is significant that students are not specifically selected for classroom groups; they consist of everyone who is already in the class. As such, you can expect that there will be a variety of learning needs and styles represented in classroom groups and that students will bring a wide variety of life experiences into their participation in the group. So, planning classroom groups requires attention to offering a variety of activities and mediums for learning, and it also requires offering multiple opportunities for children to relate to the content and focus of the group.

Classroom groups also tend to be relatively large, with 25 students or more in some classrooms. Initially, you may not even know the names and personalities of all of the students in the group, especially in the beginning of the school year. The reality facing many school counselors nationally—with ever-growing counselor/student ratios—is that it may be unlikely or impossible to know students individually to the extent that they may desire. In some instances, these issues may be further complicated by the fact that not all of the students in the classroom will be equally interested in or in need of the particular content of the group. Also, classrooms typically have their own group dynamics that have developed over time and that have existed long before your entry into the room. A common challenge for school counselors leading classroom groups is more about finding a way to *enter into* the existing group. This highlights the importance of establishing your own set of norms and rules, which will be discussed in more detail in Chapter 6.

Since classroom group membership is not based on screening or on any one student's individual needs, screening and membership issues for classroom groups is less about who is in and who is out of the group and more about making the group work for the variety of student members. In general, classroom group plans, then, need to be appropriate for the size of the group and they should account for the process of getting to know the students initially. The plans should also vary from week to week as they must accommodate an assortment of interest and ability levels so that the group is engaging. To these ends, we suggest that you continually ask yourself: "How will I make this relevant and engaging for *all* of the students in the group?" (See *Ethical Standards for School Counselors* [ASCA, 2004], Preamble and A.1.b for reference to this issue of relevancy.) As mentioned, you will need to consider ways in which student interest will be captured and be vigilant in finding content, materials, and ways to work that honor the unique and different interests and backgrounds of the variety of students present in the group. Here we reference the concept of windows and mirrors.

An important first step in making the classroom group relevant and engaging for all students is to get to know the students early on. Spending time in the classroom with the regular teacher in advance of your work with the students can introduce you to the dynamics that are present in the group, and it will give you some insight regarding what works for whom, and when. We realize that visiting the regular classroom for an observation is not a regular practice of most school counselors, but we still hold firm that it is an important first step for effective planning for classroom (and counseling) group work. School counselors should not feel pressured to begin their classroom groups before they are ready. No classroom teacher starts the first day of classes with a sole focus on content—teachers typically begin their classrooms each year with a process that allows for getting to know one another. This practice can benefit the school counselor as well. Finally, and related to this issue of feeling pressured to begin classroom group work, we emphasize that classroom group work should never put school counselors in the role of "substitute teacher." The purpose of classroom group work in schools is instructional, not convenience.

You can also get to know the students prior to planning the first classroom group session by asking teachers to share their knowledge about particular group dynamics, trouble spots, and strategies for managing difficult behaviors. Also, be prepared to use tools such as name-tags, icebreakers, and other getting-to-know-you activities in some of the early group sessions. It is appropriate to inform students that while they already know each other's names, you are new to the group and it will take a little time to get to know everyone.

Counseling Group Membership

Small counseling groups in schools are also designed to promote the development of social, emotional, behavioral, and academic skills. However, counseling groups are typically designed to address specific issues, problems, and/or needs that are common to a small group of students (Schmidt, 2007; Sciarra, 2004; Stone & Dahir, 2006). Examples of these kinds of groups include a counseling group for third and fourth graders whose parents are recently or currently in the process of divorce, a counseling group for kindergarten children who are struggling with being away from home for the first time, and a group for high school students who are feeling stressed about academics or the college application process.

Because the content of counseling groups tends to be designed around the specific needs of its members, these groups differ from classroom groups in that they tend to encourage more personal sharing among members (Sink, 2005) and students in these groups are more likely to be emotionally engaged in the topic. Membership in counseling groups is based on a screening process so that the students are appropriate for the particular group and so that the group addresses the specific and individual group member needs. This screening involves informing students of the purpose of the group and gathering information about the student and his or her experiences related to the intended topic of the group. It also involves informed consent and student asset—all of which will be discussed later. Putting effort into selection positions the group for success. Many excellent texts exist that address inclusion and exclusion criteria for small group membership, albeit most of these address these criteria for adult members. Here we review the most pertinent processes to consider while selecting members for your groups.

Let us start by saying that the commonsense adage "members who want to be in groups make for better groups" is usually true. Moreover, every group is not good for every student. For example, if you decide to offer a counseling group for early elementary school students on getting along with others, it is important to invite students who are trying to get along with others—congruent with the focus of the group. If you unwisely invite students who appear intent on making others miserable (e.g., instigating fighting, belittling others, bullying) or who lack the requisite social skills or abilities to read social cues, these students are unlikely to benefit from inclusion in the group. Answering the question "Who is this group for?" will guide decisions regarding potential group membership.

One other process, which affects member selection is worthy of introduction here: School counselors are literally blessed with the easiest access to children in need of professional counseling services in the entire realm of the allied mental health professions. That being said, it is our belief that many (rather than few) small groups should be designed and led throughout the academic calendar to meet the unique needs of as many children as possible. One crowded (say 15 members), long-running (say 4 months) counseling group is far less beneficial than several 6-member, 8-session counseling groups with a carefully composed membership. This combines the adages "less is more" and "more is better" in a very user-friendly approach to offering the right group to the right students at the right time. Planning groups in this way also avoids a problematic tendency to have one group attend to too many issues. It is better to select members, work together toward specified goals, and once attained, terminate. If there are other goals, perhaps a second group is in order.

Finally, we want to address the issue of member homogeneity here as well. Even though students are selected for participation in small groups because they all have a connection to the issue or topic that is the focus of the group, these students will be different from each other in a variety of other ways. So, for example, while all of the students in a grief group may share the common experience of loss, they may be different in the ways in which they experienced the loss, and the ways that their families responded to the loss. There may well be differences in other areas as well, such as in reading level, the degree to which they are introverted or extraverted, and with regard to other abilities, skills, and characteristics. Therefore, planning for small groups must also account for differences among group members, and it must also attend to some of the unique learning and participation styles that all members bring to the group. To this end, the suggestions in the previous section with regard to planning for a diverse membership in classroom groups are also pertinent to this discussion on planning small counseling groups.

CASE STUDY 1.1

Engaging a Variety of Students

Ms. Boise, a high school counselor, and Ms. Hulsen, the school athletic director, were planning a 5-week athletic team captains leadership group for all of the fall varsity sports team's captains (football, soccer, field hockey, and cross country) that school year. The plan was for the group to meet every third week during the season in the evening, with pizza and soda available, so the captains could attend after their afternoon practice times. The leaders planned to use (very roughly) a leadership curriculum that the school counselor had been exposed to at a professional development conference. In planning the group, the leaders recognized that the leadership asset inventory that they hoped to use would be difficult for the two English language learners (ELL) who were the co-captains of the boys soccer and cross-country teams that year. They also recognized that many of the captains would come to the first group meeting with a high level of apprehension and skepticism about the purpose and utility of the group. In addition, even though between the two of them they knew all the students who were invited to be in the group, neither leader knew every student who was invited to be in the group. Similarly, while all of the students probably knew who their peers were, many of them did not know each other very well. Ms. Boise and Ms. Hulsen were not sure how well the students would initially work together in the group.

The leaders planned to begin the first session slowly with some getting-to-know-you activities over pizza. Next, they planned to have the students work in triads (captains of a different teams would be assigned to work together in the triads) to brainstorm the challenges of being a captain to peers. They decided this initial session would help them identify the natural helpers and stronger leaders in the group. They also hoped that the first session would help them decide how to pair the students for the next session when they would be using the leadership survey in order to limit unwanted exposure of the ELL students' reading difficulties.

After the first meeting, the leaders decided that they would identify alternative activities that could substitute for the reader-dependent curriculum they intended to use.

In addition, they immediately recognized the importance of identifying an athlete in the larger community who was from a minority group and who could be a guest member or visitor to serve as a role model and mirror for the two minority-group team captains. Finally, they also planned to seek consultation on leading a discussion regarding the complexities of race relations on the athletic field.

Reflection Questions

1. What are some ways that survey instruments can be used that will promote the team leaders' group cohesion rather than just promoting individuals working in the group essentially alone? How might you modify reading-heavy curriculum so that it could be used successfully with individuals who have difficulties in reading?
2. How can group leaders provide mirrors for nonminority students in relatively homogeneous groups or school communities?
3. In what ways might you address the topic of race relations on the field with this group of team captains?

DIVERSITY IN MEMBERSHIP

Even when issues around race, class, and status are not explicitly stated as goals for a particular group, these issues are always present within student interactions, student–teacher interactions, and in school–community relations (see *Ethical Standards for School Counselors* [ASCA, 2004], A.1.b., E.2.a–d and *ASGW Best Practice Guidelines* [ASGW, 2007], A.7., B.3 for the need to address these issues in the group). That is, they always are present in every group. Cultural racism, which refers to the messages and images in society that reinforce the notion of White privilege, "is like smog in the air" according to Tatum (1997, p. 6):

> Sometimes it is so thick it is visible, other times it is less apparent, but always, day in and day out, we are breathing it in. None of us would introduce ourselves as "smog-breathers" (and most of us don't want to be described as prejudiced), but if we live in a smoggy place, how can we avoid breathing the air? (Tatum, p. 6)

Counselors need to be intentional about constructing groups so that *all* members have a place and have an opportunity for identification and for growth in the group—this is what we mean by planning for *windows and mirrors*. We sometimes like to think that "diversity issues" are variables that smooth over with inclusion; on the contrary, inclusion does not happen if these issues are smoothed over. Classroom groups with a diverse membership have the potential to offer a rich array of perspectives into the learning process. That potential is realized, however, only when students feel that they have a place in the group and that their voice is wanted, worthy, and respected. It is the responsibility of the group leader to create a safe space for all members of the group.

Small counseling groups can also offer countless opportunities for students to see the realities of the lives of others and to grapple with the importance of context in perspective-taking, even when these are not the explicit focus of the group. This windowing that can happen in a counseling group is one of the inherent benefits of using group work as a medium for learning in schools. Small groups can also provide a venue for offering students mirrors to see themselves as strong individuals and to support healthy development. However, because identity characteristics associated with race, ethnicity, gender, socio-economic status, sexual orientation, age, and physical and mental ability exist in polarized contexts of status/advantage/privilege, a minority voice in a group of dominant-group-others can easily be silenced. A student who stands apart on one aspect of the above-mentioned characteristics may not *feel*—and may not *be*—safe in the group. As a result, students whose experiences in life are different from the others in the group may feel censured or may censure themselves, thus rendering the group not just unhelpful, but potentially harmful. Again, we emphasize that it is the responsibility of the group leader to assure that all members feel safe and that all members are safe in their groups.

Given the complexity around these issues of diverse group membership, leaders must give careful consideration of homogeneous versus heterogeneous grouping. In some groups, this issue will be more critical than in others. For example, if the purpose of the group is to provide an opportunity for students to talk about the inherent stressors of living in a dominant/subordinate society, it may be more beneficial for racially minority students to be in the group with others who share their minority status and without dominant-culture peers. As Tatum (1997) points out, many minority teens will gravitate toward this type of natural grouping anyway, thus providing insight into "Why are all the black kids sitting together in the cafeteria?" (i.e., the title of Tatum's 1997 book). Although it might be informative for dominant group members to witness the experiences of the minority group members, the more critical issues are (a) the purpose of the group—who it is designed for and why—and (b) safety for the minority members. We would argue that the goal of teaching students in the dominant group about the issues of power and privilege is an important goal for all schools to embrace, but it should never come at the expense of those members of minority and potentially disenfranchised groups. Heterogeneous groups that focus on this issue must be carefully constructed with thoughtful consideration of who is in the group, as well as with clear articulation of the goals, with informed consent, and with skillful management of the group.

In other cases, the diversity characteristic that separates some students from others may be less salient than the issue that is the subject of the group. In these cases, heterogeneous grouping may be very appropriate. For example, it may be appropriate for a student who uses a wheelchair to be in a group focused on anxiety reduction strategies; of course, excluding the student from this group because of the disability is obviously inappropriate. In these situations, race, socio-economic status (SES), or other characteristics do not disappear—we can never take the stand that differences do not exist. They should be introduced into the group as they are relevant to the topic, the discussion, and the needs of the group members. Therefore, in the case of the student who uses a wheelchair, discussing the stress of using a wheelchair in school may be relevant in the group and certainly is not something that should be squelched because it might be uncomfortable for the members or for the leader to talk about. It may even be—and probably is—appropriate for the group leader to bring up, because this factor is already obvious in the group.

We recommend asking these questions when planning group membership:

1. How will member configuration support the contributions of the student whose identity characteristics might set him up for feeling silenced or dominated by others?

2. Who in this group will serve as a mirror for another group member? Who will serve as a window?
3. How can I be sure that the window does not stand alone in the group?
4. Who will support the contributions of members who do not come to the group with cultural capitol in this school community?
5. What other ways (besides in membership selection) can I introduce windows and mirrors for all of the students in this group?

DEVELOPMENTAL ISSUES

Nowhere in the counseling profession is developmental range more apparent than in elementary, middle, and secondary school counseling programs. The distance between a kindergartener and a third grader seems immense, and just look at the physical differences visible in any middle school! Along these lines, it is tempting but shortsighted to imagine that all students in a fifth-grade classroom will be developmentally identical. Therefore, we suggest designing your classroom sessions in terms of the standard bell-curve distribution. Because the fifth-grade classes' cognitive development will likely span from those who are far more similar to fourth graders to those expected to find in sixth graders, designing a classroom group lesson that attempts to meet this wide range of cognitive developmental levels is much more likely to be successful. It seems too obvious to emphasize that school counselors must take these developmental differences seriously.

What does this actually mean to you as a group leader?

- Tailor your vocabulary to challenge those at the lower developmental end, but also engage those "nearly sixth grade" students.
- Be certain that your directions and examples are selected from across this developmental span. For example, you might use a popular cartoon-network character along with a more sophisticated movie character to make your point or to use as an example.
- Attempt to subgroup and regroup members within the group. It is often true that classroom teachers are extremely adept at grouping (consider reading groups, math groups, and activity-based learning modules). Do not hesitate to ask for teachers' insights into how to subgroup members and use developmental readiness to your advantage in group.
- There is often great utility in cross-grade membership for counseling groups in schools. For example, at times the membership of several fourth graders in a group of mostly third graders whose behavior is immature can have a strong positive effect. Of course, members should be selected for group inclusion only if their needs match the learning goals; therefore, mixed-age grouping is appropriate only when it meets the learning needs of *all* potential group members.

THE ETHICS OF PARTICIPATION

Because membership in counseling groups is leader-invited and participation is voluntary (rather than a part of the overall curriculum for students, which is the case in classroom groups), issues of *informed consent* and member *assent* are relevant to the discussion here. Most school districts require specific parental permission for their child to participate in a counseling group, so it is always incumbent on you to know your school policy in this regard. Although law (policy) supplants ethics, it does not give school counselors permission to perform unethically. We cite the *Ethical Standards for School Counselors* (ASCA, 2004), the *ACA Code of Ethics and Standards of Practice* (ACA, 2005), and the *ASGW Best Practice Guidelines* (ASGW, 2007) as our ethical roadmaps in negotiating quandaries that arise from our attempts to balance school-specific needs and our ethical obligations. However, a brief example and comment is warranted here: If you intend to lead a small time-limited, supportive counseling group with students who are experiencing their parents' divorces, it might be quite challenging to obtain parental permission due to custody issues. We suggest asking yourself these questions: (a) From which parent does the counselor ask permission? (b) Can the parents function cooperatively in order to grant permission that would be in their child's best interest? (c) Are there good reasons for why seeking permission from one or the other is unwise? These are good questions. However, the message is clear: Follow policy. In doing so, it is wise to know that policy affects the type of groups you may elect to lead and it can affect the membership of your counseling groups.

Remember that students cannot grant legal consent for participation in many school-related activities, as this is a privilege afforded only to adults (and in some circumstances emancipated adolescents). However, students of all ages can (and should) be asked to assent—meaning that they have a voice in whether they would like to be members of any counseling group. Seeking assent from students to be in a counseling group requires, of course, that the purpose and process of a counseling group be presented in developmentally appropriate language so that those who are invited to be members of the group can determine if they wish to make that commitment. To this end, you should plan a pre-group informational meeting where invited students are informed (individually or in a small group) about the group and invited to join. (For specific ethical codes and guidelines on this topic, see *ACA Code of Ethics and Standards of Practice* [ACA, 2005] A.2.a & d, B.5.b. & 6.d, and D.1.c; *Ethical Standards for School Counselors* [ASCA, 2004] A.2 & 6, B.1 & 2; and *ASGW Best Practice Guidelines* [ASGW, 2007] A.7.)

Of course, you should always respect students' decisions to participate or decline membership in the group. In the long run, you do not want to have a counseling group that was formed by coercion (in its many overt and subtle forms). Students who are able to make an informed decision about being in a group are likely to stick with the group, support its established goals, and be active participants in the process. Those that are assigned membership without assent are likely to create an atmosphere where defense, reluctance, anger, and all other methods of being cantankerous will flourish. The bottom line is that you must think carefully about the ethics of counseling group membership, and articulate these implications carefully to members, parents, teachers, and administrators so that all are equally informed.

ESTABLISHING PROGRAM RELEVANCY

The content of classroom as well as counseling groups, is often subject to questioning from parents, guardians, and administration. Though these individuals rarely doubt our process, they sometimes wonder whether some topics really are school "business." We firmly believe that the litmus test to relevance is always found in the answer to this question: Does this group assist its members in maximizing their chances for success in school? If this question is applied to say, a counseling group for students whose parents are recently divorced, and the goal of the group is to assist students in navigating such a difficult personal adjustment, then we believe that the group would probably be very appropriate—in fact ideal. Sometimes parents who are in this situation need the support of the school counselor in assisting their children through such challenging times.

A second issue of appropriateness is raised in this classroom group example: Imagine a 4-week classroom group focused on respect (for everyone in the class). It is not difficult to envision a parent questioning why his or her "very respectful" son or daughter would need lessons in respect. Our position is that respect is not an either/or characteristic. We believe that even the most respectful of students benefit from thoughtful discussion about the meaning of respect (and who actually defines it), the nuances around how respect is communicated, and why respectful people do not always act in respectful ways. This example illustrates the need for articulating a compelling rationale for well-designed group work in schools.

Effective Communication Between School Counselors and Others

We now look briefly at the intersection of classroom and counseling groups—school counseling services in general—on one hand, and teachers, administrators, and school boards on the other.

School counselor autonomy is a mixed blessing. We, as school counselors, are often left to do our "thing," and although good school counseling programs are inextricably linked to the overall vision and mission of their schools and their school unions or districts, people often do not understand what we do. School counselors should not operate behind a veil—allowing only a few to know what exactly they do. As is clearly articulated in the Preamble of the *Ethical Standards for School Counselors* (ASCA, 2004), the rights of privacy, as well as respect and dignity, are fundamental, but this should not be viewed in any way as implicit permission to practice in secret. Rather, transparency, publication, and public understanding are almost always preferred. For example, a teacher who is giving up his classroom so that the counselor might work with his students should be afforded the opportunity to know what will take place in his classroom during his absence. It is inconvenient for teachers to shuffle their belongings out of their "office" and into a workroom while the school counselor moves in and, unfortunately, we have witnessed busy or otherwise occupied school counselors not extend the courtesy of explanation to these teachers who have been inconvenienced. Communicating to others the intent of your work goes a long way in avoiding misunderstandings and helps foster collaborative relationships. For example, if you are presenting a series of lessons on academic success, an under-informed classroom teacher might surmise that you see some flaw in his class, thus rendering it in need of counseling. Although this could not be further from the truth, unless explained, the potential for misunderstanding is grave. There is tension here, of course, as the information to be shared needs to be carefully and thoughtfully considered. Maintaining confidentiality around student disclosures is a fundamental aspect of the practice of counseling, and confidentiality must be maintained regarding student issues. The information to be shared with others should focus on very general content issues and any sharing of student information must be limited to a brief as-needed professional exchange of information or otherwise by parental consent (and student assent). (For more on this, see *ACA Code of Ethics and Standards of Practice* [2005] D.1; *Ethical Standards for School Counselors* [ASCA, 2004] C.1., D.1.)

In general, school administrators need to know what is going on in their classrooms, their building, and their district. They expect to be able to articulate to a concerned or inquisitive parent or school-board member everything that is taking place under their supervision—which is a weighty and untenable position. So, it is beneficial to administrators that you keep them generally informed of what is happening in your groups, as appropriate.

A variety of methods can be used to inform not only the administration but also the parents and guardians of the children and adolescents you serve. Many school counselors send home newsletters with information about their services and programs. To cut down on the cost of mailing, some school districts, unions, and school counselors are now using school websites to communicate effectively by posting regular updates, news briefs, and invitation electronically. Please do not misunderstand this public communication as unethical—of course that which is confidential must remain confidential. However, it is appropriate to keep our administration and the school community informed on all that we do (within the confines of our ethical obligation to confidentiality). (For specific relevant codes related to confidentiality, consult the *ACA Code of Ethics and Standards of Practice* [2005] and the *Ethical Standards for School Counselors* [ASCA, 2004]).

Mentioning confidentiality raises an important point to address here: It is unlikely that a student can expect that no one will know that he or she is spending time with the school counselor—individually or in small groups. Therefore, it is always prudent to discuss with students what they might communicate directly to their teachers about their counseling sessions. At times, students might ask you for help in communicating their needs—which they often believe will not be easy to speak to a teacher about—on a strictly need-to-know basis. This applies to communication with parents as well. An example of successful communication between Mrs. Ahadi, a sixth-grade science teacher, and Ms. Lebowitz, a middle school counselor, is outlined in *Case Study 1.2*.

CASE STUDY 1.2
Negotiating What to Say

Pavan is a sixth-grade student newly transferred from a school in another state. His science teacher had mentioned at a sixth-grade team meeting (faculty, administrator, counselor, school nurse) that she was worried that Pavan was making a poor adjustment to the new school. Others concurred and Ms. Lebowitz, the school counselor, agreed that she would meet with him and reinvite him to a new student group that he turned down initially.

When Ms. Lebowitz met with Pavan in a short screening and invitation session, she mentioned that Mrs. Ahadi had expressed concern for him. Pavan appreciated her concern and told Ms. Lebowitz that he really liked Mrs. Ahadi, but that he did not know how to tell her "what was going on." Ms. Lebowitz agreed that this might be something that he would like to bring to the group—to learn how other students were communicating with their teachers about their difficulties. She also asked Pavan's permission to allow her to mention to Mrs. Ahadi that he had accepted an invitation to participate in the group. Pavan told her that would be great.

The result ended in rich discussion group lasting several sessions, empowerment for Pavan (and several others), rehearsal of how to approach teachers (including very funny role-playing by the counseling group members), and a plan for Pavan to talk to Mrs. Ahadi and his other teachers. Pavan's counseling revealed incredibly difficult family dynamics following his parent's separation, which prompted his moving. As a result of sharing these feelings and rehearsing how and what to share with his teachers, Mrs. Ahadi very willingly offered to help Pavan in whatever way she could. Pavan was making the transition into his new school with extra-appreciated care.

However, the story continues. Mrs. Ahadi sought out Ms. Lebowitz in the hall one morning and asked with good intention, as well as with some sense of urgency, "What exactly is going on with that family? How can a mother uproot such a sweet kid? How selfish and horrible divorce is—and . . ." to which Ms. Lebowitz listened and replied, "You really have such strong feelings about this and really care deeply for Pavan, but you know that what Pavan talks about in group is not open for me to share with you. It appears obvious though that Pavan seems to really value you and your class. I'm so thankful that you raised your concern for him with the team."

Reflection Questions

1. In this case study, the school counselor invited Pavan to join a counseling group and initially he declined. She then approached him a second time, inviting him again. Was this being too pushy or was it appropriate?
2. At what point—if any—would it be appropriate to share with the teacher what you know about a student so that she can better support him or her in the classroom?

Curiosity, passion, and concern do not warrant breaking confidence—not even a little bit. Case Study 1.2 demonstrates that we are able to include and coordinate services with teachers and uphold our ethical responsibilities simultaneously. The reward of clear and open communication with others almost always works to our benefit and the benefit of our students.

CHAPTER 2

Developing and Writing Group Plans

THE LANGUAGE OF GROUP PLANNING

Many counselors, leading groups in schools, are required by their school administrators to complete *lesson plans* for their groups, much in the same way that teachers are required to do so. Of course, the term *lesson plan* immediately gets us thinking about teaching. But do not be fooled by this terminology; a lesson plan really is, in its simplest sense, a plan for the group. A *lesson* is the instructional component of learning (Price & Nelson, 1999) and a *lesson plan* is the written outline of the learning goals and objectives and how those goals and objectives will be carried out in the group. So, while some counselors may balk at having to create lesson plans, being well-prepared is a precursor to successful group work, whether that group is conducted in a classroom or a small group format, in or out of schools, with children, adolescents, and even with adults! As you will see, planning is a continual refrain throughout this text.

Although we use the term *lesson plans* in some of the discussion that follows, you might find more professional comfort in using the term *session plans*. We encourage you to adopt a nomenclature that best suits your philosophical orientation, the demands of your job in its setting, or that is most comfortable to you. We prefer not to get caught up in terminology—we think that debate, if necessary, is better suited for some other venue. Instead, in this text we have chosen to focus on the important elements that should be included in written group plans. Our structure of this discussion begins in this chapter with a thorough discussion about how to draft goals and objectives, being thoughtful about incorporating complex learning tasks into the plans for the group. It also includes discussion regarding attention to diversity issues, how to stimulate meaning-making, and finally, tips for actually writing group plans. In Chapter 3, *Planning for Implementation*, the focus is on planning so that the group will be facilitated in a way that addresses the goals and objectives for group. In the final Chapter 4 of Part 1, *Designing Assessments*, we offer a discussion on selecting an appropriate measure for assessing the extent to which the intended goals and objectives have been met in the group.

GROUP GOALS AND OBJECTIVES

Group planning typically includes a statement of the goals and objectives of the group, as well as an articulation of how the group leader will facilitate the group to meet these goals and objectives. When used in the context of group work, *goals* generally refer to what the leader hopes members will gain from the experience of being in the group; they are the outcome expectations for the group. Goals provide a direction and long-term plan for the group (Price & Nelson, 1999). According to Corey and Corey (2006), goal setting is at the core of group counseling because "in the absence of a clear understanding about the purpose of a group and meaningful goals for members, much needless floundering can occur" (p. 145). Group goals are entwined in group membership and goals become the source of designing outcome measures of group effectiveness.

Group *objectives*, on the other hand, typically refer to more specific and short-term instructional (or therapeutic) outcome expectations for the group (Price & Nelson, 1999). We think of them as the steps or parts that lead to the larger group goal. In teacher language, the objective is what the teacher hopes to accomplish at the end of a particular lesson. In counselor-led groups, the group objectives refer to the intended learning expectations for a particular group session. So, while group goals refer to what the leader hopes to accomplish over time after a number of group sessions, group objectives tend to be narrower in focus, referring to the intended outcome of a particular group session.

Classroom Groups

In classroom groups, *goals* tend to be based on the focus of the curricular content rather than specific individual group member needs. The curriculum used by school counselors is typically determined by the district and/or school. The American School Counseling Association endorses these key instructional domains for developmental school counseling curricula: academic, career (vocational), and personal/social development (see the *ASCA National Model*, American School Counselor Association [ASCA], 2005). Many schools and school districts have aligned their comprehensive school counseling programs to this *ASCA National Model* (ASCA, 2005) and numerous publications exist for helping school counselors align goals and objectives to the domains and standards outlined in the Model. The ASCA domains are fairly broad, as they refer to general areas of focus rather than specific goals, objectives, or intervention outcomes. The standards, competencies, and indicators that are listed within the three domain areas in the *ASCA National Model*, however, are more appropriate examples of goals for classroom groups because they are smaller and fairly specific (these are included in the Appendix of the *ASCA National Model*, 2005). Finally, the American School Counselor Association articulates school counselor responsibilities to students and schools, which also shape the content of group work conducted by school counselors (specifically, see *Ethical Standards for School Counselors* [ASCA, 2004] A.1.b., D.1. a, c, & d). These standards emphasize that school counseling programs, of which group work is a part, are a vital component—not extraneous, not expendable—of the school, the school system, and the community.

Again borrowing from what we have learned from the teaching profession, we suggest that classroom group goals be stated in terms of what the leader expects to accomplish *at the end of multiple classroom group lessons*. Because they refer to learning expectations for multiple classroom group lessons, we sometimes refer to them as *unit goals*. For example, the unit goals for the Elementary Level Classroom Group Plan sample in Appendix A are: Students will understand the ways in which students bully others and the implications of bullying behavior. Students will learn and use strategies for responding to bullying. Students will understand the ways in which students bully others and the implications of bullying behavior.

In classroom group work, *objectives* are the outcome statements that direct the specific interventions *that will be used in each group session*. They direct the details and steps that are arranged sequentially and aimed towards meeting the broader curricular unit goals. For example, the individual lesson objectives for the first lesson in the Elementary Level Classroom Group Plan sample in Appendix A are: Students will learn the three types of bullying. Students will learn the three roles in bullying behavior ("bully shoes"). Students will identify/express their feelings. All of these objectives fit in a sequence and address some aspect of the larger unit goals. Notice how these are specific and sequential.

Typically, a single classroom group lesson would be aimed at one or two specific objectives, whereas the regular meetings collectively address the larger proposed group goal. Teacher language may be helpful here in promoting this concept: One might think of the classroom group goal as an instructional unit goal. Using this nomenclature, each lesson is designed towards one or a few specific learning objectives that are sequenced to meet larger curricular unit instructional goals.

In addition to working from a planned comprehensive developmental curriculum, we expect that school counselors will also be responsive to the immediate needs of the classroom, schools, and communities in which they work (Goodnough, Perusse, & Erford, 2003). Thus, the importance of maintaining flexibility with regard to how curricular goals and objectives are decided and how they are implemented in the group is underscored here. Classroom group goals and objectives should address the particular needs of a particular classroom at a particular point in time.

Allow us also to point out another important issue related to goals and objectives in school groups. While classroom group goals and objectives are not typically designed around the needs of one individual or specific student, comprehensive developmental school counseling programs always focus on relevant developmental issues, often in the areas of personal and social development. We would venture to say that there will always be at least a few individuals in every classroom group who are especially in need of developing their personal self-management and social skills. So, while classroom group work is not designed to meet the individual needs of specific students, it is likely that your classroom group will address the individual and specific needs of some of the students in the group. For example, in a local school, learning to resolve conflicts was an identified curricular goal for the fourth grade in that school's comprehensive school counseling program. There were several students in the two fourth-grade classrooms in that school who were particularly challenged by managing themselves when in disagreement with others. For two of these students, the acquisition of conflict resolution and self-management skills were documented Individualized Education Plan (IEP) goals. In this situation, the classroom group goals and objectives overlapped with the individual needs and goals of these particular students in the group. Our point is that while classroom groups are typically not designed around the individual needs of a particular student in the group, it will likely be the case that individual student needs are met by the classroom group curriculum.

Finally, even though students are not likely to be directly involved in the development of classroom group goals and objectives, they can and should be encouraged and given opportunities to provide input into what they are learning and how it is (or is not) relevant to them (Kerr & Nelson, 1998). This input can be elicited in the beginning of the school year, at the beginning or end of a particular topic, or periodically as curricular objectives change throughout the year. On a larger level, student, teacher, and parent input should always be solicited in the curriculum goal setting process for developmental school counseling programs in the school and district. School counselors often create advisory boards and make good use of consultation with peers to this end. Communicating often and effectively with parents, guardians, as well as teachers, administrators, and the school board is paramount to program success.

Counseling Groups

In counseling groups, *goals* and *objectives* are typically developed in response to a common need or concern that is shared by the individuals for whom the group is planned. That is, the focus of the group is usually established to meet the needs of the group members rather than a pre-determined curriculum. For example, a group may be formed for a small number of students who have difficulties getting along with others. The goal of this group might be to strengthen friendship skills. Objectives for the specific group sessions in this group might include: learning how to use I-messages, respectful disagreement, giving feedback, and working through conflicts. To risk being redundant, notice here how these four objectives are skills that, once developed, will assist students in attaining the counseling group's goal—that of developing friendship skills. In this hypothetical group, we might plan for each objective to be the focus of a single group session. Week 1: I-Messages, Week 2: Respectful Disagreement, etc. A second example: The objectives of a counseling high school counseling group with a goal of developing a career interests are: learning about careers, exploring personal-career interests, and planning for education. As these examples illustrate, these smaller *objectives* typically detail the work towards meeting the larger goals for the group.

Counseling groups, of course, may also be planned to address specific curricular or learning needs that are identified in the school or district comprehensive developmental school counseling program, and they may be aligned with the domains and standards mentioned in the *ASCA National Model* (American School Counselor Association [ASCA], 2005). For example, a counseling group in a local middle school was developed for a small group of students to help them identify an awareness of their personal abilities, skills, motivations, and attitudes. This group goal is directly taken from the *ASCA National Model* Standard A in the Career Domain (ASCA). Objectives within this goal statement included having the students learn about their interpersonal style, as well as to explore personal and career or vocational interests. Numerous activities were used strategically towards these specific objectives. A second example is the high school group mentioned above that focuses on career-related goals and objectives. That group may be one that is held year after year and one in which every student eventually cycles through, but none-the-less, it is conducted as a small counseling group with a psychoeducational focus, and it should be responsive to the particular members of the group each time it is conducted. The *Ethical Standards for School Counselors* (ASCA, 2004) outlines ethical practice guidelines relevant to the planning of services and programs (specifically see sections A.1.b, D.1. a, c, & d).

Finally, we mention here a common disconnect between many group courses in graduate school and actual group work practice in school settings. Very often, group counseling is taught experientially in graduate school with members of the class/group bringing different issues with varying senses of urgency, apprehension, anxiety—all valued in an interpersonal growth experience. These training groups require intense cognitive complexity, abstract reasoning abilities, and they entail an implicit interest and possible fascination with interpersonal communication as a means toward intrapersonal insight. However, the group objectives that are a part of one's training to be a group leader, might be hard won by third graders or outright off-putting to seventh graders. Therefore, while we take no umbrage to conducting personal growth groups in schools (in fact, we support their use when appropriate and well-screened members are able and willing to participate), we do envision the distance between a first-grade counseling group for children who are challenged by being away from home for so long each day; a personal growth group with high school seniors who are making that developmental leap into future career plans, with all its existential and practical anxiety; and the interpersonal groups used for counselors-in-training. These are very different groups, indeed! We invite you to consider the important elements that transfer between these different types of groups, especially in terms of group leader skills (which will be the focus in Part 2), but do not assume that the particular type of group experience you had in grad school is the type of group you will be conducting with youth in schools. School counselors always approach group planning with a focus on the needs of the individuals who will be in those groups.

Bloom's Taxonomy

Whenever possible, group plans—objective statements, particularly—should take into consideration the type of learning expectation that you have for your group. That is, it is important to think through the desired complexity level of the learning that will be addressed in the objectives you have planned for your group. For example, objectives can embody simple learning tasks such as rote memorization or more complex tasks such as the application of a particular concept into practice. Note that this level of detail is more appropriate for group objectives than for goal statements. Bloom's *Taxonomy of Educational Objectives* (Bloom, 1956), a classic borrowed from teacher education, is the often-cited framework for thinking about the process of learning. This taxonomy identifies six levels of learning that can be incorporated into various learning tasks, so as to promote complex learning accomplishment. These levels are:

1. *Knowledge.* This refers to the process of finding out, discovering, and recalling information. Knowledge learning tasks tend to focus on the acquisition of specific information.

2. *Comprehension.* This refers to developing understanding, grasping meaning, and interpreting the information presented. Comprehension-focused learning tasks tend to invite students to think about or make sense of the information that is presented.

3. *Application.* This refers to making use of information, such as applying the information or steps to a problem. Learning tasks focused on application provide students with an opportunity to practice something that has been learned or to apply information to solve a problem.

4. *Analysis.* This refers to taking apart information and examining the relationships and themes that lie within. Learning tasks designed to promote analysis invite students to deconstruct or critically examine new information.

5. *Synthesis.* This refers to the creative or divergent application of the information, or putting the information together in a new way. In lessons planned to address this dimension of learning, students may be invited to compare or apply information from one context to another.

6. *Evaluation.* This refers to inviting students to be critical consumers of information by judging outcomes and supporting their ideas with reason. Learning objectives, focused on evaluation, invite students to consider the validity of the information presented and to think about how it fits with other knowledge, information, or experiences they may have had.

While all of these levels of learning may not be incorporated into each and every group plan, Bloom's taxonomy offers a helpful way of thinking about sequenced learning objectives so that each lesson builds upon the previous one and allows for a rich and varied in depth and scope in the learning process.

Positive Interdependence and Individual Accountability

Johnson and Johnson's (2004) Cooperative Learning model encourages the creation of group learning environments that have components of positive interdependence *and* individual accountability. *Positive interdependence* refers to a learning task in which group performance is highlighted and individual accomplishment is a function of how well the group does (Johnson, Johnson, & Holubec, 1994). *Individual accountability*, on the other hand, is focused on individual performance and/or achievement rather than on a collective group goal or performance (Johnson, Johnson, & Holubec, 1994).

Positive interdependence can be facilitated by requiring students to work together on tasks that are oriented towards collective group success. For example, a challenge exercise where all of the students must make it across the room walking on mats that are spaced apart requires the group to plan how they will accomplish the task together. It also requires that all of the students be involved in the task in order for it to be realized. Assigning student roles in these tasks can facilitate group interaction and is also an excellent way to neutralize social status differences among group members (see Cohen, 1994, for more on how to work with social status hierarchies in classroom group work). For example, having one student in the group be "materials manager," responsible for getting the materials before and after the activity, another being the "note-taker," helps engage all students by giving them an important role in the group.

Learning tasks that focus on *individual accountability* require students to individually demonstrate learning or proficiency in some way. A good way to facilitate individual accountability in counseling and classroom groups is to encourage individual goal setting. By inviting students to consider what they think will be personally relevant to them with regard to a particular topic or task, each student is able to work towards attaining his or her unique goal. Individual goal setting can be formalized by asking students to document their personal goals and having the leader review them with the students periodically or at the end of the group. It also can happen more informally and in a more abbreviated way by asking students to consider what they might hope or expect to learn from a particular activity as that activity is being introduced.

The relevance of these ideas to planning group objectives is its emphasis on the ways in which the group can be designed to meet the needs of the individual in the group, as well as the needs of the group as a whole. If you are asked to work with a group with the purpose of developing cohesion or helping the members work together on a particular task, for example, writing objectives and planning activities that emphasize positive interdependence might take priority over individual accountability. However, we, like Johnson and Johnson (2004), believe that a dual focus on individual accountability and group interdependence is worthy of consideration for most groups that are designed for children and run in schools, as this dual focus on interpersonal and intrapersonal is at the crux of socially appropriate functioning.

Types of Learning Experiences

In Cohen and Smith's (1976) conceptual model for group leader interventions, which we discuss in more detail in Chapter 6, the term *type* is used in reference to the ways in which group leaders engage members in the group. Cohen and Smith identify three types of interventions that are typically used in groups: conceptual, experiential, and structural. We reference intervention type in our discussion here to talk about the ways in which you can plan for different kinds of learning experiences in the group.

In the Cohen and Smith (1976) model, leader interventions that focus on helping members conceptualize or make meaning around a significant issue or idea are *conceptual* interventions. These interventions focus on information, concepts, ideas—on thinking. They inspire students to think, consider, and explore new ideas.

Experiential type interventions (Cohen & Smith, 1976) focus on the experience (feeling, thoughts, or behaviors) that group members have while they are in the group. When the content or topic of the group elicits feelings or causes specific behaviors and when the group leader draws attention to these experiences, the intervention is experiential. Similarly, when the leader draws attention to the ways in which students are interacting with each other, the focus is on the experience of the members—it is an experiential intervention. Once you plan to discuss this experience—to think about it or make meaning of it—however, the shift is back towards thinking and this new intervention would be conceptual.

Finally, in the Cohen and Smith (1976) model, interventions that make use of planned activities, exercises, structured tasks or interventions that change the physical movement patterns of members in the group are called *structural* interventions. These kinds of interventions are likely to stimulate thinking, but they may also elicit feelings and new behaviors. They are often used when a different kind of interaction is needed in the group, and they can be especially helpful in stimulating interest and shifting the group when it seems that a problem may be developing.

A fourth type of learning that can be stimulated in the group, and this does not come from Cohen and Smith's model, is *personal application*. Personal application refers to the extent to which students can relate material to their own beliefs, feelings, and experiences. Providing opportunities for students to relate personally to the material offered in the group helps establish relevancy and also stimulates investment in the content. We encourage you to develop group plans that address all four of these areas, so as to offer broad and textured opportunities for learning in the group.

ADDRESSING DIVERSITY ISSUES

Clearly articulated group goals and objectives direct group focus so that it is purposeful. If your intent is to provide windows and mirrors through the topic area and/or in the process or interactions among group members, then writing this into the group goals and objectives will help assure that it will happen. Indeed, offering students an exposure to ideas and experiences that sit just outside of what is familiar (windows) and helping them make meaning of these new experiences, as well as providing opportunities for students to see their own experiences reflected back and validated (mirrors) fits with learning goals in almost every area of development. Articulating this focus in group plans provides the map for how to lead the group in this direction.

When the topic of the group is intended to offer windows and mirrors into the experiences or lives of others, Bloom's *Taxonomy of Educational Objectives* (Bloom, 1956) can be used to plan sequential learning objectives. As you will recall, the first level in the Taxonomy is knowledge. A general goal that students will learn new ideas and specific information with regard to the lives of others or that students become aware of power, privilege, and injustice in the community or world around them, are all examples of group goals that might begin with a focus on knowledge level learning. *Case Study 2.3* illustrates how exposure to the new information offered at a knowledge level of instruction is used to provide a window to the experiences of individuals who experience discrimination.

CASE STUDY 2.3

Window Goals

The goals for all of the classroom groups in this semi-urban elementary school include the expectation that students will learn about perspectives that are different than their own and that they will develop acceptance and appreciation across differences. The rationale for this goal is linked with the state harassment law, which articulates the wide range of protected categories that are addressed by this particular protective legislation. Part of the comprehensive developmental program in the school also includes helping students understand what is meant by a "protected category," and why one group may warrant special protections under the law.

Working towards this goal, students in the fifth grade study the concept of family with the objective of understanding that different individuals have different experiences of family. This includes children who are living with aunts and uncles, as well as with foster families, same-sex parents, heterosexual couples, and divorced and blended families. In carrying out this objective, the counselor used the film and discussion series, *That's a Family* (Cohen, 2002; Logan, Chasnoff, & Cohen, 2002) to expose children to multiple family types. She also used the book, *And Tango Makes Three* (Richardson &

Parnell, 2005), which exposes children to the true story of two male penguins at the Central Park Zoo who fall in love and raise a baby penguin together.

Reflection Questions

1. Consider the elementary school you are most familiar with. Can you imagine that school community's response to this particular fifth-grade classroom group topic?
2. With a commitment to offering windows and mirrors for all students, this example emphasizes the point that social context brings so much to bear when constructing curriculum—when planning and preparing for counselor lead classroom groups. Consider all that contributes to a community's expectations for its school counselors. What are the risks of offering this curriculum? What are the risks of not attending to these diversity issues in your school community? (We also address these questions in our discussion below.)
3. What administrative and community supports would be necessary to conduct a curriculum such as this? What preparations are needed?

While the activities in Case Study 2.3 expose children to new knowledge, Bloom's Taxonomy (1956) reminds us that learning is enriched when it encompasses the other levels (comprehension, application, analysis, synthesis, and evaluation) as well. Written plans that specifically outline discussion questions and comments that bring forth these other levels of learning invite students to examine the information presented at an ever-increasing level of cognitive complexity. For example, in Case Study 2.3, discussion after the film and book can help students connect the new information about different family types to social-context issues such as societal norms, or to school-experienced behaviors such as bullying and teasing. Students might be asked to think about how they make decisions about others based on judgments, thus learning how to critically evaluate information that is presented to them. All of these represent higher level learning tasks, according to the Bloom Taxonomy.

We emphasize that the content of the group described in Case Study 2.3 is not—and should not be—designed to encourage students to adopt values that are different than their own; it is designed to have students become aware that there are other perspectives and other ways of experiencing the world. As Style (1998) says, "For me, the beauty of the classroom gathering lies in its possibility for seeing new varieties of Beauty [*Sic*]" (p. 150). Opening up the content in the group to account for the experiences of a diverse population of students, of course, also allows individuals with less social capital, who are members of under-privileged groups, or who are members of groups that are potentially marginalized in larger society, to witness their own experiences as having a place in the group. Representation communicates that their truths are respected as valid rather than minimized or ignored. This validation lies at the heart of Style's (1998) concept of mirrors. She points out that traditionally, school curricula privileges dominate culture experiences and views, relegating individuals from minority groups repeated experiences of windows of others' lives (i.e., windows into the world of privileged accounts and experiences) and little validation of what is their own truth and experience. McIntosh (1998) reminds us that acknowledging privilege—that is, acknowledging one's personal privilege and acknowledging the ways in which privilege works its way into curriculum in institutions of education—makes one newly accountable for the power that it grants those of us in positions of power. We would argue that planning curriculum that offers windows and mirrors to all students in the room sets a precedent for privileging the voices of every member of the group.

This discussion about windows and mirrors has brought up some very controversial ideas—intentionally on our part. We realize that acknowledging same sex partnerships, for example, may be deemed "unspeakable" in some communities. Perhaps, it is also unspeakable from the lips of some counselors and group leaders? To this discussion, we add two very important points. The first is about the role of counselors as advocates and agents of change. Bemak and Chung (2005) lament that school counselors "similar to disenfranchised students, have been in some cases inadvertent victims of the systems in which they work, adopting values and practices conducive to bringing about categorical discrepancies in achievement" (p. 197). Indeed, there is a loud call in the profession for school counselors to take on the role of agents of change in their schools, their communities, in the lives of the children and families they serve (American School Counseling Association, 2005; Trusty & Brown, 2005). "It is critical," Bemak and Chung (2005) conclude, "for school counselors to become advocates who challenge old paradigms and power structures" (p. 197).

Second, we remind you of the very important duty we have as counselors to assure safety for all students in our schools. As we mentioned before, challenging inappropriate structures of power and privilege is an important goal for all schools to embrace, but it should never come at the expense of compromising the safety of minority and potentially marginalized students. It is the job of the adults in the school to facilitate important discussions and to provide meaningful learning experiences and it is also their responsibility to do so in a caring, respectful, thoughtful, and, especially, a safe way.

INTENTIONAL MEANING-MAKING

When we talk about the concept of *meaning-making*, we refer to an aspect of the learning where concepts and ideas are transformed into meaningful information that the learner can make sense of and then build upon, act on, or somehow become moved or changed. Piaget (1972) used the terms *assimilation* and *accommodation* in reference to how individuals make meaning or learn from new material. Assimilation involves incorporating new ideas into existing cognitive structures, and accommodation means changing those cognitive structures as a result of the new information. Learning requires a balance or, in Piaget's terms, *equilibrium*, between these processes. Vygotsky (1978) moved our understandings about cognitive development further. He emphasized the roles of language and culture in cognitive development, arguing that all cognitive functions originate in and are products of social interactions. That is, learning is not merely an active process, as Piaget explained, but it is also a social process. Explaining this social constructionist perspective, Burr (1995) says:

> It is through the daily interactions between people in the course of social life that our versions of knowledge become fabricated . . . what we regard as 'truth' . . . is a product not of objective observation of the world, but of social processes and interactions in which people are constantly engaged with each other. (p. 4)

In our notion of meaning-making, we convey a social constructionist premise about learning: Knowledge is not merely transmitted to individuals—it is constructed and re-constructed in a learning process. Learning implies an active engagement by and with the learner. When talking about group leadership, we focus on the important role of the group leader in facilitating the process of meaning-making (Wheelan, 1990). We should add, Lieberman, Yalom, and Miles (1973) argued long ago, and most group leaders still agree, that helping group members make sense of what is happening in the group as being linked to positive group outcomes. Group work affords particular opportunities for students to be engaged in meaning-making because it provides a venue for members to "negotiate and re-negotiate" meanings together (this concept of negotiating meanings together comes from Bruner, 1990, p. 67). Here we discuss how leaders can intentionally facilitate the construction of meaning by working with mental models and through spiraling.

Mental Models

Tileston (2004) highlights the ways in which learners use *mental models* for understanding new concepts and ideas. A mental model is a cognitive representation that is formed from existing information and experience and becomes a referent for thinking and reasoning. When individuals are able to link new concepts to a cache of existing knowledge or experience, understanding is facilitated. Mental models serve as a base from which meaning is constructed.

Group leaders can stimulate the use of mental models for learning new concepts in a variety of ways. While planning for groups, for example, leaders can sequence sessions according to a logical order and verbally remap that sequence at the beginning of each session, so as to help students see the connections between existing and new. Similarly, students can be asked to talk through the steps they have used to acquire a particular skill or to map the history of how they got to a particular idea. In addition, leaders can present information in a variety of ways and using visual and oral cues. Tileston's (2004) suggestion that teachers (group leaders) pause periodically and invite students to stop, think, and consider, allows students the time that they need to make these connections between new information and existing experience and knowledge. In the planning stage of the group, these interventions require that the leader select appropriate materials and that they plan an appropriate amount of time to stimulate for meaning-making in these ways.

Spiral Learning

Learning does not happen through single exposure to information; students must study new information over and over again to understand it. Bateson (1994) proposed that "lessons too complex to grasp in a single occurrence spiral past again and again, small examples gradually revealing greater and greater implications . . . Spiral learning moves through complexity with partial understanding, allowing for later returns" (pp. 30–31). So, providing students with multiple and varied exposures to information is an important way of facilitating meaning.

Learning objectives can be spiraled in group work in a variety of ways. For example, presenting information to students and then having them engage in an activity where they must apply that information, spirals students through a topic two times.

Providing progressively complex learning tasks (i.e., comprehension, application, analysis, synthesis, and evaluation) offers repeated and varied exposures to information in a planned and meaningful way. For example, after teaching a new concept, you can assign students to work together on a project that requires application of the concept. Encouraging students to discuss the topic as they are working creates additional passes through the information. Structuring these discussions by asking strategic questions stimulates critical thought and draws attention to certain aspects of the topic that are particularly worthy of consideration. Finally, asking the students to personally reflect on the material spirals them, again, through the information or topic.

Spiral learning stimulates and engages students in slightly different ways with each exposure, providing students with multiple opportunities to make meaning and learn about the material. Planning learning opportunities in these ways will stimulate complex learning, increase the likelihood that group goals and objectives will be met, and offers strong promise for the application and retention of learning. Notice how the learning tasks and processing questions in *Case Study 2.4* spiral students through the material in a way that enhances meaning-making.

CASE STUDY 2.4

Meaning-Making

Mrs. Morrissey, a middle school counselor, planned to facilitate meaning-making in her counseling group focusing on conflict mediation. During the first two group sessions on the topic, students were taught some basic communication skills and a conflict mediation process. For the next 2 weeks, students were assigned to work in small groups to draft a real life conflict scenario that they would then mediate. During the fifth and sixth weeks, students would perform their conflicts and mediations for the others. After each conflict scenario, Mrs. Morrissey intended to spiral student learning in a processing discussion facilitated by these questions:

- Why is it important to ask the protagonists (the central character) to share their opposing positions in the conflict before moving on to the brainstorming options phase of the process?
- How was it for you to use these strategies? What did and did not work? How come?
- Have you ever tried to use these strategies in real life?
- What might be/are the strengths and pitfalls when you try to use them in real world settings? How might you have to adapt them? What other skills might you need to call into play?
- What other strategies have you used to mediate conflict in the past and how have they worked?
- What is the hardest part of mediating conflict in real live situations? Can these skills help? What else will you need to be successful?

These questions, of course, had no correct answer. They were designed to provide students with a repeated exposure to the concepts and to invite them, as much as possible, to consider the ideas in juxtaposition to their own lives. The leader's expectation was that students would be engaged in the learning and more likely to use the conflict resolution steps in their own lives if they were repeatedly exposed to them and had the opportunity to practice them in the group.

Reflection Questions

1. Think about the process Mrs. Morrissey led these middle school students through, especially each enactment. If you were asked by Mrs. Morrissey to bring a real life conflict to the group for mediation—what would you select to share? Once you have picked a scenario that you would share—go through the sample of questions provided above asking yourself where your personal strengths and weaknesses lie in conflict mediation. Second, ask yourself how the strategies for personal meaning-making that Mrs. Morrissey teaches might benefit you regarding the conflict you shared.
2. Do you see challenges ahead given that each student will likely take something unique from a counseling group?
3. What would be the most difficult scenario you can imagine resulting from Mrs. Morrissey's question of these middle school students: "Can these skills work?" "Would you use these skills to mediate conflict in your personal life?"

WRITING THE PLAN

Before we get started talking about the actual writing of group plans, we offer a few guiding comments about this section. First, we introduce a goal and objective-writing process that is essentially the same for both classroom and counseling group types. While the differences between these two group types are important, these differences revolve largely around the content and direction of these two group types rather than around how goals and objectives are stated and written. Second, you may notice that we make liberal use of teacher terminology and sometimes refer to teaching practice in this discussion. While we firmly believe that there are profound differences between what school counselors and what teachers do, we also believe that the teaching profession has much to offer professional school counselors about planning for groups.

A Framework for Writing Group Plans

It makes sense to write group plans in a format that is comprehensive and that also is accessible in the moment of leading the group. School counselors are often running from one task to another, so having all the information for leading the group available and in one place is critical. Group plans also need to be simple to read. In the midst of conducting your group, you will want to have your attention on the group, not on trying to decipher the plan that you wrote in the plan.

A simple yet comprehensive group-planning format is outlined in two parts below (Figures 2.1 and 2.2). The first part is the *Unit/Overall Plan* (see Figure 2.1). This part of the plan is an outline for what will be accomplished through the group experience over the course of multiple group sessions. It does not include the specific activities that will be used each week. The second part of the plan is the *Lesson/Session Plan* (see Figure 2.2). It is an outline of each individual or weekly classroom lesson or counseling group session. So, while the Unit Plan offers a general overview of the group, the specific lessons or sessions will be outlined in the Lesson/Session Plans. These latter plans detail the specifics of what

> • Topic:
> • Grade/Class:
> • Approximate number of students:
> • Rationale (if appropriate):
> • Goals for Unit:
> • Number of Lessons in Unit:
> • Unit Assessment Plan:

FIGURE 2.1   Format for Group Plans: Unit/Overall Plan

> • Week/Session Number:
> • Grade/Class or Group Name/Topic:
> • Time:
> • Lesson/Session Objective:
> • Plan:
> • Materials:

FIGURE 2.2   Format for Group Plans: Lesson/Session Plan

will happen in each group meeting. You will notice that this format is used in the sample classroom and group plans included in Appendices A, B, and C. A sample unit and one lesson/session plan for elementary classroom and counseling groups are in Appendix A, for middle school groups are in Appendix B, and for high school groups are in Appendix C.

Remember that the Unit Plan (Figure 2.1) outlines what will occur in the group over time. It begins with general information about the group: the grade or age and number of students, topic of the group, and the rationale. It also outlines the goals, the number of lessons or sessions expected to address the topic, and a plan for how the goals will be assessed. All of this will be discussed in more detail shortly.

Each Lesson/Session Plan (Figure 2.2) outlines what will happen each week or each group session. There will be a number of lesson or session plans in each unit. The Lesson/Session Plan should include the specific objective or objectives for each session, an outline of how the objectives will be met (the implementation plan), the materials and advanced preparation that will be required, and any special considerations that are notable. Below, we discuss in more detail how to write the rationale, goals, objectives, and the plan for the assessment of the unit. While it may seem like a tremendous amount of time is required for drafting these plans, we assert that careful group planning is a key component of assuring that your group will be effective, and it is ethical group practice (see *ASGW Best Practice Guidelines* [ASGW, 2007]).

The Rationale

The group rationale simply refers to the articulated reason for the existence of the group. When the group goals fit with the curricular components of the school or district developmental school-counseling plan, this plan is typically referenced in a rationale statement. This is likely to be the case for much of the classroom group work that happens in schools. School counselors also sometimes plan their classroom and small counseling groups in line with the student competencies articulated in the *ASCA National Model* (ASCA, 2005). For example, you will notice that the classroom group plans in Appendices A–C reference a fictitious comprehensive school counseling program district plan, as well as the *ASCA National Model* (ASCA, 2005). Referencing any or all of these documents, as appropriate, strengthens program accountability. In some cases, school districts do not have specific curricular plans for the school-counseling program but they do have specific benchmarks or student competencies that are targeted. For example, a school district may establish a target benchmark of fewer than 10% unexcused absences per quarter in each school. Designing a classroom group intervention with the goal of decreasing classroom absences for a particular class with high truancy would fit within this broader district mission.

In the case of counseling groups, the rationale may be a few sentences indicating the problem that gave rise to the need for the group and an explanation of how the group is intended to address the problem. For example, a counseling group plan designed for students whose parents were divorcing included this rationale: Student's experiences of divorce are generally linked to feelings of loneliness, depression, and anxiety. For some students, these feelings interfere with their ability to complete schoolwork, get along with their peers, and benefit from the potential opportunities that exist in the school environment. This counseling group is intended to provide students with an opportunity to make meaning of their divorce experience and develop strategies for managing the stress in their lives so that they can be attentive and participatory in constructive ways at school.

Of course, some small counseling groups also address issues that are articulated in school or district curricular plans, so references to these would also be warranted. The counseling group sample unit plans in Appendices A–C include a short narrative explanation, as well as reference to particular standards. The rationale that is included in your group plan should be appropriate to the expectations of your particular school setting.

Writing the Goals and Objectives

You will want to begin the classroom and small counseling group planning process by identifying the goals for the group in the Unit Plan. Written goals should begin with students as the subject (e.g., "The students will . . ."), they should be stated in positive language since they articulate an expected accomplishment, and they should be written as a complete sentence. Consider these examples: Students will learn conflict management skills. Students will have a better understanding of the grief process. Students will identify three ways to de-escalate themselves when they are angry. Note the goal statements in the sample unit plans for the classroom and counseling group in Appendices A–C.

To enhance your ability to later determine if the goal has been met, each goal should be written in clear, observable, measurable language as much as possible. Keep in mind that when you are able to demonstrate that the goals of a group are being met, the greater support you will likely have from parents, teachers, and your administration. To determine if a goal is specific and measurable, you can ask yourself: "How will I know if this goal has been accomplished?" Be careful in your selection of the verb for each goal. For example, "Student will *recognize* . . ." is more challenging to assess than "Students will *demonstrate* . . ."

For each goal statement, a number of specific objectives should be identified. These identify the sequential learning steps that are parts of the larger unit group goal and often are the focus of each individual group session or lesson. Objectives should be written in language that is specific, measurable, realistic, and appropriate given the opportunities and constraints of the setting and resources. Just like goals, objectives should be stated in complete sentences with the students as the subject. When goals and objectives are clearly written in concrete and, if possible, behavioral terminology, it is easier to plan strategies to realize their accomplishment (Price & Nelson, 1999). The assessment plan, which we introduce in detail in Chapter 4, is also born from clearly articulated group goals and/or objectives.

As mentioned, classroom and counseling groups are sometimes planned in response to student difficulties or group problems. We realize that it can be challenging to articulate a goal or objective in positive language when we are faced with glaring problems—at those times it seems that all we can think of is what we do not want! Asking yourself, "What would the student be doing if this problem was not here?" is one way to side-step problem-saturated thinking. Also, drawing on your counselor knowledge about student development can help shift problem language into tangible or working goals for group planning. *Case Study* 2.5 illuminates how to shift into appropriate goal-setting language. In this case study, the math teacher asked the counselor for help with regard to a particular issue in her class. While the teacher was able to identify a legitimate concern, translating it into a desired outcome accomplishment (i.e., a goal) was a bit challenging. The counselor needed to know what the teacher hoped she would accomplish in the group before she could actually plan the intervention. In this case, the counselor's knowledge about the learning process and about anxiety helped her develop an appropriate goal statement and also helped her identify the smaller group objectives that would be used towards accomplishing the goal.

CASE STUDY 2.5

Writing Group Goals and Objectives

A math teacher in a middle school asked the school counselor to work with her students because they were "very anxious" about their upcoming final exams. When the counselor asked what the teacher hoped would be accomplished in the classroom group, the teacher said, "Could you help make them be less anxious?"

The counselor wanted to have a sense of what the students would be doing or experiencing if they were not anxious during the test. She wanted to know what "less anxious" looked like. When she asked the teacher clarifying questions, the teacher expressed that the students would be able to do better on the test if they could focus on the test rather than on their anxiety about it.

Drawing from this and her own knowledge in the area of academic skills, the counselor developed a classroom group goal that the students would acquire test-taking skills. This goal was broken down in to these three smaller objectives: learning self-calming strategies, learning multiple-choice test response strategies, and learning proper study habits. They were written as follows:

> *Goal:* Students will acquire test-taking skills.
> > *Objective 1:* Students will learn and use self-calming strategies when they are anxious.

Objective 2: Students will learn and apply multiple-choice test response strategies.

Objective 3: Students will develop and demonstrate helpful study habits.

Plans were developed for this classroom group so that each objective was addressed as a separate group session and the group ran for three sequential weeks for 30 of the 90 minutes in the classroom math block.

Reflection Questions

1. Given the math teacher's request for the counselor to assist these math students decrease their anxiety, do you feel that the goal the counselor established is acceptable? Do you see how the school counselor both clarified and made her objectives measurable for the group?

2. When you read this case carefully, you will note that the counselor took the math teacher's lead an agreed to support all students in this class not only the anxious ones. Discuss how the use of group work uniquely makes this possible, and consequently what an individualized response might have engendered in this particular response.

It is also important to write goals and objectives that are realistic and attainable. Ask yourself, "Is this goal/objective realistic for these students, given their developmental level and the time and resource limitations?" In reference back to Case Study 2.5, a school counseling intervention geared towards the goal of, say, helping "all of the students pass their math exams at a 90% level or higher," is an admirable goal, but probably not realistic for many classes. More importantly to this discussion, we point out that this goal is inappropriate because it is not within the expertise area of the school counselor to prepare the students to pass a math exam. A goal more related to math anxiety, however, is more within the realm of what school counselors are trained to do. Therefore, it is important to articulate goals and objectives that can be reasonably accomplished and that are appropriate to the training and role of the school counselor. Goals and objectives must accurately reflect what you realistically and ethically are able to do in the group (see *Ethical Standards for School Counselors* [ASCA, 2004] A.1.b & 3.a).

Finally, we advocate for goal and objective statements to be written in generic and "materials free" language. This is not to say that the lesson plan should not include the names of the specific materials that will be used, but we emphasize that *the goals and objectives should be stated materials-free*. The reason for this is so that the leader can understand what the student is expected to learn without having to track down specific materials. For example, a goal (or objective) that students will complete the *Best-Ever Career Interest Inventory* does not clearly articulate the more accurate desired goal of students developing a list of current, personal career interests. Even if the *Best-Ever Career Interest Inventory* will be used to achieve this goal of awareness around career interests, it is best considered as a means towards a goal, but not the goal itself. Having said this, you should include the names (and locations) of all materials that will be used in the weekly plan for the group in the implementation part of the plan, but this will be addressed later. You will notice reference to specific materials in sample group plans in Appendices A–C.

CHAPTER 3

Planning for Implementation

Thus far, our discussion has been on planning group content. That is, our focus has been on how to plan groups so that they are conducted according to a sound rationale and specific goals and objectives. In this chapter, we discuss planning for how the group will be managed so that those intended goals and objectives will be realized. More specifically, the implementation plan refers to the details of what you will do in the group each week, lesson, or session. This corresponds to the sample classroom group lesson plans and counseling group session plans for the elementary, middle, and high school groups in Appendices A, B, and C.

You will notice that the level of detail in the implementation plans varies widely among the sample plans found in Appendices A, B, and C. This is intentional on our part. We want to communicate that there is considerable room for variability in how group implementation plans are written. A number of variables should be considered in determining how much detail really is needed in the implementation plan. First is group leader style. While some leaders like to write down what exactly they should say at various places in the group session, others may prefer to just note the topic, general theme, or to include a prompt for what to say. Second, the topic of the group will determine the level of detail needed in the implementation plan. It is probably a good idea to use a good bit of detail when planning for the delivery of complex content and topics that are less familiar to you. More familiar or easy content may not require such detail. Third, if you are planning well in advance of when you will be conducting the group, a greater level of detail might be a good idea to help you remember your intentions when you finally implement the group plan. Fourth, the level of detail needed in the implementation plan also depends on the level of structure needed in the group. In general, we recommend using a fairly high degree of detail in the implementation plan when working with younger children and when working in a group of students with whom you are not familiar. We also recommend including more details in plans for groups with students who have difficulties regulating themselves, and when there are complicated group dynamics that interfere with the ability of some individuals or some groups to function together towards intended learning goals. This higher level of detail will help you keep on track when there are distractions and when you'll need to attend more carefully to group management.

Having clearly positioned ourselves as advocates for careful group planning, we also caution that working well in groups, especially groups with students, requires flexibility and willingness to change and adapt along with the needs and circumstances of the group. Implementation plans are only useful as guidelines; when they are used as law, the group can become more about the counselor's ideas and her need for conformity than about the member's experience. This can be a dangerous formula for disaster. There is great power and value in following the path the students chart rather than steering them back to where you wanted them to be. This concept is delicate, of course, as we would hate for the reader to misinterpret this to mean that a school counselor should stray with every distraction in the group. Know where you are going (i.e., the plan) but do not allow the plan to cause you to lose other spontaneous and equally important opportunities for students' growth. We will return again to this discussion on spontaneity in Chapter 6.

WRITING THE IMPLEMENTATION PLAN

We recommend using a sequential approach to writing the implementation plan, beginning with an introduction to the topic. You can write out the specific words you will use to introduce the session or just note the themes or relevant prompts. We suggest that your plan also include a learning map and strategies to immediately inspire student interest and participation (these ideas are discussed in more detail in Chapter 6, as part of the discussion about leading the group).

After the introduction, the plan should include a description of the group tasks, process, activities, or exercises that will be used to address the learning objectives in each session. They should be arranged sequentially according to how they will be introduced in the group. We recommend planning to use a variety of learning tasks and processes when working with children and young teens, and also with large groups. This is because varying the ways in which students are engaged in the group is a good antidote to distractibility. Here again, the level of detail needed in the implementation plan around activities will vary from plan to plan and from leader to leader. Some leaders prefer to write out the step-by-step instructions, whereas others find a more minimal approach more desirable. In cases where more minimal notes are preferred, we suggest that the plan at least include the name of a material that will be used, as well as a note regarding the relevant themes that are addressed through the use of the activity. If you are using a particular section of a popular film, video, or book, the intervention plan should indicate the name of the film to be used, where it is located (e.g., X film is in the school library), the specific cue spot in the film (e.g., 34 minutes from start at the beginning of the scene X), and how long the clip should be played. Finally, you may also want to articulate the amount of time that should be used in the group for the activity, as well how much time will be used for processing the activity (to facilitate meaning-making). The specific processing questions or discussion points that will be used should also be outlined in the implementation plan, even if the activity itself did not require much detailed explanation. This is particularly important for groups where there is some reluctance for members to speak out. A more thorough discussion on processing group activities is included later in this chapter.

Finally, the implementation plan should also make mention of the ways in which you will close the group each session. While undue attention need not be drawn to the final moments of the group, it is important to spend at least 5 minutes in the group summarizing the learning that has occurred. Inviting students to think about what they have learned at the end of each group session stimulates student thought processes for integrating the learning and is also useful as a tool for assessing the extent to which students reached the intended session objectives. Much can be lost in terms of meaning-making if you run out of time and do not give this part of the process adequate attention. Some group leaders prefer to ritualize closings—rounds are particularly good for this task—so that students are clear about the expectations around this part of the group. When the time does not allow for extensive student input at the end of the group, you can offer a summary of what happened, linking what has happened to the intended learning objectives for the session. Either way, the implementation plan should outline the closure process that will be used.

USING ACTIVITIES IN GROUPS

Well-selected activities can promote learning in a nonthreatening way and they often stimulate motivation and engagement among students (Gladding, 2003). Activities also provide opportunities for assessing members in action with each other, they tend to increase the comfort level, and activities can set a tone of having fun in the group (Jacobs, Mason, & Harvill, 2005; Kees & Jacobs, 1990). However, it is important to emphasize that school counselors must not assume that just reading a story to students or engaging a group of students in a fun activity promotes learning and change. Group activities need to be carefully selected and facilitated in a way that promotes the intended goals and objectives of the group. In this section, we will discuss the selection of group activities, the important work of processing group activities so that meaning-making is enhanced, and the timing of when and how to use activities.

Activity Selection

A wide variety of activities can be used in classroom and counseling groups with children and adolescents. For example, Gladding (2003) recommends using puppets, music, and artistic activities to promote self-understanding and to help children understand others. Kees and Jacobs (1990) and Smead (1995) recommend using written exercises (e.g., sentence completions, journals, listings), movement exercises (e.g., family/classroom sculpting, trust exercises, relaxation training, high-low level adventure-based activities, dance), arts and crafts activities (e.g., drawings, collages, clay sculpting), readings (e.g., read by leader/read by members), music, fantasy exercises and guided imagery exercises, group decision-making, consensus exercises or challenges, and rounds in groups with people of all ages.

What makes a particular activity appropriate for a particular group is the match between the activity, the goals and objectives of the group, and the particular make-up of the group. This requires general knowledge of developmental milestones or expectations for students of various ages. It also requires particular attention to the cognitive, language, and social abilities of the group members, as well as the cultural understandings and experiences of the students and the community in which they belong. For example, a school counselor we know was once besieged by disgruntled parents when he led a middle school classroom group through a guided imagery—a few parents initially interpreted the activity as some form of hypnosis. Although this was an innocent misunderstanding, the principal of the school was not amused by the "miscommunication." Being clear about the goals for the group, particularly with regard to the level (i.e., Bloom's Taxonomy [Bloom, 1956]) and type of learning (i.e., cognitive, affective, behavioral) that is intended, can guide activity selection. We recommend asking yourself these questions to assess the appropriateness of a particularly activity, exercise, or discussion for a particular group:

1. What is the purpose (i.e., the objective) of this group session?
2. What level of learning (i.e., Bloom's Taxonomy) do I want the students to achieve?
3. What kinds of learning activities have I used in the past? How have the students responded to those activities? How does this activity fit with those that I have used in the past/plan to use in the future?
4. What kinds of discussions and activities are engaging for students this age? What activities would be embarrassing, too risky, or too boring for these students?
5. How much time do I need for this discussion/activity and how much time do I have in the group?

In order to be sure that the materials and activities you are intending to use in the group are appropriate, you should become very familiar with how they work *before* introducing them. That is, it is critical that you read the books, play the games, and preview all DVDs or videos in advance of using them in the group. Also, do not forget to assure that they are available (along with projection equipment) on the day you want to use them. Finally, we want to point out that it is very important for you to be careful to select and facilitate activities that are within your own experience and ability level. Do not lead group exercises that you are not trained or experienced in leading or that require more supervision or skilled facilitation than you can provide in the school setting.

Making Activities Meaningful

It is crucial to keep in mind that planned group activities are a *means* for addressing a particular goal or objective, they are not the goal or objective. So, while activities may make groups fun, they are used in groups in order to advance intended learning goals and objectives. A critical component of teaching centers on helping students acquire a conceptual understanding of the material presented (Bloom, 1956; Tileson, 2004). Here, again, we are referring to the process of meaning-making, which happens throughout (before, during, and/or after) the activity. Group leaders and researchers, Lieberman, Yalom, and Miles (1973), use the term *meaning attribution* in reference to ways in which group leaders help group members make meaning from what is happening in the group. They emphasize the group leader's task of facilitating the group process so that group members are engaged in making meaning from what is happening in the group. We have already discussed (in Chapter 2) ways in which meaning-making is facilitated through careful group planning. Here we emphasize that meaning-making must accompany group activities and exercises, and that the implementation plan is where meaning-making efforts will be documented.

Meaning-making notations should indicate how students will make connections between their experience in the activity and the intended learning objective. This is most effectively done through a series of processing questions, which will be discussed shortly. Below are Luckner and Nadler's (1997) suggestions for ways in which group leaders can facilitate meaning-making discussions (ways to process activities) in the group.

- *Framing*   Providing information prior to the activity to help participants be aware of what is to come and to provoke anticipatory thought. Also, framing may include contracting within the group or establishing individual contracts.
- *Large Group Discussion*   This may occur in an open forum, through asking questions such as the processing questions mentioned below, and by using rounds.
- *Journal Writing and Written Activity Sheets*   This type of processing promotes personal rather than public exploration. However, Luckner and Nadler suggest that the expectation be set that individuals will be asked to share some of their personal reflections with others as well.
- *Dyads or Small Groups*   Inviting students to discuss an activity in twos or in small groups promotes interpersonal interaction and may be less threatening and less time consuming than processing in the larger group.
- *Isolation*   Providing time for group members to have a chance to think for themselves can be very helpful, especially if the group activity or exercise was very intense. Individuals can be invited to think, journal, or even use drawings to process or reflect individually on their experiences. Sometimes it is helpful to pair individual thinking time with another format of group sharing so that individuals are also encouraged to share their experiences and learn from each other.
- *Videotaping*   Producing a video recording of a particular learning or group experience offers a creative format for processing a group activity.
- *Process Observers*   Inviting an individual to observe the group activity and comment on his or her observations is a powerful tool for stimulating meaning-making and reflective discussions.

Processing Questions

Processing questions—questions that are designed to encourage group members to reflect, analyze, and discuss their experience in a particular activity (Kees & Jacob, 1990; Luckner & Nadler, 1997; Smead, 1995)—are often used in groups to scaffold meaning-making and to help students make connections between activities and learning goals and objectives. Processing questions facilitate the transfer of learning from experiences in the group to outside applications or situations, and they help provide closure after a group exercise or activity (Kees & Jacobs, 1990). Group activities can be processed in a variety of ways, but Smead suggests that the focus of processing discussions be in these four areas: intrapersonal learning (i.e., an examination of the individual member's experience), interpersonal experience (i.e., what happened between members of the group), new thoughts or learning (i.e., a focus on what was learned in the group), and application (i.e., a focus on how the new information or knowledge will be used).

As mentioned earlier, the specific questions that you will use in the group to process the activities or learning should be clearly outlined in the implementation plan. You will notice this is the case in the classroom and counseling group lesson/session plans in Appendix A, and in the classroom plan in Appendix B. We recommend using this structure provided by Kees and Jacobs (1990) for processing group activities:

1. *Process the Exercise Itself*   Ask members to discuss what happened in the exercise/activity.
2. *Reflect on Member's Experience*   Ask members to share their reactions to the exercise.
3. *Reflect on How the Experience Affects Group Process*   Ask members to reflect on how the group worked in the experience. Prompts may include: "How did all of us interact during the exercise?" "What did you learn about someone else in the class during the exercise?"
4. *Move to a More Personal Level of Processing*   Ask members what they personally felt/learned/experienced by participating in the exercise. Prompts may include: "What did you notice/learn about yourself as a result of this experience?" "What has this activity caused you to be more aware of now?"
5. *Transfer of Learning*   Ask members to think about how their experience in the exercise relates to other aspects of their life. Prompts may include: "What are you taking from this exercise about working with others (for example) to the playground with you when you leave here?" "What are you willing to work on this week with regard to what you have learned today in here?"

Timing the Delivery of Activities

Equally important to the selection of activities is the timing of their introduction. Some group activities build on concepts learned in earlier group sessions, whereas others serve as an introduction to a particular concept or learning focus. Therefore, it is important to consider how particular activities fit together and how they are paced in the overall unit plan.

The level of risk required for participation in a particular activity is an important consideration when planning activities, particularly in larger classroom groups and when working with children and adolescents. While some activities are excellent for fostering group cohesiveness and trust, others require trust and cohesiveness for them to work well in the group. We encourage group leaders to consider their ethical obligations in selecting and implementing activities with their groups in both counseling and classrooms. Risk is individually defined by members in groups; it is imperative that counselors realize that although an activity may appear emotionally safe (and, of course, physically safe), circumstances such a personal history or social capital can affect a student's sense of vulnerability in the group and thus, the student's ability to participate in the group activity. For example, Shelia, a ninth-grade student participating in a Student Leadership Summer Academy that was designed by the administration and the counseling department, had what some might refer to as a panic attack during an activity. She was participating in a trust walk with a peer when she, as the blindfolded partner, began to scream and tear at the blindfold, and then ran from her partner frantically. Even though Shelia had consented to participate in the activity and even though she was a superb young student leader, something about the activity triggered an unexpected abreaction. Once the school counselor and a wonderful ninth-grade peer in the group managed to calm Sheila down, she was able to recover from the panic attack and get back with the group. Shelia agreed to spend some time with the counselor afterward and to talk with her parents about her experience. The outcome was beneficial, but our purpose here is to insist that contingencies be made for such unexpected events, that alternatives always be presented to student participants in any activity, and that school counselors ensure that sufficient resources (in this case other professionals) be available (for more on issues related to student safety, see the *Ethical Standards for School Counselors*, [ASCA, 2004]).

Another challenging aspect of planning activities is being able to accurately predict how long a particular activity will take. When activities are extremely engaging or when they require careful attention or management, it can be easy to lose track of the time. When this happens, the intended learning from the activity is easily lost in the scramble to rush through the ending or wrap-up quickly. Rushing through an activity so that it can be completed in a short amount of time may render the activity ineffective, so be sure that you have enough time in the group to use the activity appropriately. Of course, this means having enough time to process the group activity as well. As mentioned, writing in the implementation plan the expected time you will need for each activity, as well as how much time you will allot for its processing, will help you keep the group on task. While some group leaders indicate the number of minutes should be used for the activity, others prefer to indicate the actual clock time to begin each section of the plan. In some cases, you may need to negotiate for more time for a particular group session if the activity warrants additional time. Alternatively, you may need to consider dividing the activity into two group sessions if extra time is needed. Some counselors have been able to work with classroom teachers to integrate their learning objectives into some of the activities or lessons that are being used by the teacher, thus having more time for some of the longer activities. This scenario is exemplified in Case Study 6.12 later in this text.

PLANNING FOR DEVELOPMENTAL, GRADE-RELATED, AND SPECIAL NEEDS

As we noted in Chapters 1 and 2, school counselors must be knowledgeable about the developmental readiness of students in both classroom and counseling groups. As an illustration, allow us to draw a parallel between leading groups and teaching math. A competent classroom teacher will recognize that within a classroom there will be those students for whom the material, say learning their multiplication facts, will be accomplished quickly and often seeming effortlessly. Others will inevitably take much longer to accomplish the same task—and with great struggle. This range, although well within the developmental range of "normal," can produce numerous effects. For example, students who wiz through memorization of multiplication tables may chastise students who "hold the class up," while students who struggle may find inappropriate humor or oppositional behaviors preferable to "looking slow" in the eyes of their peers. The consequences of these variations are obvious. The teacher must be vigilant and responsive to the wide range of abilities, achievements, and behaviors in order to best meet the needs of everyone in the classroom. This is true for the school counselor as well; we must develop a keen awareness of the range of students within the group, and the implementation plan must be responsive to the unique make up of each specific group.

One of the most difficult aspects of planning for groups is to determine what "the most appropriate" instruction is. This is particularly true for planning classroom groups, where there is likely more variation in the membership than in counseling groups. The curricular content and the instructional practices that are used in the group should be designed to ensure that all students are meaningfully engaged at an appropriate level of difficulty and in ways that relate to their own lives or lived experiences. This includes assuring that the content is inclusive with respect to the various cultures represented in the group and that instruction is in line with the cognitive and developmental needs of the students. Intuitively, most would concur that schools in the United States are quite diverse with regard to ability, achievement, race, ethnicity, social class, and developmental/life experiences. So, planning needs to be appropriate for and attentive to a diverse student body; it must provide windows and mirrors for all students in the group. As mentioned before, it is never appropriate, even in seemingly heterogeneous groups, to assume that diversity does not matter. The heterogeneity of the group of students in counseling and classroom groups should never be ignored.

When school counselor-to-student ratios are ideal, we like to believe that the counselor will have the opportunity to know his or her students—in terms of abilities and achievements. However, when school counselors contend with outrageously high numbers of students on their rosters, it is appropriate to consult with the students' teachers in order to acquire an understanding of various experiences, abilities, and achievements of the students who will be in the groups. We also recommend that you use your community and school resources to become familiar with the cultures that are represented in the student body of your school. One might ask why this is important. The answer is compelling: School counselors have to take into consideration who is present in the group and what will maximize every child's experience as they participate in the group. Remember, the school counselor's clientele is every student in the school.

Along with within-classroom differences, there often are enormous between-classroom differences across seemingly similar groups of students. A classroom group lesson that works masterfully in one second-grade classroom may bomb in another right across the hall. School counselors must develop flexibility and quick decision-making as a part of their group skills. When we were practicing school counselors, we both went into all of our classroom groups with a contingency plan—what we would consider trying if it was obvious that what we had planned was failing. We encourage you to always have a Plan B in writing for every group you run (notice the contingency planning in the Middle Level Counseling Group Session Plan in Appendix B).

Such advanced planning and flexibility is required as events inevitably arise that will thwart the direction of the group and your anticipation of what you expected to accomplish during that specific session. It is our position that working in groups always requires a precarious balance between staying with the session objective and moving in a direction that one or more members needs to move. Key here, for both classroom and counseling groups, is acknowledging that groups of all kinds are dynamic. We must recognize as naïve the thought that we, as leaders, have full control over what transpires within our groups.

Allow us now to briefly discuss an often overlooked but important topic for school counselors: working effectively with children with special needs in classroom and counseling groups. Although we are confident that children with special needs frequently benefit from individual interaction with school counselors, we fear that groups, even diversely heterogeneous groups, sometimes underserve children with special needs. School counselors should embrace the rich opportunities that participation in groups can afford children with cognitive, physical, and emotional/psychological needs and also notice that inclusion of children with special needs provides rich opportunities for other students in the group. However, adequate inclusion does not happen without careful planning.

Key to fully welcoming students with special needs into classroom or counseling groups is ensuring that accommodations are made so that these students will have the best opportunity to benefit from the group experience. All too often, we have seen children with special needs present but unnoticed in classrooms. At the risk of oversimplification, we urge counselors to begin by noticing differences. As we advocate throughout this text, often utilizing the metaphor of windows and mirrors, recognizing the unique contribution of a full-range of student abilities—cognitive, physical, and emotional—affords the potential for true value-added experiences in groups. For this to happen, school counselors should be adequately informed about the special needs, as well as the learning styles and strengths that these students will bring to the group. Fortunately, many students with special needs have carefully articulated assessment results and learning plans that are available to help determine the best way to engage, support, and challenge them in the classroom and group environments. These documents should be reviewed by the counselor when she is planning the group.

ACCOMMODATING GROUP STAGES

Awareness that groups progress through observable stages or phases is helpful in developing goals, objectives, and in planning assessments. The work of Tuckman (1965), Gazda (1989), Gladding (2003), Corey (2007), Trotzer (1999), and Yalom (2005)—all afford group counselors with a variety of stage models. We believe that these models provide a valuable framework for anticipating how groups develop over time and should be considered when constructing group lesson or session plans.

Group stage theories can help with the sequencing of weekly plans. The juxtaposition of stage models to group planning allows you to consider the group dynamics that are typically associated with various stages or phases of the group development in your plans for the group each week. For example, it is wise to ask yourself what tasks of *forming* or *exploring* will need to be met in the plans for the early sessions. Later, you will want to enact the kinds of plans that will help students work through the theoretical *storming* process. Such attention benefits the group members as learners in both classroom and counseling groups.

Stage models also can help with anticipating group member responses and potential challenges that may arise. For example, stage models help you anticipate that members may be reluctant to speak out in earlier sessions, particularly when the topic is uncomfortable for them. Planning for early group sessions must take this level of discomfort into consideration. Stage theory helps us understand that in later group sessions, conflict among group members may be an indication that they are engaged in the material and willing to take risks and try new things. This knowledge can help us avoid scapegoating one member of the group as the instigator for the conflict in the group.

In summary, keen understanding and careful planning requires sequencing of content overlaid on the stages of predictable group development. These two mutually supportive concepts are imperative for the successful planning and leading of groups in school.

DIFFERENCES BETWEEN CLASSROOM AND COUNSELING IMPLEMENTATION PLANS

It is easy to see that classroom groups necessitate a different kind of planning than counseling groups. These differences are in both the content of the group, as well as in the ways in which the group will be managed (i.e., the implementation plan). However, you cannot assume that all classroom groups should be planned and managed in one way and that counseling group plans are qualitatively different. Plans need to be responsive to the particularities of the group—the membership (ages as well as personalities), topic, goals, and size. These can vary even within each group type.

The major difference in classroom and counseling group planning has to do with the issue of *structure*. School counselors sometimes tend to ascribe a great deal of content, try to address multiple outcomes, and are very structured in how students will engage with each other, the leader, and the content, in classroom groups. On the other hand, plans for counseling groups sometimes tend to be rather sparse when it comes to content, intended outcomes, and plans for engaging students with each other and around the topic. It may be that school counselors are wary of interfering too much with structure or direction in the process of leading smaller counseling groups and that they overly structure classroom groups in fear that the larger numbers of students in these groups require a higher level of regulation. Interestingly, process sometimes seems to hold some great magic in counseling groups and it is often overlooked as an important learning and management tool in the larger classroom groups. Our position is that both group types must have sufficient structure, that structure includes attending to group content as well as group process, and the degree to which structure is needed in a particular group depends on multiple group variables—not just group type.

In both counseling and classroom groups, students need to be clear about the expectations for the group and the group needs to be facilitated in a way that allows students to fully participate and have the opportunity to meet the intended goals. It is up to the leader to structure the group towards these ends. Sometimes, this means that students need explicit instruction, they need to be engaged in planned activities followed by specific processing questions, and that norms around participation need to be shaped carefully by group rules. In other groups, the goals and objectives might be better addressed by offering a more open structure where students are invited to participate in a discussion around a topic without being asked to participate in a specific activity or exercise. In these latter groups, the leader may attempt to make her presence much less visible, structuring the group so that the students are engaged with each other (and not so much the leader) around the topic or material. Again, we suggest that all of these plans around structure be based on the content and the membership of the group, rather than the specific group type (i.e., classroom or counseling group). Simply put: Some groups need more structure than others.

Allow us to add a final important point here: Plans are not prisons. As we stated earlier, we do not advocate that you adhere so austerely to your plans so as to rob students of the spontaneity that can flourish in classrooms and counseling groups. While thoughtful planning allows counselors to facilitate the overall direction of the group (toward the desired outcome), it is the creativity of the group leader and the student members that provide serendipity. We would be naïve to believe that only one road leads to a desired end point. *Case Study 3.6* offers two examples of the importance of being flexible in groups.

CASE STUDY 3.6

Flexibility in Planning

Consider these two case studies regarding flexibility within well-designed plans. The first brings to life a classroom group in the middle school and the second is about an elementary school counseling group.

Middle School Classroom Group

In a sixth-grade classroom group, the lesson focused on addressing diversity issues as part of a planned character curriculum in the middle school. As the students were working cooperatively but with low-energy on a well-planned exercise about quality characteristics, one student raised concerns about what role quality characteristics played in the upcoming student government elections. What if the current slate of nominees for class officers—this annual election was taken very seriously by many of the middle school students—had someone who "doesn't have very good quality character"? The student, careful not to name-names, quickly added, "What if we knew something about one of the candidates for eighth-grade president that isn't so good?"

With this question, the counselor allowed the lesson to take a new direction and take on new life. Students suddenly seemed to be passionate and energetic, so the school counselor who was leading the group activity chose to veer purposely from her intended lesson toward this new, spontaneous and exciting example of quality characteristics. The students were willing to make the discussion hypothetical to avoid talking about someone who was not present in the group—a norm agreed upon earlier. Notice, however, that the lesson's overarching objective—to generate examples of quality character—was not abandoned. It was simply attained by following a theme that better captivated the students' attention. The end result was a most successful lesson—one reached by being flexible yet adhering to the lesson's objectives and goal.

Elementary School Counseling Group

A counseling group had met for approximately 4 sessions with a group goal around physical fitness. Most of these fourth and fifth graders had poor performance evaluations in Physical Education for a wide variety of reasons. The specific objective for this particular group session was to build a list of physical activities as alternatives to inactivity—it was called "The To Do List."

At the beginning of the lesson, one student seemed to be the brunt of others' giggles and subtle mocking about how she had outgrown the clothes she was wearing that day. Although the counselor loved the lesson they had planned for the day (a counselor and an intern were co-leading the group), it was obvious that their plan was better postponed and the issues real and in-the-moment should take the stage. The To Do List was pushed aside as the subject of the taunts gave voice to something most if not all members had experienced first-hand. Consequently, the discussion was rich and beneficial. The original group goal was kept in sight, but the ways in which the group would reach it proved to be flexible and beneficial.

Reflection Questions

1. Did it seem like a good idea to you to postpone the plans in the middle school group rather than proceed with the activity planned for the group that day?
2. What is the risk of not addressing the issue that came up in the elementary school group? What, specifically, might you say in the group if you were the leader to address this situation and focus the group on attending to this important issue in the group?

REMEMBERING WINDOWS AND MIRRORS

In Chapters 1 and 2, we forcefully argue for the importance of planning groups so that they provide opportunities for students to see a world of experiences that are new and to help students make meaning from those new perspectives—windows, and also to plan for group opportunities for students to see their own experiences and beliefs valued and respected—mirrors. As mentioned, written goals and objectives help assure that a particular focus will be addressed in the group, while the intervention plan describes how.

Case Study 2.3 in Chapter 2 offered a glimpse into how one school counselor was able to incorporate window and mirror experiences into her fifth-grade classroom group. Here we add to this discussion by emphasizing that even when the focus of the group is not explicitly related to diversity issues, the importance of providing windows and mirrors remains. For example, in a stress management group, multiple ways of experiencing and managing stress may window new possibilities or mirror the lived experiences of some students in the group. College preparation panels that include members of diverse racial, social, and other potentially marginalized groups provide opportunities for windows and mirrors for students in groups that are traditionally not represented in those forums. School counselors should always be aware of which windows and mirrors are being offered in the group experiences they have planned and which ones remain closed or obscured.

ATTENDING TO PHYSICAL SPACE

Plans for groups in schools must take into consideration the physical space of the room that will be used for the group. This is particularly important as many school counselors are faced with the challenge of conducting classroom groups in other teacher's classrooms or sharing a group room with another professional in the school. Variables to consider when planning an appropriate space for your group work include insuring that students will be relatively comfortable in the room (e.g., they are not hungry, not cold, familiar with the materials around the room), students can adequately see you and each other (as appropriate) when they are in the group, the room is relatively free of distractions, and you also will want to be sure that there is enough space in the room for the kind of activities that you have planned.

Planning how the physical space will be used in the group also means being sure that the activities that you have planned for the group are appropriate for the setting in which you will be working. Remember that some activities have the potential to be noisy or otherwise distracting to the classrooms nearby. Unique physical space needs may require creative group planning efforts, including seeking out alternative settings when necessary. Sometimes counselors choose to work outdoors when they are using activities that require a lot of space or that make a lot of noise. If that is the case, you will want to be sure that the outdoor space is really available and not disruptive to others in the building, and you will also want to be sure to follow school policies for taking students out of the building. Also, if you are planning to work outdoors or in any other space that is not your own regular work space for the group, you will probably want to be sure that you have a "rainy day" plan for your group in case circumstances change.

Of course, when you conduct classroom group lessons in someone else's space, it is important to respect your guest status in that room. Being a guest requires you to be vigilant that the room is clean and in order at the end of the group, that others' belongings are not disrupted, and that you give the room back promptly at the end of your allotted time. Following these simple guest rules will go a long way towards fostering collaborative relationships between you and the others who teach the students in your group.

KEEPING IMPLEMENTATION ETHICAL

We close this chapter drawing your attention to a very important aspect of group leadership: ethics. When a school counselor is working with a group (as compared to when he or she is working with an individual student), she or he must consider how the process, as well as the content, will affect everyone in the room. This requires strong understanding of the student members who are in the group. For example, a school counselor wished to videotape a classroom lesson (as he had done previously), so he might gain feedback on the lesson from fellow counselors with whom he met once a month for peer supervision. The videotaping of students in learning situations is approved for academic purposes (i.e., teacher evaluation, student assessment) in this counselor's school district with the caveat that parents/guardians must be notified beforehand. In order to videotape this particular classroom lesson, he sent a notification home. One parent, for undisclosed reasons, asked that her daughter not be videotaped under any circumstances. Although the school counselor believed it would be easy to simply excuse the child from this particular lesson, he spoke with the building principal who asked that he instead pick another class to record rather than excusing this individual from the class for this 30 minute lesson. The building principal's decision was a surprise to the counselor, but her respect of the parent's wishes gave a very important directive to the counselor. This exemplifies the importance of ensuring proper clearance, proper notification, and keeping key individuals "in the loop." In this case, without careful regard to the school policies, the outcome could have been very unpleasant. Examples like this one should be used to encourage school counselors to advocate for counselor-friendly school policies, as well as clarity around school counseling's code of ethics.

As was mentioned earlier in this chapter, our intent may be innocent (e.g., recall the school counselor who used guided imagery) but without caution and prudent education of everyone involved, intent matters little. We highly recommend that counselors keep careful watch of the professional literature and position statements from local, state, and national professional organizations that support the wide-range of processes appropriate for use by school counselors in striving to attain the goals and objectives of the groups they lead.

We want to reiterate the point made earlier that it is the school counselor's ethical obligation to uphold the privacy and the confidentiality of the students and families with whom we work, as appropriate, within our capacity as ethical school counseling professionals (for definitive direction on confidentiality, see *ACA Code of Ethics and Standards of Practice* [ACA, 2005]; *Ethical Standards for School Counselors* [ASCA, 2004]; and *ASGW Best Practice Guidelines* [ASGW, 2007]). We remind school counselors to ensure confidentiality around all that is discussed in small counseling groups (except, of course, around issues of duty to warn). Because confidentiality is more easily compromised in larger classroom groups, it is the counselor's responsibility to assure that students set appropriate boundaries around the content of their sharing, so that they are not disclosing information that is not appropriate for the group. Classrooms are not confidential. More clearly to the point: Your intentions to invite students to personally share in the group must also include appropriate protection for that sharing. Also, remember that minor children (with whom we work as school counselors) cannot grant legal consent, so we must make every effort to keep perfectly clear the policies within school districts regarding informing parents and guardians about the activities of the school counselor.

CHAPTER **4**

Designing Assessments

Assessing whether the intended goals and/or objectives for the group have been met is a critical component of the group planning process. This is aligned with current practice in the field of counseling, which emphasizes the importance of using data-driven assessment measures to evaluate learning or client change and also advocates for the use of assessment for assuring school counseling program accountability (Cobia & Henderson, 2007; Corey & Corey, 2006; Gladding, 2003; Johnson, Johnson, & Downs, 2006; Sexton, Whiston, Bleuer, & Walz, 1997; Whiston, 2007; Whiston & Sexton, 1998). Counseling group outcome data can be used to provide clinical information regarding specific students, identify the effectiveness of particular interventions, and determine areas of needed change (Cobia & Henderson, 2007; Whiston, 2007). More broadly, in the area of accountability, group assessment measures can direct school counseling program goals and objectives, help engage school personnel in decision-making, expose access and equity issues, and it can help provide input for decisions regarding how to direct limited resources to needed areas (Cobia & Henderson, 2007; Whiston, 2007).

Focusing here on assessing the work that happens in classroom and counseling groups, it should be clear that having well articulated outcome expectations that are linked to specific assessment measures provides valuable formative and summative feedback about the group. Feedback from assessment helps the leader determine whether the goals and objectives were appropriate and attainable, whether group was the best mode of intervention for all of the individuals in that group, and whether the pace of the group was effective in meeting the intended learning goals and objectives. If the specific goals for the group have been accomplished, you can move ahead with new material. If through assessment you find that a goal has not been met, however, you may need to review a particular content area again or devise new strategies for accomplishing the intended learning. None of this can happen without an assessment plan. For example, when Mr. Ellis decided to compose a counseling group to address the shared struggle several sixth-, seventh-, and eighth-grade students appeared to be having with issues related to weekend visits to their non-custodial parents' homes, he designed the group to address these goals: (a) members will have strategies to lessen the effects of stress that builds prior to their leaving; (b) members will have strategies to smooth their adjustment back home; and (c) members will be able to share (articulate) with others those stresses they associate with out-of-town parent visits. Several outcome measures were designed so that the students could rate their progress in attaining these three goals. One measure was a self-report scaling question following each session designed to determine how well the group helped students attain each goal. That formative feedback from this assessment was largely very positive and Mr. Ellis was pleased and certain that he would run this type of group again. At the end of the group in a summative evaluation, he asked the students if they could suggest that anything be done differently in the group and if so, what. Unanimously, every member suggested that the groups be segregated by grade (i.e., a separate group for sixth, seventh or eighth graders)—because, generally, the stresses were very different for members in each grade. Not until the summative feedback did Mr. Ellis learn that the group was a wonderful success—but it could be better. In future groups, he would implement the suggestions for single grade membership in these groups.

TYPES OF OUTCOME ASSESSMENT MEASURES

We suggest that assessment measures be linked to group goals, rather than to session objectives. This is because the goals clearly articulate the intent of the group, whereas the objectives are more specific to the steps rather than outcomes. Also, linking assessment to the goals enables you to keep focused on the larger intent of the group and it simplifies the assessment process. Of course, it is often the case that the assessment of a particular goal will focus directly on a specific objective. For example, the *Ways of Bullies True/False Assessment* outlined in the Classroom Unit Plan in Appendix A is directly related to the group objective that students will learn the three types of bullying. In this case, learning about the three types of bullying is a key aspect of "understanding the ways in which students bully others and the implications of bully behavior" (as per the plan), so it makes sense that assessment plan focuses on this particular objective. We just emphasize to focus on your identified group goals rather than the specific objectives when creating your assessment plan.

It is important to think carefully about how you will assess the goals for your group. A poor match between assessment tool and intended learning outcomes can yield outcome data that is either invalid or just not very helpful. We believe that Brenner, Curbow, and Legro's (1995) proximal-distal continuum for assessing health status outcomes offers a helpful framework that can also be used by school counselors in determining appropriate measures for outcome assessment in their group work. This framework identifies desired outcome information on a continuum—proximal and distal outcomes—and proposes that the type of instruments used for assessment match the type of outcome information desired. *Proximal outcomes* refer to those objective signs and symptoms that are *closely related* to a particular intervention and, in this case, to group goals (Trusty & Brown, 2005). For example, asking students who participated in a 3-week group on mindfulness training conducted in a classroom group for students with test anxiety to rate their anxiety prior to taking a test at two points of time (before participation in the 3-week group and after the group has ended) would be a measure of a proximal outcome. This is because this specific measurement protocol offers pre-post comparison data related to the specific goal of decreased anxiety and it is connected to a specific strategic intervention that is used in the group. *Distal outcomes*, on the other hand, refer to the more *broad outcomes* that might be distantly related to a specific intervention. Examples of distal outcomes in Brenner, Curbow, and Legro's work (in the area of health) include mobility, role performance, and life satisfaction. In the field of counseling, Trusty and Brown suggest that increased academic achievement would be an example of a distal outcome for a school counseling group intervention because academic achievement is related to and dependent on numerous factors and, therefore, only distally related to the influence of a particular group experience.

Brenner, Curbow, and Legro (1995) and Trusty and Brown (2005) conclude that assessment measures that focus on proximal outcomes are more likely to yield valid results and meaningful information regarding program efficacy (than those that focus on distal outcomes). This is because proximal outcomes and their measures are directly related to the specific goals and interventions used in the group, and they are outcomes that are less likely to be affected by other intervening and spurious variables. We introduce this discussion on distal and proximal outcomes here as it relates to the ways in which you should think about planning group goals and how they should be measured. When selecting an assessment measure, it is important to be clear about the intent of the goal being measured and to select a measurement tool that provides the most accurate measurement of that goal. Again, Trusty and Brown (2005) assert that proximal outcomes offer more meaningful information regarding the effectiveness of strategic interventions and, in the long run, are more effective in constructing a knowledge base regarding school counseling program effectiveness, especially in the area of academic achievement-related goals.

Self-Report Measures

Tests are sometimes thought to be the best way to assess learning, but we encourage you to think more broadly and creatively about assessment in group work. Assessment really can occur in a variety of ways. For example, Johnson, Johnson, and Downs (2006) point out that data can be collected verbally (e.g., articulation of what has been learned), in writing (e.g., tests, worksheets, behavior reporting), and through demonstration (e.g., role play, real-life applications). A variety of assessment measures are used in the various sample classroom and counseling group plans in Appendices A, B, and C. For example, the Unit Plan for the Elementary Classroom Group in Appendix A proposes pre-post tests, student articulation of learning, and role-play demonstration as data sources for outcome assessment. The assessment plans for the Middle School Counseling Group (Overall) Plan in Appendix B include participation in discussions, completion of questionnaires, and a follow-up discussion with the referring teachers.

Verbal student self-report of learning can occur in a many ways. Students can verbally respond to questions about the subject matter individually or in a group discussion or they can participate in a brief verbal interview about what they have learned. Students can also indicate their learning in written form. Examples of written assessments include having students in the group write a reflective comment or essay, complete a report, or by taking an objective assessment, such as a questionnaire, checklist, test, or quiz. As an example, the High School Classroom Group Plan in Appendix C (see the Unit Plan) uses a questionnaire that will be given to students (and their parents) at the end of the unit.

It is important to point out that all of these types of assessment measures mentioned so far typically gather evidence regarding cognitive learning—that is, what students report to have learned. They are limited, however, in the extent to which they can produce data regarding the application of a particular learning principle. Such evidence cannot attest to a student's ability to perform or *do* what they have learned. Observational assessment may be a better way to assess behavioral change as a result of a group experience (although observational assessments are conducted by others so they are not self-report measures).

Before moving on to a discussion of other types of assessment measures, we want to emphasize the value of *using* student feedback to determine the extent to which the group has been a rewarding and effective experience for students. Here we want to point out that if you are planning to conduct an assessment of the group experience (which you should), you should do so with an openness and willingness to make changes, as appropriate, if that is warranted from the feedback. Remember, students vote with their behavior and their feet; no groups are effective when students do not want to participate.

Assessment by Others

Teachers and counselors are frequently called upon to produce data or testimony regarding student learning outcomes. For example, a teacher can be asked if a student is using the specific skills discussed in a counseling group and a counselor can observe a student's participation in a group activity or role play in the group. These kinds of performance assessments are most likely to focus on behavioral indicators of success—the demonstration of a specific skill—because *behavior* is what others can most easily see. For example, the Unit Plan for the Elementary School Counseling Group in Appendix A indicates that a teacher survey will be used to help assess one of the objectives in this particular classroom group unit. Other methods for generating outcome data include observing students in the group or the regular classroom or the playground and using checklist or observation reports.

The limitation of assessment measures that rely on behavioral performance as a measure of student accomplishment is that if a student displays a poor performance, it remains unresolved whether cognitive learning actually occurred or if the difficulty was just in the application process. Another limitation of using this type of assessment tool is that teachers sometimes feel overwhelmed with a large amount of paperwork that they have to complete in the regular course of their job, so they may not be open to completing a survey. In these cases, some counselors use a short informal interview with the teacher to gather their observation data. If you use an interview in this way, it is important to carefully document what has been reported.

Parents and guardians, too, can offer interesting insights about student learning. Their window of assessment typically offers a perspective that sits outside of the immediate learning environment. The data provided by parents may help assess the transfer of learning or the application of knowledge or skills in another setting. However, it can be helpful to put some structure around the kind of information you are seeking from parents, so that the data they provide is appropriate to the kind of outcome data you are seeking. The High School Classroom Group Career Life Planning Unit Plan in Appendix C indicates that a parent survey will be used at the end of the group to assess the accomplishment of the third curricular goal for this unit. Of course, not all parents will be available or willing to complete this type of survey instrument. However, we encourage school counselors to endeavor to collect outcome assessment information from parents both because of its value in determining the transfer of learning, but also for its value in strengthening parental involvement in the school and for building public confidence in the work that happens in comprehensive school counseling programs. As Whiston (2007) points out, parental involvement is related to student success in counseling, especially for low or under-achieving students.

Distal Measures

There are also numerous other ways to assess learning, growth, and change: student grade point average (GPA), class/course progress/failure, attendance and truancy rates, vandalism incidents, discipline referrals, parental involvement, teacher attendance rates, standardized test scores, extracurricular activity and community service involvement, higher education choice data (Johnson, Johnson, & Downs, 2006), and various rating scales (Corey & Corey, 2006; Gladding, 2003). Keep in mind that most of these measures are distal outcome measures. That is, the outcomes indicated in these assessment results cannot be linked solely to the intervention that you provided—they are outcomes that are related to numerous variables. For this reason, they may not be the best assessment tools to use for the purposes of measuring group goal accomplishment. We recommend using them in conjunction with other more proximal measures.

SELECTING APPROPRIATE MEASURES

We have already presented multiple avenues for collecting outcome data (e.g., student, teacher, counselor, parents) and we reiterate that it is important to be clear about the intended goal when selecting an assessment. Here we will address the ways in which you can be intentional about selecting an assessment measure that addresses the specific learning *domain* (e.g., cognitive, behavioral, affective) that is intended in your goals. For example, giving students a multiple choice test on the conflict mediation steps will help identify how well the students have memorized the conflict mediation skills taught, but will not yield data about how well the students *used* the steps to resolve conflict in a role play or as observed in the "real world." So, if the group goals and related outcome questions are action kinds of questions (i.e., questions that seek to determine how well the students did something) then the outcome measure should examine action (i.e., behavior). In this example, it is probably most appropriate to offer two assessment measures—one to assess whether the content learning (i.e., mediation steps) was accomplished and one to assess behavioral performance (i.e., if they could implement the steps). Learning in the cognitive domain might best be assessed through a multiple choice or write-in questionnaire or test. However, the second part of the goal—that the steps be implemented—will require a different assessment measure.

Assessing Cognitive Goals

Bloom's Taxonomy (Bloom, 1956) can be used to consider the nature of cognitively-oriented learning tasks for the purpose of selecting an appropriate assessment measure.

Lower level learning tasks which focus on facts and developing conceptual understandings (i.e., knowledge and comprehension) lend themselves well to verbal or written student self-report assessment tools. For example, the first few lessons in the *You and Me: Bully Free* Classroom Group Plan in Appendix A focus on having students learn specific bully facts. These are easily assessed in the true-false quiz (*The Ways of Bullies True/False Assessment*) that is administered in lessons 1 and 6. That instrument is included in the Appendix as well.

Higher-level cognitive learning tasks, such as critical thinking and application tasks (i.e., application, analysis, synthesis, and evaluation), are sometimes best assessed by monitoring the student's participation in a group discussion, observing the student in a naturalistic setting, or the creation of or participation in a project or report. This is exemplified in the Middle Level Classroom Group Unit Plan in Appendix B, where assessment consists of observing student participation in discussion and student reflection questions. Similarly, counselor observation of the input given by group members is used to assess some of the goals in the Middle Level Counseling Group Overall Plan in Appendix B. Teacher, counselor, parent, and/or administrator input can also be used to assess some of the higher level learning goals. Standardized tests, disciplinary referrals, attendance rates, and progress reports may also yield data that corroborates evidence of higher level goal achievement, depending on the specific goal or objective assessed, but recall that these distal assessment tools are not easily tied to any single specific intervention efforts, so caution is advised when using them to justify program results. These distal measures are probably best used in combination with other more proximal outcome measures.

Assessing Affective Goals

Group goals that focus on affective learning are notably difficult to assess (Gronlund, 2000), so articulating affective-oriented goals in the clearest and most concrete language possible helps with assessment planning.[1] We caution against making definitive interpretations about student affect that are gleaned from observations; arguably an important way to determine how someone feels or what they value or believe is to ask them. Student self-report and observation are probably the best sources of information regarding student feelings, motivations, and attitudes. The reflection questions in the Middle Level *Body Image* Classroom Group Unit in Appendix B were designed to surface emotional responses from students regarding body image and could be used to assess affective learning.

Assessing Behavioral Goals

Some groups focus on having students learn or perform a specific skill or behave differently. These kinds of groups that focus on skill development require more than cognitive understanding about a particular skill or topic; they require performance or demonstration. Therefore, having students demonstrate the skills in a role play or observing the student in the class, on the playground, or in halls, are ways to assess these performance goals. The counselor observation of the student role play exercises in

---

[1] It is worth mentioning that in the 1950s Bloom also developed an affective taxonomy, however, it has not endured as well as his Cognitive Taxonomy. Nevertheless, school counselors may find the hierarchy Bloom presents interesting. A reputable source for accessing this taxonomy is www.thesocialvoice.com/bloomtheory2.html

the *You and Me: Bully Free* Elementary Classroom Group Unit Plan in Appendix A is an example of using observation of student performance as a behavioral assessment measure. A better assessment method would be to observe the students in non-structured time at school to determine whether they were actually using the skills taught in the group. However, this type of assessment is difficult to conduct in a systematic way in many schools, largely due to the high number of demands on teachers and counselors. Therefore, many counselors rely on anecdotal data to assess whether these skills are being performed outside of the classroom where they were taught. Finally, another assessment that would allude to the performance of these skills outside of the instructional setting would be to collect bully referrals prior to and after instruction. However, be careful in using this type of distal measure for assessment as there are likely multiple variables affecting these referrals.

We reiterate that it is much more effective to plan for assessment when the specific assessment criteria are identified in advance. For example, if the teacher reports that the students in a group are "doing better," you will need to know what specifically is happening that is considered to be "better," and, perhaps, how that is a change from what happened before. So, the group plan must have a clear articulation of the goal being assessed, the criteria upon which the assessment will be made, and an outline of the specific tools that will be used for the assessment to occur. We also recommend combining assessment measures so that you are able to use a variety of data to determine whether the group has been effective in promoting learning or change.

DIVERSITY-WISE ASSESSMENT

Every discussion of assessment should, at some point, address the issue of assessment bias and fairness—both with regard to the way in which the assessment has been conducted and also with regard to the ways in which assessment information is used. The issue of test bias in educational and psychology professional communities has long focused on race, gender, and SES/class group differences in standardized assessment results (for more on this, we suggest reviewing the FairTest website www.fairtest.org) and unfair practices of student placement or tracking that follows. This debate continues to raise questions about whether racial, gender, and SES differences in standardized assessment results are due to flaws in assessment instruments themselves or, instead, due to flaws in educational and community settings that are inherently unfair and unequal. This debate compels us to further examine these types of assessment measures to gather outcome data, as they may not provide an adequate assessment of our group goals—at least not for all of the students in our groups. It also encourages us to question the use of these instruments for other purposes in schools.

Sternberg (2007) offers a list of lessons he has learned regarding the use of assessment instruments with a diverse student body. He points out that the very act of assessment has very real effects on student performance, largely because the meaning of assessment varies across cultures. He also points out that the very definition of smart or intelligent behavior is culture-bound. This reminds us to be careful when we use the term *test*, for example, as this term may conjure expectations that are not consistent with our intent of evaluating the effectiveness of certain group interventions. Instead, students may feel that their particular performance on the test has more significance than we had intended. Related to this, being aware of what is valued as important or smart in various subcultures in the school is important in planning group goals and in select-ing appropriate assessment tools. Sternberg also points out that individuals from differ-ent cultures may think about concepts and problems differently than how they are conceptualized in instruction and assessment instruments. Therefore, inviting students to explain or describe their understandings may be particularly helpful with a diverse population of students.

Sternberg (2007) reminds us that students will do better on assessments of material that is familiar and meaningful to them, and similarly, many children learn contextually important and practical skills, sometimes at the expense of academic skills. While this statement seems obvious, the implications are important. Assessment results that fail to demonstrate concept proficiency—that the objective of the group has not been met—may say more about the community of the learners than about any individ-ual within that community. Group content that is far from the experience of the mem-bers of the group will probably require more time and instruction. Stenberg also points out that academic failure can reflect factors other than ability, including poor health, a lack of understanding of the requirements of the assessment tasks, and instruction that is inconsistent with one's culture. All of these variables must be considered when inter-preting the results of assessment measures.

With regard to the non-standardized assessment measures, it is important to con-sider the extent to which a minority student feels comfortable or safe in the group and with the counselor, and how this issue of safety affects assessment. For example, will a minority student feel as safe as majority students when asked to provide *honest* feedback to the teacher or counselor? If the feedback is genuinely appreciative and com-plimentary about the group, perhaps so, but what if that genuine feedback is critical? Would the student, for example, be able to say that the group was boring and useless? Obviously, responses that are constructed to please the counselor are not likely to yield accurate assessment information.

Counselor bias—the tendency to offer preference towards a particular individual or perspective—also affects assessment results. If the counselor ignores or dismisses assessment data from some students (e.g., a student who did poorly in the group/on the post-test "because" he has a difficult home situation), then the potential for using that feedback to enhance the group experience is compromised. Also, when assessment measures fail to take into consideration cultural differences in self-expression—for exam-ple, cultural norms about the expression of sadness, anger, or self-praise—the informa-tion yielded by such assessments will be misunderstood at best, incorrect at worst.

In summary, assessment results are accurate only to the extent that the instruments used are valid and reliable, that those asked to participate in the assessment process can offer accurate and objective observations and feedback, and only to the extent to which the data gathered is valued. All of these variables point to the subtle nuances of outcome assessment and remind us to be sure that assessment is offered in a manner that is both safe and transparent, and that all students have an equal (although perhaps not the same) opportunity to learn and to demonstrate that learning has been achieved.

A final issue of importance related to diversity-wise assessment is for the group leader to assess the extent to which the group experience was beneficial in terms of pro-viding mirrors to students who may feel marginalized in the group, even if this was not an articulated group goal. That is, we suggest that you also always assess whether stu-dents in your group whose identity characteristics have the potential to put them in subordinate or less powerful positions in the school community have had an opportunity to see themselves represented, respected, and valued in the group community. Similarly, we suggest that you assess the extent to which non-minority students have had an opportunity to learn about and have been pushed to respect multiple perspectives and lifestyles—windows—through the group experience. These questions can be assessed in a variety of ways using self- and other-report measures.

THE ETHICS OF ASSESSMENT

School counselors answer to professional and ethical obligations to demonstrate accountability for the intended outcomes of groups they run, as well as to the ways in which they measure those outcomes. Our professional codes of ethics offer some guidelines for our work with assessment measures. In the *Ethical Standards for School Counselors* (ASCA, 2004) we read, "The professional school counselor adheres to all professional standards regarding selecting, administering and interpreting assessment measures" (excerpt from A.9.a, see Appendix E). No one would argue that *all professional standards* is a lofty responsibility, and our recommendation is to consult with professional peers whenever possible with regard to selecting and using appropriate assessment measures. Section E, Evaluation, Assessment, and Interpretation of The American Counseling Association *Code of Ethics and Standards of Practice* (ACA, 2005) further compels counselors to take "into account the client personal and cultural context [and] . . . promote the well-being of individual clients or groups of clients by developing and using appropriate educational, psychological, and career assessment instruments" (Section E. Introduction). Clearly, our cautions regarding the selection of appropriate assessment instruments—both with regard to the match between goal and assessment measure, and also with regard to the appropriateness of using a particular measure with a particular student body, are warranted.

Here we also offer a reminder that the anonymity of classroom members and small group counseling group members in the reporting of any outcome data or analyses gained through those assessment measures must also be assured (for more on the ethical positions and standards regarding confidentiality, see Appendices E and F). Assessment data must be gathered by methods that protect the privacy of families as well as students. Although we realize that anecdotes are powerful testimony to the work school counselors perform, we are never at liberty to share a story that might be identifiable. The sanctity of anonymity is a cornerstone upon which our reputations form in our school. We must be vigilant not to share someone else's story as we describe our services.

USING ASSESSMENT RESULTS RESPONSIBLY

It is affirming when the feedback from assessment indicates that the students have learned. However, we know that not all students learn what we hope they will learn and not all students learn in the ways that are consistent with our group plan. It is important to keep in mind that assessment is not just something we do to determine *whether* learning has occurred. As Cobia and Henderson (2007) tell us, the "purpose of the evaluation is to determine the extent to which program goals are being met and provide information that will lead to program improvement" (p. 70). This reminds us to account for our program strengths as well as our program weaknesses. Where we are ineffective, we are obliged to improve.

An assessment plan conceived from the very beginning—developed well before we sit down with students—provides us with direction for growth. Quality assessment processes are ones which help determine *which aspects* of the intended goals and objectives have been met and *what additional effort or instruction* is needed to meet those goals and objectives. In short, assessment provides feedback for use in future planning efforts.

To illustrate the importance of assessment for program improvement, we offer the following example. A multiple-choice assessment in one classroom group revealed that 80% of the students were able to identify the steps for conflict resolution. However, when the counselor used an observational assessment rubric to assess whether students could apply the skills that they learned in role plays, far fewer of those 80% actually used the conflict resolution steps they had learned. This latter assessment measure helped the counselor determine that more focus was needed on the application of the conflict mediation steps in the group. To this end, he decided to spend 3 more weeks on practice sessions and to incorporate more processing discussions and group feedback rounds into the group following the practice sessions. At the end of these final 3 weeks, students were able to use the steps more consistently in the role plays. However, verbal and written comments were also used as assessment data, and they revealed that students felt that peer pressure inhibited their use of conflict mediation skills. This information led the group leader to focus on peer pressure as a larger goal for the next classroom group plan. Again, assessment data is most useful when it is used to further group instructional goals and objectives.

Beyond being useful to the group leader, assessment information can also be very useful to the student participants themselves. We suggest that whenever possible, group leaders should share their assessment results with the students in their groups. This allows students the opportunity to reflect on their learning, feel they are a part of their learning process (i.e., that they help construct learning, it does not just happen to them), and it provides an avenue for the leader to gain valuable student insights about the group process and for future directions with the group.

Sharing assessment outcomes with parents, teachers, and school administration is also helpful for obtaining feedback and for establishing the importance of the work accomplished through classroom and counseling groups. Of course and as already mentioned, any reporting of group assessment data to public sources (parents, teachers, administrators) should be provided in a way that protects individual students rights for confidentiality (see the Preamble and Section A.2 in the *Ethical Standards for School Counselors* [ASCA, 2004]). School counselors typically distribute assessment information in newsletters, quarterly or annual reports, and in meetings with particular interested or invested parties (such as the parents of a student in the group). The capstone to this chapter is that assessment not only provides data for accountability, it also offers quality feedback for all who are involved with meeting the educational needs of students in schools.

CHAPTER 5

Leader Decision-Making from a Clear Philosophical Position

DEVELOPING A PHILOSOPHICAL POSITION

Learning and personal growth do not just happen because students are together in a room with a common goal; learning happens as a result of intentional facilitation on the part of the group leader. Paradoxically, having a clear foundation from which to lead allows the group leader a certain degree of flexibility when working in the group.

When things go wrong in a group, leaders sometimes scurry to identify and label a particular student as the problem and they remedy the problem by removing or changing that individual who is deemed culpable. In response to this, we raise two points that are fundamental to the position we take in this chapter. First, it is important to keep in mind that most difficulties that arise in groups are not because of any one individual but because of a group dynamic that is problematic for one or many individuals in that group. When group leaders are able to manage groups so that students are engaged, supported to learn, and given opportunities and feedback with regard to regulating their own behavior, growth and learning can happen for all students in the group and problems and misbehavior will be kept at a minimum. Second, we want to point out that not all "problems" in the group are problematic. That is, learning can happen when things go "wrong" in the group. Learning from challenge can happen if the group leader is intentional about harvesting learning opportunities when they present themselves. *Case Study 5.7* illustrates the value of these two points.

CASE STUDY 5.7

A Group Versus an Individual Problem

Patrick, an active boy with a 3-year reputation of being "challenging" (according to his teachers), was invited to participate in a 10-week counseling group. The group goal was "being the best we can be." The school counselor's screening and invitation process predicted that although Patrick might be a "handful" in the classroom, he seemed to really be interested in participating in the group.

At the end of the first group session, which was extremely challenging to manage, the counselor concluded that she had "seen the light" and that she had "made a huge mistake" inviting Patrick into the group. Patrick's in-group behaviors demanded nearly constant attention; he was fidgety, loud, and bossy; and he seemed disinterested in engaging in the work of the group. Strangely, though, he seemed keenly aware of both the counselor's and his peer's frustrations with him in the group.

Initially and quite understandably, we can see how the leader's attention immediately focused on Patrick being a bad fit for this group. In fact, the counselor framed this "disaster" as a nearly insurmountable—and decided that if Patrick was not removed from the group, the remaining nine sessions would be a failure.

After consulting with a colleague, the school counselor considered this situation in light of what is known about how behaviors influence and are influenced by group dynamics, and she began to focus on what Patrick might bring to the group—with all his challenges intact. Rather than blaming or lamenting, the counselor asked herself how the dynamic around Patrick's behavior could stimulate learning for all of the members in the group. After all, she surmised, Patrick was present in similar fashion with everyone in the third grade every day, so what she was experiencing in the group was an everyday occurrence in the regular classroom and in other settings in the school. As you might imagine, Patrick had perfect attendance! With these thoughts in mind, she decided to hold off on removing him from the group, at least for one more week.

In the subsequent group session, the counselor focused on processing Patrick's behavior in the here-and-now, using exactly what was happening in group instead of attempting to control Patrick's behaviors or others' reactions to him. For example, at one point in the group, Alina asked for the counselor's assistance to put a book away. At that moment, Patrick jumped up, approached the counselor with a display of a picture that he had been drawing, and asked her if she liked it. Alina called over again, asking for assistance a second time. Patrick turned to her, commanding: "Put that away yourself, can't you see that she is helping me?" With this, the counselor stopped the group, saying, "We are working on communicating respect in this group. Has anyone noticed a communication that has happened in here that may have felt disrespectful to another person in the room?" She followed with a thorough processing of the interchange, directing Alina and Patrick to speak to one another about the interaction that had just transpired.

While Patrick's problem-behavior became a major focus of the group members' interest—a real, in-the-present enactment of "becoming the best we can be"—students developed skills (with group leader direction) in offering feedback to each other. These exchanges offered students an opportunity to consider the importance of self-regulation for developing friendships. In the end, the group was a grand success and although Patrick's behaviors in group were initially seen as disastrous, both he and the other members of the group demonstrated marked gains on both objective measures (in group and in the classroom) and the members' subjective report on how participating in the group benefited them.

Reflection Questions

1. When, if ever, is it appropriate to dismiss a student from the group in response to his or her disruptive behavior patterns? What personal values or personal and internalized rules of conduct might rise up from deep inside to direct your action to dismiss a student?
2. If the focus of the group is not on interpersonal interactions or communication issues, would it be appropriate to process the disruptions in this way?

Authoritative Leadership

We use the term *position* to talk about the philosophical and relational stance from which group leader's lead. It is a term that is used by social constructionist writers to convey the social and cultural ways in which identities are produced (Burr, 1995). In this context, we highlight the ways in which group identities are produced. Namely, we want to talk about how the counselor's presence in a group sets a tone for how the group will function—for how the group will come to be.

The different ways in which the group leader interacts and relates to group members forms a norm in the group. This norm produces group dynamics that further define rules, roles, member interactions, and it impacts on if and how group goals are being met. For example, if the group leader enters into the group in ways that communicate disinterest in the group members or disinterest in the goals or activities in the group, then the students are likely to be unengaged, they may feel unimportant or unvalued, and they are not likely to be invested in the group or in the intended learning opportunities. On the other hand, if the leader truly values the students in the group, really believes that they have important and valuable ideas, and believes that the members are capable of learning from each other in the group, then these beliefs and principles will be the norm in the group, and students are likely to conduct themselves accordingly.

The group leader position we advocate for, in both counseling and classroom groups, is best characterized as *authoritative* leadership. Authoritative leadership is a term that is used in the teaching and parenting literature to describe an educational-oriented approach whereby the leader is clearly in charge or in control of the group, but leads in a fair, warm, and caring way (Hughes, 2002). We urge readers not to mistake "authoritative" for authoritarian—the two are distinctly different and we see little if any merit in school counselors being authoritarian!

While it is sometimes difficult to translate a philosophical stance into observable behaviors, Larrivee (2005) suggests that authoritative group leaders convey a sense of being in charge of and caring for members by being attentive; by offering specific and direct comments, suggestions, instructions, and feedback; and through modeling. Authoritative group leaders articulate reasoned expectations for the group, encourage verbal interchange among members, encourage student self-regulation, and are flexible in how they lead the group (Hughes, 2002; Ingersol, 1996). They have high and appropriate expectations for group members, they intervene to help members make appropriate choices whenever possible, they provide ample opportunities for success in the group, and they establish and enforce fair rules in the group, making the reasons for these rules transparent when appropriate (Larrivee, 2005). In contrast, an *authoritarian* leader dictates and controls most activities in the group with little input from group members ("Authoritarian leadership," n.d.) and in groups with authoritarian leadership, there is a clear and hierarchical division between group leaders and group members.

As illustrated in *Case Study 5.8*, authoritative group leaders like Mr. Herrera assert appropriate limits and controls and also encourage independence, verbal dialogue, and debate. The focus of authoritative actions is always on communicating the belief that each individual in the group is capable, and to support each and every student (sometimes differently) so that those capabilities come forward.

CASE STUDY 5.8

Authoritative Leadership

In a sixth-grade classroom group early on in the school year, school counselor Mr. Herrera noticed that in group discussions, students consistently raised their hands and waited for him to call on them before they would speak. They looked at him rather than at each other when they spoke, and their comments did not take into consideration what was stated before them. Along with this, the pacing was odd—it was as if the group discussion was regulated through him. The regular classroom norm of raising hands before talking was probably very effective for some of the academic discussions that happened in that classroom, but Mr. Herrera thought that it interfered with student's abilities to more naturally enter into a discussion with each other in this group. He wanted students to feel more in charge of the group process, while also keeping in mind his role in leading the group towards the intended goals.

After two group sessions, Mr. Herrera decided to present his observation to the group. He started with "it seems that many of you have important things to say when we have discussions, but I'm thinking that it might work better if we didn't have to raise our hands to speak. That way, you could all talk to each other and not have to wait for me to call on you."

The students all agreed with this proposal, and were ready to jump in and give it a go.

"However," Mr. Herrera added, "I'm thinking that it might be a good idea to talk about how we can make this change from hand-raising to non-hand-raising, and still be sure that everyone has a chance to speak if they want to. Sometimes when people just call out, they forget to clear a space for others to speak, and they get so focused on what they want to say, they forget to listen to others. Any thoughts on how we might do this successfully?" he asked.

As the group moved into a discussion about this, Mr. Herrera intentionally worked to draw out some of the quiet members and he reminded some of the more verbose members to hold back so that others could speak. In these ways, he was able to model the kinds of behaviors he expected from the members.

As the discussion came to a close, Mr. Herrera asked students to reflect on how the group managed the discussion they just had, and if there were some ways that they could do better with this in the future. This question led to an interesting discussion about how some students were quieter in the group and others were louder. They moved into talking about ways in which they would notice the quieter voices and how to respectfully notice when they felt that someone was too domineering in the group. Some of the more active students seemed committed to make a space for others in the group, and the quieter students agreed to try to participate more in discussions.

In the end, the group decided that they would share spontaneously in group discussions rather than raise their hands before speaking. With the help of Mr. Herrera, the following expectations were outlined: (a) that student contributions be relevant to the discussion, (b) that they not be hurtful to other members of the group, (c) that students should not dominate the discussion (i.e., they should take turns and remember to clear a space for others), and (d) that everyone try to participate in group discussions.

Reflection Questions

1. Is it a good idea to allow students to call out answers in the group? Might this lead to disorganization and loud behavior in the group?
2. It can sometimes be difficult for children (adults too) to navigate gracefully between two or more distinct norms or different sets of expectations. In this case, Mr. Herrera asks his students to behave differently than they are accustomed to. Discuss with one or more of your classmates how gaining mastery of this skill— negotiating two sets of classroom norms and expectations—might prepare students to take this skill into real life situations. That is, the dual norms in the two classrooms may mirror differences between broader norms including local norms "at home and in school" or cultural norms "in my neighborhood we never do this or that," or societal norms, "from the country where I was born and this country." What other ways might the group leader work intentionally to help students become adaptable in this regard?
3. Can you imagine a classroom teacher who might take umbrage to "that potential chaos in MY CLASSROOM"? Work with a partner to discuss ways you as a school counselor might help this particular teacher "clear a space" for your different way of doing things. What defenses and what buttons might be pushed by a teacher who might not welcome your way of doing things?

While it may seem that such a lengthy discussion about raising hands in the group in Case Study 5.8 might be excessive if not tangential, we would argue that time spent early on in discussing group norms and creating appropriate rules and expectations is time well spent. In this case, not only did this discussion help to facilitate a group process that seemed appropriate for this group, but it also created an opportunity for individuals in the group to think about the ways in which they and their peers interact with one another and contribute to collective discussions.

In the weeks that followed, Mr. Herrera had to remind the group members of the rules from time to time and, as one might expect, he occasionally had to respectfully cut-off a student from long and winding stories. He also worked to find specific roles for members who seemed challenged to find a way to participate in the group. For example, he assigned students to be co-leaders in group discussions and he introduced other roles for students, including a time manager and materials captain. In these ways, he was able to capitalize on the strengths of all of the students and also step back from being too actively controlling of the group.

A Discipline Philosophy

It seems that at some point or another, most discussions about the role of school counselors raise questions about the position of school counselors with regard to *discipline*. Some school counselors report being hesitant to "discipline" students in their schools because they believe that doing so will compromise their ability to adequately develop counseling relationships with those students at a later time. Or, they believe this precarious dual role will baffle students who will not be able to see the distinct differences between counselor and teacher. We know many school counselors, however, who have been able to adopt a school presence that is consistent and effective across the various roles they assume in schools, including classroom and small group work. They, like us, believe that discipline is about setting limits and that setting limits is not something that is inherently bad nor is it something that necessarily compromises their ability to develop supportive counseling relationships with students. As Jones and Jones (2001) say, "The main issue is not whether teachers should be less warm or friendly, but that they must simultaneously assert both their right to be treated with respect and their responsibility for ensuring that students treat each other with kindness" (p. 83).

We offer a metaphor for thinking about discipline as a guardrail: Imagine a road without guardrails that bridges across a deep canyon. Crossing this road would be difficult and very scary for many drivers—unable to clearly see where the edge of the road ends and where the fall begins. Putting guardrails on this road, however, would lessen the anxiety and make the journey across the canyon easier to travel. Like guardrails that provide drivers with a clear and secure barrier so that their vehicles can cross the canyon safely, limits allow students to know how close they are to the edge and protect them from falling off. Note that in this metaphor cars are not supposed to crash into the guardrail to prevent them from falling into the abyss. Rather, the guardrail, like clear limits that uphold and enforce the rules and responsibilities of being a member of the school, when this is needed, is intended to alert that the abyss is very real. Students learn, both from direct experience and word of mouth in the school, that they need not test strong and secure limits. (Although, of course, some will!)

When the term discipline is synonymous with setting limits, then it is like the metaphoric guardrail that provides safety for crossing through difficult places. We would argue that when limits are set with a focus on learning and imposed in ways that respect the integrity of others—as they always should be—then yes, school counselors, like all professionals in schools, are in the position of disciplining students in their schools. You will notice that the interventions included in Chapter 7, *Responding to Problems in the Group*, illustrate the philosophical position that we advocate here.

A few caveats warrant mention here. First, remember not all roads have guardrails. Only some roads need that extra protection. Guardrails should only be put along the roads that need them. This is true, too, for leaders who set limits in the group. Second, remember that guardrails do not attempt to steer individuals across the canyon. Group leaders should give students every opportunity to steer themselves successfully toward their desired destinations—the guardrails are just on the periphery to assure that the student is doing so safely. Third, well-marked guardrails allow for safe passage, but they do not usurp personal responsibility or self-control. Drivers still must work within the safety zone. Finally, we point out that consequences for venturing out beyond the rail must be clear, fair, and without discipline in a draconian sense. This is a delicate balance at times. Remember Patrick from earlier in this chapter? The school counselor had subjective urges of telling him to "sit down, pay attention, and don't ruin this group for those who really want to be here!" but that would have been "grabbing hold of the wheel" rather than maintaining the guardrails and allowing both Patrick and other members of the group to navigate the road appropriately and successfully. If, however, dangers arose in the group due to Patrick's behavior, the counselor would have needed to intervene more actively and these actions likely would have included imposing consequences for his inappropriate behavior (see more on this in Chapter 7). This is consistent with authoritative group leadership.

Taking a Stand on Diversity Issues

The concept of *windows* and *mirrors* is more than a practice of addressing diversity issues in schools. It is a philosophy that is centered around a respect for multiple perspectives and an understanding of how context, especially social context, constructs the lens though which one sees the world. It is a philosophy that honors and celebrates the unique talents of a diverse body of students and that does not minimize or become "color blind" to differences.

When one truly steps into these understandings, one begins to become acutely aware of the ways in which group member identities such as socio-economic conditions, race, disability, sexual orientation, gender identity, to name only a few, are made visible by social status markings. The effects of these social status markings are apparent in classrooms, schools, and larger communities. When an institution's or a community's ways of thinking or ways of acting systematically privilege one perspective or one group over another, discrimination results. We would argue that embracing a windows and mirrors philosophy goes well beyond merely understanding these concepts; it requires taking a stand against these kinds of markings and taking a stand against discrimination when it presents itself in your groups, as well as in your school community.

Taking a stand, with regard to group work, begins with assuming an active role in planning and facilitating groups so that the voices of all are heard and respected, and so that all members in the groups have equal access to knowledge and growth opportunities. It also compels us to work for change by actively helping students understand the very real effects of attitudes and behaviors that are hurtful or discriminatory to others and not being afraid to challenge inappropriate behaviors or attitudes. It means addressing uncomfortable issues and modeling how to have hard conversations. It means exposing students to that which is new and different, inviting reflection on and meaning-making from those experiences, and stimulating critical thought. It means never tolerating remarks or behaviors that are hurtful. Embracing a windows and mirrors philosophy means positioning yourself to be a voice and an advocate for every member of the school community. The leadership skills outlined in Chapter 6 are tools that we advocate using for carrying out these critical leadership actions in groups.

COUNSELING AND CLASSROOM LEADERSHIP APPROACHES

If there was a specific and limited set of skills and a discrete knowledge base for leading classroom groups and a parallel but different set for leading counseling groups, then leading these groups would be fairly simple—you do one thing for one group type and something different for the other type of group. Unfortunately, we honestly believe that this is not the case; leading groups is not that simple. However, the good news is that the set of leader skills and the knowledge base for leading both of these types of groups is essentially the same. The difference lies in their application.

So, while successful leadership of classroom and counseling groups does not require two (or more) distinctly separate sets of group leader skills, the ways in which group work skills are put into practice in each group type varies considerably. (For a thorough discussion of these issues and more, see ASGW Professional Standards for the Training of Group Workers, 2000, at http://www.asgw.org/PDF/training_standards .pdf) Adaptation of the group work skills and knowledge presented in this book will be needed as you switch back and forth between both groups in your school. Again we return to Case Study 5.7. In the small counseling group format, the counselor was able to rely more fully on Patrick's peer group members to offer both supportive and corrective feedback when his group behavior reached the point of being dangerously close to the "guard rail." If similar problems had surfaced in a classroom group setting, the same counselor might have needed to use many more management functions (possibly including, although no one ever likes to imagine this, asking Patrick to accompany her out into the hall where the conditions for him to remain in the group would be outlined in clear and firm language). Here we discuss ways in which these two group types are similar and how they are different.

Similarities in Leading School Counseling and Classroom Groups

Group work theories, we believe, offer a fairly consistent foundation for understanding how both counseling and classroom groups function. The theories that outline group stages, for example, describe a similar developmental schema for both groups: the theoretical warm-up, action, and closure stages are present in both classroom and counseling groups (although what they might look like when observed in each group, may be somewhat different). Both group types require the group leader to be mindful—and *planful*—about the ways in which groups are structured over time and how group dynamics change over the life of the group.

A second similarity is that the outcomes of both counseling and classroom of groups in schools emphasize personal as well as social growth and development. This seems intuitively correct; school counselors' expertise is in human development and psychology, and youth development in the areas of social and personal growth occupies a large amount of their attention and concern. In most schools, these areas of development are not systematically addressed anywhere else in the curriculum. We argue that learning how to be and how to be with others (personal and social skills) is, fundamentally and ethically, a part of academic, personal, and social-cultural goals (for more on this, see *Ethical Standards for School Counselors* [ASCA, 2004], A.1.b, A.3.b). Both counseling and classroom groups offer an important venue for advancing personal and social growth, whether or not this agenda is specifically the focus of the content learning goals of the particular group. Both group types require a leadership approach that attends to social and personal skills by managing both group process and group content.

Another similarity between counseling and classroom groups has to do with the context in which both groups are conducted: schools. There is a way of being present in a school that is unwavering in its commitment to learning and development, but decidedly focused on academic achievement. Unfortunately, sometimes this comes at the expense of development in the other domains of personal, social, and career/vocational development. This attitude also sometimes alludes to a mentality (we use this word intentionally, but not in a derogatory sense) of managing large numbers of diverse individuals in the most efficient way possible. We caution that learning extends beyond academics and that efficiency does not always equate to effectiveness. Dogmatic commitment to one domain of learning and decision-making that is based solely on practicality may not always lead to just and appropriate action. With regard to group work, both classroom and counseling groups should be structured from identified learning needs and appropriate methods of meeting those needs. School counselors sometimes need to advocate for their work to be based on sound principles of instruction rather than convenience.

In summary, even though the purposes, the memberships, and goals for these two different types of group conducted by counselors in schools are often vastly different, the fundamental counseling and group skills used by group leaders are essentially the same for conducting both counseling and classroom groups in schools. This point foreshadows the executive function leadership skills discussed in Chapter 6, as well as the problem response strategies included in Chapters 7 and 8.

Differences in Leading Classroom and Counseling Groups

Of course, classroom and counseling groups are different. They likely differ in their purposes (their goals and objectives), in the number and make up of their members, in how their goals and objectives are accomplished, and in how each group is facilitated by the group leader. These differences compel us to think about how group leader skills and style will need to adapt as the leader switches back and forth between these two distinct group purposes.

Let us start with *structure* and *directiveness*. Structure refers to a group process that is organized and predictable. That is, where the leader has determined, in advance, what will happen how and when in the group. Nonstructured groups are organized around spontaneous group member input, structured groups are not. We think of structure as existing on a continuum where group members are allowed differing amounts of freedom to determine the pace, content, and process of what is happening in the group. Directiveness refers to the ways in which the group leader is actively involved in structuring group process in order to accomplish the goals and objectives in the group. In both cases, we are talking about the ways in which the group is planned so that students are directed towards learning a specific content and how the leader intervenes to direct student attention and behavior during the group.

Predictably, classroom groups tend to require higher levels of directiveness and structure more frequently than do smaller counseling groups. This is due to multiple factors. Perhaps, most significantly, the larger classroom groups have representation from a wider range of students than the more homogenous smaller counseling groups, so there is more potential for divergent attention and behaviors—particularly when there is a mismatch between content and student interest or need. Some participants may be less engaged than others.

It would be naïve to assume, however, that structure and directiveness are only required in larger classroom groups. Indeed, for many counseling groups the leader must be exceptionally clear, extremely structured, and every bit as directive as when she leads a classroom group. This is particularly the case in initial group sessions where structure is needed to establish group norms, especially with regard to confidentiality and when outlining leader expectations for the group (DeLucia-Waack, 2006). Also, in both group types, leaders typically structure the group process so as to provide some kind of summation of the learning that has occurred at the end of the group (DeLucia-Waack, 2006). Kline (2003) reminds us that while groups do not always need directive structuring, the leader must be ready to provide direction in every group when needed. In the end, it is not simply a matter of whether one is directive or not; but rather, different situations call for different levels of directiveness on the part of the group leader. The same is true for structure in the group.

Another difference between the counseling and classroom groups is that classroom groups often do not deliver the metaphorical *depth* that counseling groups can elicit. We tread on thin ice here, as we try to further explicate this notion of depth from the professional discourses of what is considered therapeutic in counseling and what is considered appropriate for the school context. Our reference to depth here refers to the extent to which a particular issue can be personally explored in the group. To clarify, our use of *depth* does not connote the more colloquial and sophomoric status of "not useful" that is typically relegated to this term in some professional circles. The bottom line is that classroom groups that focus on delivering curriculum in the areas of academic, personal, social, and career domains tend to offer a broad-scope educationally-focused group experience that only secondarily (and only sometimes) provide opportunities for extensive personal exploration. The curricular focus of classroom group work definitely has the potential to be beneficial to students, especially when there is a logical connection between the goal of the group and the group delivery plan (Trusty & Brown, 2005), but it is often not what we might call *deep*. Again, this is not to say that students do not explore issues in depth in classroom groups—it is just that they will probably not personally engage with the material in classroom groups in the same way that they might in the smaller counseling groups.

This notion of depth has huge implications on the leadership style and decisions for counselors leading classroom and counseling groups. Leadership interventions for classroom groups tend to be aimed primarily at eliciting broad, intellectual engagement with ideas and experiences. They sometimes also offer opportunities for meaningful, careful, and personal reflection and exploration, too, of course. Counseling groups, on the other hand, would more intentionally and more regularly invite meaningful personal exploration and personal reflection. It follows that group leader interventions such as cutting off, focusing, shifting the focus, open-ended questions, reflections, and immediacy (see Appendix D for a more complete list and explanations of these terms), would be used to structure student engagement differently and at different times in each of these group types.

Finally, the use of structured activities is typically different in classroom and counseling groups. In general, structured activities are used to illustrate major concepts, elicit student engagement, and to offer an opportunity to put ideas into practice. They are likely to be used more frequently in the larger classroom groups than in counseling groups, because student engagement is likely to need more structuring in these larger classroom groups. Of course, this does not mean that these activities are not used—or should not be used—in the smaller counseling groups. It is just that smaller counseling groups are sometimes able to use a less-structured format to better accomplish their goals and objectives. This less structured format can be more tailored to the needs of the individuals in smaller counseling groups (i.e., students can talk about their own experiences rather than what is elicited in the activity) and often invites a more personal level of exploration. Activities or exercises sometimes simply cannot provide the individual and personal focus and attention to the issues that are meaningful to students in small counseling groups.

NAVIGATING SOCIAL ISSUES AND SCHOOL CULTURE

As previously mentioned, it is challenging to write a text on the implementation of group work in schools because there are so many school-related variables that affect the ways in which students engage in groups in this particular setting. In the following sections, we will discuss two critical school-related issues. First, we will identify some of the social skills that are critical for students to be able to meaningfully engage in group work. We also discuss the role of group leaders in facilitating the development of these skills. Second, we will address the ways in which issues of difference are structured into social status orderings that potentially inhibit healthy group functioning. The important role of the group leader in bringing forth the strengths of all students in the group is highlighted in these discussions.

School Social Skill Development

"It is a great mistake to assume that children (or adults) know how to work with each other in a constructive collegial fashion," says Cohen (1994, p. 39). Indeed, participating in group work requires of students some very basic interpersonal skills. At the very least, students need to be able to express themselves, communicate with others, and regulate their own behavior enough to establish the most basic interaction with peers in the group. Unfortunately, not all students have these skills. (The *Ethical Standards for School Counselors* [ASCA 2004], Preamble, A.1.b., D.1.g statements calling for school counselors to be attuned to the diverse needs of the students and families that they serve is relevant here.)

When working with students in groups—regardless of the content of the group—you will likely need to teach and support the development of the interpersonal skills necessary for group participation. Brophy (1999) refers to this as *socializing students into learning communities*. A socialization process does occur in elementary schools where children develop skills such as staying with the group, taking turns, sharing, asking questions of group members, using quiet voices (Jones & Jones, 2001), and appropriate ways to enter into group discussions and activities. These are skills that are taught and coached by elementary teachers, counselors, and administrators to provide young students with the basic requisites for participating in classroom learning. Upper elementary and middle level students are typically coached to listen, encourage, and check out their understandings with others, so as to participate more constructively in classroom

discussions. Older students learn to offer critical feedback (please do not misread critical feedback as criticism or hurtful feedback) with regard to content and to engage in
constructive feedback exchange with peers. They are encouraged to offer meaningful
contributions to advance discussions (e.g., additive comments), to respond thoughtfully to others, and to monitor their own behavior in regard to group expectations and
learning tasks (e.g., self-regulation). We call these interpersonal skills *school social skills*
because they are the skills that are needed by students to benefit from the many and
varied group venues utilized for learning in schools. Paradoxically, school social skills
are requisite skills for participating in groups; yet, they are developed over time by participation in groups. Since these skills do not come naturally to many students, school
personnel are always working on teaching, shaping, scaffolding, and coaching the
development of these critical school social skills.

Let's take a look at some of the many ways in which teachers facilitate the development of school social skills in their classrooms. Teachers cue students to pay attention
and they are sometimes directive in asking students questions and inviting them to
examine what others have said in order to encourage and support critical thinking.
Teachers shape student responses by asking students to summarize and paraphrase
what they are saying so that their point is highlighted, or they may ask a peer to paraphrase what they have heard in order to encourage appropriate listening skills. Some
teachers ask students to connect what they are saying to what has been said previously
by another peer; this emphasizes the flow and continuity in the class construction of
meaning. For a higher level of cognitive participation, teachers invite students to articulate their thought processes and require them to offer facts or provide evidence to support their ideas. All of these teaching behaviors serve to help students enter into
discussions and connect with others in intellectual thought and dialogue. They are
ways to ensure that students are meaningfully engaged in learning.

A large portion of school and district developmental guidance plans focus on
helping students acquire these school social skills in an interpersonal communication
skills curriculum. However, just because curriculum has covered these skills, you cannot assume that all of the students in your school will be able to *use* them. Learning
these skills takes time and practice—and that happens in school classrooms, halls, and
playgrounds. It is important to remember that the school counseling program social
and personal skill curriculum cannot be a curriculum that runs parallel to other academic curricula in schools. The school social skill curriculum is something that should
span multiple settings and will be actively nurtured throughout the school day. Every
aspect of what happens in schools and all members of the school community must
work in concert to create socially skilled students.

Finally, we emphasize that a student's lack of school social skills should not be
used as the sole measure for screening students out of participating in groups. One
might consider that students who display a paucity of school social skills are in greater
need for opportunities to develop and strengthen them than others. While we agree that
some groups may not be appropriate for some students, all groups should be seen as
school social skill learning opportunities. The practice of including "positive role models" in counseling groups for children who have behavior problems deserves careful
consideration in this discussion. Remember that membership in counseling groups
needs to be based on the extent to which students are in need of and are likely to
achieve growth relative to the intended learning goals and objectives of the group. So, if

the individuals who are considered to be "good role models" are likely to achieve some benefit of being in a counseling group (and the leader intentionally facilitates the direction of this learning for these students), than it may very well be appropriate for them to be in a group that is otherwise designed for students who are struggling with managing their own behaviors. Otherwise, we would argue that such placements are questionable. Similarly, groups structured for students who are seeking ways to develop friends should only include students who have higher amounts of social capital when the group is facilitated in a way that also benefits these students. That is, heterogeneity in membership is appropriate when the group is facilitated in a way that benefits all subgroups of members. We caution counselors to be sure that their planning and facilitation of groups is done in a way that is intentionally meaningful for all group members.

Status Issues in School Groups

Groups have the potential to offer youth opportunities to create the ways that they want to be with others and in the world; groups also have the power to condemn youth to the social roles that have inhibited their growth historically and in their school community. The group leader holds the reigns for leading the group to either destiny.

Meier (2002) asserts that schools matter "even more than TV" (p. 10) in telling children who they are and who they can be. Here we focus on the implicit social status perceptions that develop in schools and which are prescriptive for how students engage with others socially and around learning tasks. Early in their school careers, youth develop ideas regarding competence, popularity, and other student characteristics; the social ordering that exists in regard to these variables is an undercurrent in most school communities. Children keenly understand the unspoken hierarchical structures that relegate notions of popularity and competence according to group affiliation characteristics such as race, social class, gender, ethnic group, as well as to variables such as perceived academic ability, athleticism, and attractiveness (Cohen, 1994). Social status grouping functions in accordance to unspoken rules about member role and influence (Cohen, 1994) and most students are aware where they stand in these hierarchies. They develop notions of self that are shaped by these community and status groupings (White, 2004).

Social status positioning affects the ways in which youth feel invited into and are able to participate in group learning tasks, the relative influence that they have on others in the group, the ways in which peers treat them in the group, and their own expectations regarding performance and competence (Cohen, 1994). Low status students often do not participate in discussions and if they do, their contributions are sometimes ignored or passed over by peers in favor of contributions from higher status peers. They may not have access to learning materials, resources, or information and as a result they may be seen as passive learners or as students who do not complete tasks; or worse, that they do not really care. They are not picked for teams or small group activities, and they are sometimes characterized by their misbehavior or in stereotypical ways.

Group work offers opportunities for attacking status perceptions (Cohen, 1994). In school classroom and counseling groups this happens in some important ways. First, when the content of the group focuses on deconstruction of social conventions, such as notions about attractiveness, gender roles and behaviors, or cultural norms around drugs and alcohol, students learn the important skills of appropriate inquiry and develop the courage to become critical consumers of ideas. Second, when the group leader facilitates the group in ways that are consistent with the windows and mirrors philoso-phy (that offer every group member a valued role in the group), when tasks are interest-ing and engaging in a variety of ways, and when group tasks are organized in ways that require different abilities and different student strengths for participation, then students will come to need and value the different strengths of all of the members of the group (Cohen, 1994). This is demonstrated in the earlier Case Study 5.8 and our discussion that followed, when Mr. Hererra introduced group roles into his classroom group.

Social status differences in the group are also attacked when group norms about re-spect and fairness are developed early on and enforced by the group leader, when stu-dents are prepared for group learning by having the requisite school social skills, when group roles and tasks are made explicit for all group members, when learning tasks take into account the varied abilities of all members of the group, when students are guided to reflect on their group processes, and when the group leader is active in assigning compe-tence to all members of the group (Cohen, 1994). *Cooperative Learning* (Johnson, Johnson, & Holubec, 1994), *The Responsive Classroom* (Charney, 1991), *Complex Instruction* (Cohen, 1994), and *Experiential Learning* (Luckner & Nadler, 1997) are teaching models that offer approaches to structuring learning environments and experiences in order to enhance the strengths of all group members. The ideas and strategies that follow in Chapter 6, *Fundamentals of Leading,* are the tools that group leaders use to facilitate the group in ways that dismantle social status positioning and to equalize access to learning in the counsel-ing and classroom groups that you will be leading in your school.

Fundamentals of Leading

Among group work enthusiasts, the term *executive function* refers to the administrative aspects of running the group (Lieberman, Yalom, & Miles, 1973). It refers to managing the pacing and timing of the group to keep it on task and providing appropriate structure so that members are able to take risks and feel safe (DeLucia-Waack, 2006). In this chapter, we discuss ways in which group leaders use their executive function role to facilitate the group towards intended learning goals and objectives. We begin with a reference to basic counseling skills, as they are the tools used for establishing group climate, norms, rules, and intervention strategies. We also offer a comprehensive discussion on executive function decision-making with regard to managing group process and content. While all of these strategies are suggested primarily as ways to manage the group, they also help effective group leaders avoid problems that distract the group from achieving its goals and objectives.

BASIC COUNSELING SKILLS FOR GROUP WORK

Basic counseling skills, sometimes called *microskills* (Ivey, Pedersen, & Ivey, 2001), are the tools that group leaders use to engage group members with each other in meaningful and growth-producing ways, to help individuals construct a sense of self and self-with-others, to facilitate the learning of new skills, and to promote new knowledge (Ivey, Pedersen, & Ivey, 2001). They are also used to create a therapeutic relationship between the leader and group member, to extrapolate meaning from client's stories, and to help group members move towards learning, growth, and change. Basic counseling skills are the *how* of group leadership. They are what counselors use to direct the group in the moment of action!

In this chapter, we will describe the specific ways in which counselors intervene in groups using counseling skills. Describing counseling in terms of discrete skills may oversimplify what group leaders do, but it does provide a concrete way of talking about how they can be intentional in their work. In Appendix D, we have included a list of fundamental counseling and group-work skills that are typically used in school counseling and classroom groups.

GROUP CLIMATE

Group climate refers to the group conditions that are facilitative (or not) of growth, learning, and change. While there are many variables identified in the group-work literature that affect group climate (e.g., the type of group, the make-up of the group, the stage of the group, or group leader competence), we have singled out for discussion here some of the variables we believe are uniquely important for working with youth in groups in schools: safety, challenge, risk, cohesiveness, empathy, and caring.

The Growth Zone

The importance of creating a group climate characterized by trust, support, and safety is underscored in the group work and teacher education literature (see Corey & Corey, 2006; Kline, 2003; Larrivee, 2005; Luckner & Nadler, 1997). Broad consensus across these fields is that the group leader (i.e., the teacher or counselor) is responsible for establishing the tone of safety in the group.

Before we go on to identify some critical components of group safety, we want to point out that safety alone is not a sufficient condition for learning. Learning happens in a safe environment that also challenges individuals to grapple with new material and ideas that are just beyond their current level of understanding (Bateson, 1994; Douthit, 2008; Piaget, 1966; Vygotski, 1978). This is what Vygotski refers to as the *Zone of Proximal Development* (ZPD). It is critical to remember that working in the ZPD tends to create a sense of disequilibrium and anxiety for learners (Kline, 2003). This may be particularly apparent in classroom groups where the audience of peers can be fairly large. While encouraging risk-taking in groups can bring forth new learning, Gladding (2003) points out that "too much or too little anxiety inhibits the performance of the group and its members" (p. 116). The task of the group leader, then, is to encourage members to take appropriate risks in a way that is safe for them, despite their feeling anxious. It is a process of push and hold; by working in what Gerstein calls the *Growth Zone* (as cited in Luckner & Nadler, 1997, p. 20).

Working in the Growth Zone happens when the norms in the group encourage and support appropriate interaction among members and appropriate risk-taking. These norms are then fortified by clearly articulated rules. Even with explicit rules in place, some group members may be more reluctant than others to take risks in the group. The ways in which the group is facilitated by the group leader around reluctance is formative to appropriate risk-taking. Basic group leadership skills such as reflection, paraphrasing, immediacy, shifting and cutting off the focus, and confrontation can be used by the group leader to manage group member anxiety and to facilitate healthy risk-taking in the group. These skills are especially effective when used intentionally, which will be evident when we discuss the Intervention Cube (Cohen & Smith, 1976) later in the chapter. It is important for us to reiterate that it is the group leader's responsibility to facilitate the group so that all students are engaged and are taking appropriate learning risks, and it is also the leader's responsibility to monitor group member safety.

Cohesion

Group cohesion is one of the therapeutic factors identified by Yalom (2005) as making groups productive for members. Cohesion refers to the establishment of a place of belonging for all members in the group (Corey & Corey, 2006; Gladding, 2008; Kline, 2003). Group cohesion develops from healthy interpersonal relationships among group members and when members have a sense of commonality in connection to the purpose of the group. That is, when students are clear about why they are in a particular group and when they feel purposefully connected to the content of the group, they are likely to feel a sense of belonging. When members feel like they belong in the group, they are more likely to feel safe enough to take some risks in order to grow.

The necessity of cohesion in larger classroom groups and in task groups is questioned, sometimes. Since cohesiveness enables students to be accepting of one another, to value each other's opinions, to be open to risk-taking, and to engage in some degree of self-disclosure (Corey & Corey, 2006; Gladding, 2008; Kline, 2003)—to function in the Growth Zone, we believe that enhancing group cohesion, regardless of group type, is a worthy group leader endeavor.

Group leaders can facilitate group cohesion by using basic counseling skills (see the list of skills in Appendix D). For example, paraphrasing, reflecting, and probing questions can be used to help students identify feelings, express empathy, and to share their own experiences in the group. Linking, focusing, shifting the focus, and cutting off can be used to help group members listen and respond to each other respectfully, as well as to shape member contributions so they are purposeful. Immediacy can be used to shift conversations to what is happening in the group, which will increase interpersonal bonding among group members. Immediacy can also be used to shape conceptual conversations into personally relevant real-life discussions. *Case Study 6.9* demonstrates how group cohesion can be fostered to engage group members, and how the group leader can use basic counseling skills to facilitate powerful and meaningful discussions in a cohesive group.

CASE STUDY 6.9

Cohesion

Ms. Martinez was working in a high school classroom advisory group (i.e., a regularly meeting homeroom that has short, focused discussions on topics relevant to the high school students in the group) that was interested in forming a school-wide Gay-Straight Student Alliance (GSA). This topic was put on the agenda by the advisory group members (all of the students in the group expressed interest in discussing the topic) to be discussed in the group after a recent Gay-Lesbian-Bisexual (GLB)-related bullying incident at the school.

As the students began to discuss their perspectives on the need for the GSA, Ms. Martinez noticed that a small group of students were involved in a separate discussion in the back of the room. Apparently this was also noticed by Juan, who was actively involved in the GSA discussion. Before Ms. Martinez could intervene to redirect the small group of students in the back of the room, Juan commented loudly, "I guess this is a topic that people who aren't affected don't care about. Reminds me of our 'privilege' discussion" he said, referring to the topic of discussion in the group over the past few meetings.

Judy jumped in saying, "Sounds like some people are trying to closet our GSA."

Seeing that the off-task group of students had caused students who were more involved in the GSA discussion to feel defensive and, perhaps, even insulted, Ms. Martinez decided that she needed to have the group address this dynamic in order to regain a sense of cohesion in the group. Using immediacy, Ms. Martinez said, "Let's just stop here for a minute and look at how we're doing as a group. I notice that there is a large group of students who are involved in the GSA discussion—bringing up pros and cons and trying to figure out what to do in response to the bullying incident that happened last week on campus. I also notice that there is another group of students who seem to be involved in a separate discussion in the back of the room. I'm not sure why there are two discussions in here, but it worries me that this is causing students to feel unsafe."

"You got that right," Jenna called out.

"We're not talking about you," Felicia responded from the back of the room. "As a matter of fact, we're trying to help Jake get his homework done."

"Thanks, Jenna and Judy and Juan for letting us know how you feel, and also to you, Felicia, for letting us know what's going on back there. That helps avoid misunderstandings. I'd like for all of you in the back to stop what you're doing and listen to what I'm about to say [she stops and waits until all eyes are upon her]: It can feel really unsafe in the group when students form their own smaller group and talk about something else, especially when the larger group topic is something as sensitive as GLB issues. Whether you intend to or not, it gives the message of disinterest and disrespect. Do you see that?"

"We weren't trying to dis anyone" protested Jake, "they're just helping me with my homework."

"I hear what you're saying about not trying to make people feel bad, Jake, and I appreciate you saying that. But, as you know—as we talked about last week: Hurt happens, even when intentions are 'good.' I just want everyone to think about the topic we're discussing and how easily misperceptions can develop. Do you see what I'm saying?"

"Yeah," conceded Jake.

"Can anyone offer a solution for how to get us to a better place in here?" Ms. Martinez asked.

"No. But I didn't mean to dis you, Jenna, and Juan, and Judy." Claudia offered from the back.

"Yeah, man. Let's move on." Juan said.

"No, I'm pissed off," said Judy. "This is the kind of silencing that happens to GLB people all the time."

"Anger is going to be a pretty present feeling when we start talking out loud about forming a Gay-Straight Student Alliance," Ms. Martinez offered. "What do we want to do with it when we see it in here . . . and how should we deal with it if we form an alliance? These are important questions."

"Well," said Claudia, "we got to make sure that we don't hurt people when we get mad. I mean. Okay, anger . . . yeah, we all get that . . . but that stuff that happened last week in school—I mean, people—I think probably even Juan and Judy—really got hurt because they were friends with, you know, 'Curley' who got beat up. That's where it's bad."

"So, you're thinking that it's okay to be angry, but not to hurt people." Ms. Martinez paraphrased. "Others?" she asked, inviting perspectives from other in the group.

By focusing the incident that arose in the group and using the basic counseling skills of immediacy, paraphrasing, drawing out, and inviting students into dialogue, Ms. Martinez was able to redirect some of the students who were not engaged in discussion with those who were offended. Part of her success lay in her ability to make parallels between the incident that happened in the group and the larger topic of GLB issues, which the whole group had earlier agreed was important. In this way, the problem that arose in the group was addressed with regard to the context of the topic under discussion. This intervention focused on helping the group be cohesive while engaged in difficult conversations and provided a structure for navigating difficult conversations.

Reflection Questions

1. Can you identify specific moments in this case where there are hints that group cohesion is developing? Can you identify any obvious risks to cohesion?
2. From your experiential and cultural perspective what are signals or clues that a group (that you are a member of or that you are observing) has cohered?
3. Discuss the role of trust in cohesion. How do cultural phenomena "play out" in group formation? How might you use members' diverse cultural experiences to build cohesion? Brainstorm several examples.

It is helpful to remember that part of the task of all groups, big or small, is to figure out how to be together as a group. You will want to work towards establishing a sense of cohesiveness early on in the group and to monitor group cohesion throughout the life of the group. This is particularly important during and after critical incidents and difficult discussions in the group.

Caring

Caring is rarely discussed in the school and counseling literature. However, Noddings (1992) pointed out that "Perhaps the most important thing children can learn from us [educators] is how to interact with people and other living things" (p. 163). This initiated a critical examination of the place for caring in public education. The ways in which Noddings (1992; 1996) defines caring relationships and the ways in which she talks about caring in school communities, illuminate some of the most basic characteristics of healthy interpersonal relationships and healthy group climates. Noddings (1992; 1996) reminds us that caring relationships are at the core of learning how to get along with others and being with others in school communities. According to Noddings, caring is communicated in school groups when children extend towards others, when they engage in the lives of others (by noticing, asking, being with), and when they respond to or acknowledge the caring efforts of others (Noddings, 1992; 1996).

We agree with Noddings that interpersonal behaviors that connote caring, as defined in the ways just mentioned, are fundamental skills for interacting with others, in and out of schools. When caring is present in a group, it sets a tone for engagement and respect. Caring also brings a sense of belongingness into the group or into a school community (Lindwall & Coleman, 2008). The extent to which group leaders communicate the expectation that group members approach each other in caring ways and embrace the spirit of caring will influence how healthy and conducive to learning the group will be. We offer these suggestions for promoting caring in classroom and counseling groups:

1. Be explicit about the importance of embracing a caring norm in the group.
2. Scaffold and structure student engagement so that it is communicated from a base of empathy and caring. This means that you may need to actively intervene in some discussions to ask students to talk to one another and to respond to each other with empathy and respect.
3. Plan your groups around topics that are engaging and relevant to the lives of the students in the group in order to stimulate meaningful thought and conversation and to communicate interest in the lives of the student members. As students come to know more about the real lives of their peers, they form a foundation which will develop into meaningful relationships.
4. Help group members become self-reflective about their own efforts and experiences of caring (Henderson, 1996).
5. Remember that expressions of caring are not just for student group members. Be mindful of the ways in which you demonstrate care for students in the group and the language you use when communicating with students. The tone that is set by the group leader will become a norm in the group.
6. A caring community has no tolerance for hurtful or disrespectful behavior. It is the group leader's responsibility to monitor the group and the leader should always intervene against potentially hurtful or disrespectful interactions in the group.

Case Study 6.10 illustrates how basic counseling skills can be used to facilitate a caring norm. Counseling skills that can be used to this end include directing member to member dialogue; focusing on feelings and thoughts; using immediacy and linking student contributions; cutting off, drawing out, and shifting the focus; processing group activities in ways that link activity to the real life experiences of the students in the group; and offering conceptual interventions for meaning-making and discussion.

CASE STUDY 6.10

Establishing Caring Norms

In a small counseling group, Claudio blurted out, "Melika, shut up. You don't know anything."

The counselor, Mr. Baker, intervened, saying "Hold on. Let's pause and pay close attention to something that is happening right now. Claudio, it seems that you are angry at Melika, and telling people to shut up is hurtful. As you know, we have talked in here about the importance of being respectful to others, and trying to do that, even when we're angry."

"Well, she's stupid. She keeps telling people not to listen to me," Claudio defended himself.

"Okay, wait," Mr. Baker intervened. "Please start with how you feel and then tell Melika what you don't like about what she said. Okay? That way you can give her feedback in a way that is not accusing and hurtful. Okay? Do you think you can do that?"

"I guess," Claudio said.

"Now, wait a minute, then, Claudio," Mr. Baker continued, "I want you to think about what you are going to say for a minute while I check in with Melika." Mr. Baker realized he also had to work with Melika, so that she could hear Claudio's feedback without reacting to his first attempts, which were, indeed, hurtful.

"Melika," he said, "Claudio made a mistake in how he handled that situation. Are you in a position to work with him as he tries again?"

"I guess," Melika said, being familiar with this kind of intervention in the group when the caring norm has been broken.

"Okay, thanks, Melika, for your patience. Let's see what we can do here," Mr. Baker said as he then moved back to Claudio to correct his former outburst and to direct the two into more respectful conversation about their conflict.

Reflection Questions

1. How does Mr. Baker's handling of this situation demonstrate Noddings' concept of caring?
2. In the second paragraph of this case, how does Mr. Baker's intervention, "let's stop for a minute," exemplify structure and scaffolding?
3. Look with care at this exchange. How is it an opportunity for Mr. Baker to apply the concepts of windows and mirrors in this moment? Can you imagine yourself in this leadership role during this situation? What are you feeling? What would you need to be particularly cautious about as you intervened instead of Mr. Baker?

GROUP NORMS AND RULES

Group *norms* refer to the unwritten code of behavioral expectations that set a tone for the group. They are not typically discussed or negotiated directly among group members and often develop out of the awareness or purposefulness of the group leader (Kline, 2003). On the other hand, group *rules* are the "guidelines by which groups are run" (Gladding, 2008, p. 117). Group rules articulate the behavioral expectations for group participation; in effect, establishing the boundaries within which the group will function. As such, rules help establish a sense of safety in the group and they facilitate interaction that is conducive to learning. So, while group norms often arise outside of the awareness of the group, the leader has an important (although often unnoticed or underutilized) role in making group norms explicit. Rules are what make norms explicit. They provide clarity around the parameters for group member participation and behavior.

Working in the Growth Zone and creating a group climate that is cohesive and fosters caring requires careful structuring and monitoring of group norms and rules in order to ensure they embody these principles. In this discussion, we will focus on ways the group leader can establish and enforce rules in the group. We will also discuss how norms and rules may look different in classroom and counseling groups.

Establishing Rules

When students are engaged in the process of establishing group rules, they are able to see that the rules represent their ideas, values, and interests. This allows students to understand why rules are needed, to develop a sense of ownership of the rules, and to feel more accountable to the group rules.

It is important to initiate a discussion about group norms and rules at the beginning of the year, semester, or time together as a group and to actively involve all of the group members in the rule-setting process (Mendler, 1992; Queen, Blackwelder, & Mallen, 1997). We suggest that you begin the discussion by inviting students to identify the kind of climate they want to create in their group; you can explain to students how rules structure group climate. Then invite students to think about the kinds of rules that would enable the climate they have chosen. As students introduce suggestions regarding potential rules, it may be helpful to focus on the intent or spirit of the proposed rule, again helping students understand the connection between rules and desired norms. Invite students to consider how each rule that is introduced does or does not embody the kind of climate that they hope to create in the group.

When engaged in a rule-setting discussion in the group, remember to solicit input from all group members. Also, attempt to shape student input so that the rules are defined or described in clear, concrete, behavioral terms, as much as possible (Kerr & Nelson, 1998). This will enable students to understand the behavioral manifestations of the rules in order to have a clear sense of how to comply with them. This point is especially important when working with younger children and others who may have difficulties understanding how concepts look in practice.

It is important to set an appropriate tone in the rule-setting process. Keep in mind that explicitly naming every rule and every behavior that is expected from group members is impossible. Also, a long list of *dos and don'ts* does not facilitate a positive group climate. Endeavor to articulate rules in affirmative, positive language (i.e., what students should do, rather than what not to do) and consider limiting the initial rule-list to those rules that are truly essential (Kerr & Nelson, 1998). If necessary, other rules can be added later on an as-needed basis.

The group leader should always be prepared to introduce rules related to member safety, even if they are not introduced by the group members. One basic safety rule for *every* group is respect for others and for property. Safety rules are never negotiable by group members and they should always be strictly enforced by the group leader, regardless of group type or age of the group members. When students are pushed to take risks that are too far beyond their Growth Zone, learning is compromised and the leader's ethical responsibility for group safety may be breached. Group leaders must take their cues regarding risk and safety from each individual in the group, as well as from their own knowledge and experience.

Another issue that we believe must be broached by the leader, if it is not raised by the members of the group, is that of confidentiality (see sections Preamble, A.2, A.6.c, & A.7 in the *Ethical Standards for School Counselors* [ASCA, 2004]). Even in classroom groups, respect for others includes honoring that which is shared by other group members. It is important that your discussion around confidentiality is age-appropriate and that it also includes mention of the limits of confidentiality (in regard to safety to self and others). However, it is important to remember that confidentiality should never be assumed in classroom groups. Therefore, classrooms should not be structured as forums in which students share information that deserves the protection of confidentiality. We recommend instituting a rule about confidentiality and having a discussion about what that means, but also the leader must make sure sensitive confidential information is not shared in the group. The leader must take charge of the group in anticipation of a possible breach of this rule.

A third type of rule that may require group leader introduction is that of task orientation. Introducing a rule related to task orientation is sometimes a good way to communicate the expectation that students in the group will be focused on learning. This is particularly important in classroom groups (because they tend to be large and, therefore, require more self-regulation on the part of the group members) and in groups with younger children. Here again, as with rules related to safety and confidentiality, it is appropriate to articulate specific behaviors that are manifestations of task orientation.

After the rules for the group have been named, it is helpful to document them. Documentation serves as a clear reminder of the rules. It is particularly helpful to have the rules in writing when they differ from those of the regular teacher, if they were established early in the school year and are likely to have been forgotten, in groups with younger children, and when you anticipate that some of the group members may challenge the group rules. If having a poster of the rules is not feasible in a particular setting (e.g., when you work in other people's classroom spaces), a quick reminder of the rules at the start of the group may be more appropriate. Also, assigning the task of *keeper of the group rules* to one student (or, better yet, on a rotating basis among students), can assist in the quest of involving all members and provides an opportunity for helping students speak up when breaches occur. These interventions, of course, must be carefully structured in the group by the group leader and all students must be engaged, so it is not always one student who informs on others who break rules.

It is important to recognize that group norms and rules will vary according to the learning objective, the activities that are being used, and the composition of the group. If circumstances in the group give rise to temporary rule changes (i.e., they do not apply for one student in the group, or a particular activity warrants different rules), students need to be informed of the changes. Keep in mind that fair does not always mean equal; group rules need to be tailor-fit to the needs of the group and to the needs of the individuals in the group.

Since the group leader is responsible for monitoring the group, the authority to make rule-changes when needed, rests on the leader. The leader may want to encourage students to make rule additions or changes as well. However, regardless of who presents them, rule changes should typically be negotiated in the group unless immediate changes are necessary for member safety or in cases where confidential information might be compromised. Whenever possible, it is a good idea to explain to students why a rule has been added or changed because rule changes are easier to navigate when they are firmly grounded in an articulated set of beliefs and expectations that are perceived to be fair and just.

Finally, rule-setting processes should vary according to the age, as well as the developmental, communication, and social abilities of the students in the group. Brophy (1999) pointed out that in early grades, teachers often spend a great deal of time explaining expectations and rules to students and modeling classroom routines. However, older students sometimes feel disrespected if too much attention is given to rules and consequences and if the rules are imposed on the group rather than generated from student input. So, it is important to match rule-setting processes to the needs of the group.

Enforcing Rules

All students and all groups vary in the degree to which they will need feedback and reminders regarding rules. So, the ways in which group rules are enforced will depend on the group. When working from an authoritative position, rule enforcement is instructive, not punitive. Rules should always be enforced in respectful, fair, matter-of-fact, instructive language, in order to encourage self-regulation and avoid power struggles.

We suggest approaching rule enforcement from a least restrictive and least invasive approach, whenever possible. One of the most innocuous interventions for enforcing rules is **cueing**. Cueing refers to prompting appropriate behavior by restating directions, giving nonverbal signals, offering reminders, and standing nearby (physical proximity). Continuously scanning and monitoring the activity helps you be on the lookout for when students need cues before rules are broken, and it allows you to intervene quickly should infractions occur. Whenever possible, it is best to cue students in ways that do not draw undue attention and to focus on supporting appropriate or expected behavior instead.

Redirection is another good strategy for helping students align themselves with the rules that have been established in the group. This strategy is fairly innocuous and can be used in response to minor events in the group related to rule enforcement. We recommend these steps for redirecting student behavior so it is in alignment with the group rules:

1. *Stop what is happening in the group or stop what is happening with one individual in the group.*   For example, "Folks, we need to take a time-out here to talk about something." "Helena, I'm going to ask you to stop for a moment."
2. *Be cautious about inclusion and exclusion.*   If there are one or two *offenders* in the group, be certain that you are not inadvertently seen as taking the whole group to task for one or two individual students' behaviors. In general, it is most respectful to respond to individuals privately, particularly if they are the only ones in the group who consistently break the rules. However, there are times when it is best to use the group of peers to shape individual member behavior. These decisions must be made judiciously.
3. *Call attention to the group rule that needs to be enforced.*   Calling attention to the rule might sound like this: "We have a rule in here about respecting others in this group."
4. *Point out the incident that represented the rule-breach.*   For example, "I just heard someone in here tell someone else to 'shut up.' When we decided on the rule of respect, we talked about the words that communicate disrespect, and clearly, 'shut up' was one of them." This helps student make a clear connection between behavior (i.e., the breach) and concept (i.e., the rule).
5. *Redirect the students to more appropriate behavior and move on.*   For example, "If someone does not like what someone else says in here, please give them direct feedback, using I-messages. Do not tell them to 'shut up.' Does anyone need help using I-messages?" "Okay, let's all get back to what we were working on and remember to be respectful of everyone in this group."
6. *Reinforce appropriate behavior as soon as possible after the redirection.*   For example, "Wow, I'm hearing some very rich conversations in the small groups now. Nice work!"

When students are fairly consistently off-task, when their behavior is causing disruptions for others, and when student behavior is dangerous or grossly inappropriate, more assertive rule enforcement is probably necessary. Chapters 7 and 8 in Part III, *Responding*, offer extensive response strategies for the more serious rule-breaches that may occur in the group.

Differences in Classroom and Counseling Group Norms and Rules

The kinds of norms and rules, as well as the ways in which the rules are established and enforced in the group, can look very different in counseling and classroom groups. Here we will specify how group norms and rules may need to be adapted for application in classroom and counseling groups, with particular attention to norms around personal sharing, issues related to sharing physical space, and working in the school context.

It is sometimes difficult to find an appropriate norm around personal sharing in classroom groups. We have found that when students are met with a welcoming and caring environment, when they are given appropriate structure, and when there is a common and meaningful purpose or task, they are likely to want to talk and participate actively in the group. Sometimes, for some students, this includes sharing personal information. Indeed, this is the goal of many small counseling groups. However, in a large classroom setting, such sharing may not be as appropriate. For example, when beginning a single class lesson on the effects of bullying, Sarah—who had previously spent time in individual counseling with her school counselor—wanted to share with the class how she had first-hand experience with bullies. When Sarah began to speak, the counselor felt that what Sarah was about to share would turn the lesson from content-driven—learning about what being a bully or being bully might cause—into a personal airing of Sarah's pain and suffering. Had this been a counseling group in which Sarah was a member, her willingness to disclose would have been welcomed as a vital catalyst for the group. But in the classroom group, this level of sharing was likely to shift the focus from the intended content and might leave this particular child feeling more vulnerable than anticipated.

While counselors typically want students to engage personally with the content and activities in both group types, the sharing of information that is too personal is not appropriate when (a) there is no group member screening, (b) the large number of students in the group inhibits the leader's ability to provide individual attention to students who many need special consideration during tender conversations, and (c) when it is difficult to enforce norms around confidentiality. It follows that norms around personal sharing in classroom groups should be more conservative than those in counseling groups.

What is meant by *conservative*? The degree of conservativeness here has to do with the function and purpose of the group. School counselors, we believe, often have to navigate turbulent waters in this area. It is likely that a few students in every classroom group have sat with the school counselor for one-to-one counseling and that several have participated in a small counseling group. In these other relationships, students have learned how to function with the counselor in particular ways. But in the larger classroom group, self disclosure, giving and receiving feedback, specific attention to feelings—to name a few skills that they developed in other counseling venues—may not be encouraged nor welcomed in exactly the same way. This can be challenging for students and counselors alike. Therefore, it is important that students be given direct and explicit instruction on how they are expected to participate in the various settings (e.g., individual counseling, small counseling groups, classroom groups) in which they participate with the school counselor. Also, it is important to remember that all students—in both classroom and counseling groups—should always be allowed and supported to pass when invited to share (i.e., students can elect to not speak), as this helps to ensure member safety and shapes appropriate self-regulation around self-disclosure.

It is also important to keep confidentiality in mind here. One might forcefully assert that there is no confidentiality in classroom groups. As mentioned, it is the responsibility of the school counselor to ensure students understand how confidentiality applies in various settings. Our ethical obligations here are many. The *Ethical Standards for School Counselors* (ASCA, 2004), *ACA Code of Ethics and Standards of Practice* (ACA, 2005), and the *ASGW Best Practice Guidelines* (ASGW, 2007) each address informed consent (assent in cases of minor clients) and issues related to confidentiality in group work. These doctrines support the necessity for school counselors to be perfectly clear and developmentally sensitive about risks associated with disclosure. Group members must be informed when confidence can be upheld. Although counseling group norms are established to uphold each members' confidence, it cannot be assured in the same fashion as one-to-one counseling between the student and counselor. The bottom line is that classroom groups should not be places where sensitive disclosures are made. We would add that in our experience, students—even the very youngest of group members in classroom and counseling groups—comprehend the limitations of confidentiality when developmentally appropriate informed assent is supplied. Our reminder here is clear: Be certain that you, the school counselor, ensure that students understand the different roles of the school counselor and what those differences mean to their expected participation in classroom and counseling groups. We will come back to this important topic later in this chapter.

Other pertinent issues around norms and rules—especially in classroom groups—have to do with the ownership of the physical space in the room and with norms around activity and noise level. In many schools, classroom groups are conducted in the physical space of the regular teacher's classroom. As we know, classroom spaces often come with explicit or implicit expectations for how they will be used and how people in those spaces are to behave. The classroom teacher will have classroom group norms and rules that are consistent with what she needs to accomplish. However, the norms and rules that are appropriate for the regular classroom may not serve the kinds of experiences that you want in your classroom group. For example, the regular teacher's math curriculum may require students to work individually and quietly during the lesson. If your curriculum is focused on helping students acquire interpersonal skills, giving feedback, or being assertive, these curricular goals are much better met though active and spontaneous engagement. However, this issue of differing norms and rules around noise, activity, and space is not solely limited to what happens when counselors and teachers share a common space. In many schools, concerns about the types of activities and the norms that are encouraged in small counseling groups (especially around noise levels and "having too much fun") are also sometimes criticized. All of these conflicting ideas and practices can be especially tricky for counselors to navigate when working in schools.

In response to these issues, we want to point out, first, that it is important to keep in mind that the owner of the classroom space must always be respected when you are in that person's room. Remembering this simple fact should be a guide for how you negotiate the use of shared space. It is also important to note that noise tends to fill space quickly when there are many students in the room, and classrooms are typically located in close proximity to one another. Although you want students to feel comfortable talking and moving about the room freely, the teacher and the students next door who are taking a biology quiz may not appreciate the noise. Be flexible and remember that your group goals and delivery plan needs to suit the school setting. Little goodwill is fostered between school counselors, teachers, and building administrators when group activities disrupt others in the school community.

In order to navigate norm and rule differences between the regular classroom teacher and school counselor using her space, we recommend that you start with what is already in place. Review the existing regular classroom expectations and rules in juxtaposition to the goals that you have for your classroom group. If the rules for your classroom group need to be different, you can modify them with the students in the group by using the rule-setting process we outlined earlier. When making modifications, it is important to be explicit about the changes and to communicate with the students about why those differences exist. *Case Study 6.11* illustrates how this conversation may unfold. As previously mentioned, students can be flexible in dealing with different expectations when they understand the reasoning for them.

It is also a good idea to communicate with the regular teacher about norm and rule differences that might occur throughout the year as you work in his classroom. This is particularly important in situations where the teacher feels uncomfortable with the fact that you have changed the classroom rules, if he is not particularly happy about having you use his space, or if problems have occurred as a result of you being in his room. It can be helpful to suggest that rules shift with the content of the group, not the physical space of the room. That is, rules should be relevant to what is being taught, not where it is being taught. It can be especially helpful to reiterate your commitment to respecting the classroom space, as well as the ways in which the teacher works with the group. Be sure to work closely with the administration in the school if there are concerns about the ways in which you are working in your small counseling groups. Be prepared to explain the purpose of your group and to offer an explanation of the kind of work you are doing in that group—why your methods are appropriate to the goals and objectives to the group. It is helpful to speak in language that is clear, informative, understandable, but that does not compromise student confidentiality. Remember that the theory behind some counseling approaches (particularly the use of play media) is often misunderstood by those who are not professional counselors.

CASE STUDY 6.11

Clarifying Differences in Group Rules

School counselor, Mr. Chira, was working with the physical education teacher, Mrs. Parnel, on a low-impact adventure-based challenge activity in Mr. H's classroom group of fourth graders. The intent of the group was to help the students develop a sense of cohesion and respect in the class. Some of the students in the group were identified as "acting out" and there had been some bully incidents in the past. Goals for the group were to help students develop interpersonal skills, to help students be more respectfully assertive with peers, and to develop classroom cohesion.

The classroom group ran for an hour and a half each week for 6 weeks, with the school counselor and the physical education teacher co-leading. Since extra time was needed to fully embrace this classroom group plan, it was decided to dedicate the class PE time combined with the regularly scheduled developmental guidance classroom group time for this group. The classroom teacher, Mr. H, was also present during all of the group sessions, and participated when he felt his presence would enhance the desired result of cohesion and respect. As mentioned, the format required students to be engaged in physical activities, which were later processed in the group. Because this group allowed the children to talk and run around more freely than what was allowable for these same children in the classroom and in their regular physical education class, the group leaders wanted to be clear with the students that the norms and rules in this group would not translate to other situations in the school. To this end, Mr. Chira told the children, "When you're in this group and we're working on some of the special activities that we will be using in here, we will be able to work in ways that are different than what's allowed in your classroom and in PE. Let's talk about how this will be different. . . ." This opening led to an explicit discussion about the group norms and rules.

Later, Mrs. Parnel added, "We all know that when you're back in your regular room with Mr. H, it's important to remember to go back to the rules in that room. We know that having these two different rules might be a little confusing in the beginning, but I think we'll all get it soon. The reason that our rules are different from your teachers is that we want you to have a different kind of learning here with us. It's not that one is right and one is wrong—it's just that they are different. Okay?"

All three adults also followed up in these discussions with the students when rule breaches occurred. These follow-up conversations continued to point out that rules vary in different situations and focused on reminding the students which rules were in operation at that time and in that situation.

Reflection Questions

1. Describe how this classroom group led by two adults plus Mr. H offered a unique opportunity on multiple levels for these children.
2. What age-related concerns might this norm and rule establishment strategy hold if Mr. Chira was called into a second-grade classroom with similar issues? What if he was called to a seventh-grade classroom?

In addition to the differences in norms and rules that may exist across counseling and classroom groups, there may also be differences in how much attention is needed for the establishment and enforcement of rules. In both groups, it is wise to establish group norms right away. In the case of counseling groups, however, you probably will not need to create long lists of rules initially. Of course, rules may need to be introduced and enforced in all groups when norm breaches have occurred or when member behaviors interfere with the intended learning objectives. The counselor should not be shy about introducing rules when needed, but they are not often emphasized early on in counseling groups. However, when working with younger children, with students who have difficulties with self-regulation, and when particularly sensitive material is likely to surface, it is a probably a good idea to outline specific rules that support the norms you want to establish right at the start of the group, even in counseling groups.

In the larger classroom groups, norming, rule-setting, and responding when rules are broken is time well-spent early on in the group. Again, when enforcing rules, it can be advantageous to actively connect rules to desired conditions of group climate, especially in the early stages of the group and when working with younger children. Counselors leading classroom groups may find that they need to spend more time than they do in counseling groups reminding students of rules, and that they need to be more direct in this role.

Finally, we want to revisit the issue of confidentiality, as this is one rule that is often brought up in the norming process with very young children, adolescents, and in adult groups as well (for a meaningful look at similar issues across the lifespan, see Gladding, 2008). "What is said in group, stays in the group" is hard for many young group participants to understand, and it can be too simplistic for older and more sophisticated group members. Instead of using simple catchy statements such as these (or perhaps, in addition to using these statements), we suggest that you focus on helping group members understand the intent of confidentiality. Confidentiality, of course, is needed to create and maintain an environment where group members can share thoughts and feelings safely. When we offer children in a group the opportunity to define what will make the group a safe place to explore feelings, to share beliefs and thoughts, and to feel supported through the process, confidentiality is usually beautifully defined. Rules around confidentiality typically flow rather naturally from clear understandings about why confidentiality is so important. We do not support the use of words like "secret," or "private," to connote confidentiality, as these terms do not adequately define confidentiality. On the contrary, they suggest an inaccurate and misleading notion of what confidentiality really means. In fact, the right of confidentiality usually belongs to parents when students are in school (see *Ethical Standards for School Counselors* [ASCA, 2004] A.2.a–g, A.6.c, B.2.a–c, F.1.d).

A second point on confidentiality is important here. While rules around confidentiality are often easily stated, they are usually much more challenging to uphold. No student should ever be promised that what they share in group will stay in group—despite our very best intentions. Group leaders simply do not have the social nor the legal power to assure that confidentiality will be maintained in the group. That is why, the leader is also responsible, as mentioned earlier, for overseeing the ways in which students are invited to participate in classroom and counseling groups in schools. This means that executive function of the group leader includes assuring that the content and the level of personal sharing in the group is appropriate.

A final insight around rules in groups with children is this: Less is more. Some children would spend days creating rules that would shape their ideal fantasies about a perfect group environment, while others are immediately turned off by the mention of the word *rule*! Too many rules burden both the leader and the members. We recommend that the list of rules be short, encompassing, positive (desired behaviors not forbidden ones), and written in a grade-appropriate vocabulary. An initial list of rules for most groups may include:

- physical safety,
- respecting others,

- honoring the contributions of every member of group,
- arriving on time,
- staying through to the end, and
- maintaining behaviors appropriate for school while in group.

These rules are best discussed in ways that offer abundant personal meaning for each group member. When asked, every member of the group should be able to paraphrase, give examples of, and teach others, perhaps, what the rules mean. Until rules are adopted and demonstrated as the norms of the counseling group, it is likely that cohesion and progress will be hampered.

Establishing Culturally-Appropriate Norms and Rules

A major difference in approaching diversity issues in schools from a tourist curriculum (i.e., just noticing the customs and celebrations of a particular culture), as opposed to a windows and mirrors approach, centers on issues of respect and valuing difference (see Derman-Sparks, 1993, for more on this concept of the tourist approach to addressing multiculturalism in schools).

When working in schools, it can be very easy to water-down differences—settling for a short band of variation that never strays very far from the mean. Yet, working with groups during the initial process of establishing norms offers an excellent opportunity to explore differences, to value multiple perspectives, and to set a norm of respect. For this reason, we emphasize the importance of connecting group norms to the purpose of the group and opening up discussions so students are supported to articulate what they need in terms of group norms. These discussions must touch on cultural and other differences that exist among members.

It is critical for school counselors to be aware that individuals from diverse backgrounds come to school with various perspectives and experiences with regard to interpersonal behavior, and also with regard to permission about what can and cannot be discussed in public (i.e., in school). It is also necessary to understand the social context of minority group status. As mentioned, group members with minority group identity characteristics can easily be silenced. It is up to the leader to assure that this does not happen in norm- and rule-setting discussions. Equally important, these students may feel conflicting loyalties—whether to honor home versus school norms and expectations. The possible tension in these situations underscores the importance of the counselor himself being able to embrace multiple perspectives, being familiar with the subgroups in the school community, having the skills to carefully guide delicate conversations, and being aware of the impact of the interventions he is making in the group. (The *Ethical Standards for School Counselors* [ASCA, 2004] Preamble, A.1.c, E.2.a–d; *ASGW Best Practice Guidelines* [ASGW, 2007] Preamble, B.8; and the *ASGW Principles for Diversity-Competent Group Workers* [ASGW, 1998] all speak to these issues.)

STRATEGIES FOR STARTING THE GROUP

Here we offer a number of strategies that can be used to begin classroom and counseling groups. They focus on how to draw students into the content of the group. These strategies, you will notice, can also be effective to draw in student attention at various other times during the group process.

Generating Attention and Interest

Whether working with young people in counseling or in classroom groups, it is important to start the group in ways that awaken and capture students' interests. This is especially important when working with youth who are not motivated to be in the group and in groups with mandated participants (such as the case with students in classroom groups, since developmental guidance groups are not optional in most schools). Interest breeds motivation to be in the group; boredom can lead to misbehavior.

Cueing student attention is a good way to start the group. For example, some counselors begin their groups by raising a hand and inviting students to raise their hands when they are focused and ready to begin. Others play music, engage in a group stretch, flicker the lights, or they may even start with a count-down or use a simple statement such as "ready, set, okay let's start." We recommend that you develop your own creative way to cue student attention and establish a routine in your groups so that students will always know when to be ready to start. This is especially helpful when working with younger children and when working in a classroom group, as it is not uncommon for the school counselor to enter a classroom that is still engaged in a prior task or for some reason is not quite ready for a change of task.

Next, direct students' attention to the task at hand. Sometimes this is best done with an appropriate yet provocative statement or question, or by unveiling an interesting (and relevant) object. You can also play some music, read a short essay, or show a short video clip related to the topic. Your opening welcomes students into the learning mode.

Creating Learning Maps

After capturing student attention, offer students a brief overview of what will happen in the group that day. This kind of preview, what we call a *learning map*, situates the current topic in a learning landscape. You can do this by linking the current learning topic or experiences that will happen that session to previous learning or by explicitly connecting the topic or activities to something that is present in the group or to a real life context. These strategies of contextualizing learning help establish relevancy. Group leaders typically offer learning maps at the start of the group or when introducing new concepts or ideas.

CASE STUDY 6.12

Learning Map

Mr. Padden, who was conducting a classroom group with ninth-grade literature teacher, Mrs. Dvorshak, began the group saying, "Today we are going to spend some time talking about 'silencing behaviors.' This fits in with our discussion last week about discrimination and the book, *Warriors Don't Cry* (Beals, 1994) that we have been discussing in class with Mrs. Dvorshak (the literature teacher). Mrs. D and I noticed last week that some students dominated the discussion and others did not say very much and we wondered about this, especially after a few students wrote in their group reflection journals that they felt that they 'weren't allowed' to speak their mind in the class. Mrs. D and I have a sense that these things did not happen intentionally, but were really a product of what sometimes happens in big groups and in schools when people get used to participating in certain ways and that just becomes a norm. Today we want to start by talking about some of the ways in which Melba and the other students of color who were integrated at Little Rock High in *Warriors Don't Cry* were silenced in their school. Who can help us start off the discussion by being the scribe on the board as we come up with a community definition (i.e., classroom definition) of 'silencing' others?"

Reflection Questions

1. Partnerships between the school counselor and other professionals are often under-utilized in classroom guidance lessons. Brainstorm several potential partnerships (e.g., the counselor and the ninth-grade literature teacher Mrs. Dvorshak). What benefits for the students might emerge through working with these individuals?
2. As you have learned, "it is not uncommon for the school counselor to enter a class-room that is still engaged in a prior task." It is also common for the counselor to ar-rive in the midst of tension, disagreement, or behavioral chaos. Have a dialogue with one or more of your colleagues: How might you "enter" such a room? When should you set aside your lesson and pick up what the class is experiencing in the moment? What are pros and cons to such leadership?
3. Have you noticed instances in groups when a disproportionate amount of time is al-lotted to the warm-up, the ice-breaker, the introduction? Such leadership error is un-doubtedly unintentional, but nevertheless, it bites into the time remaining for the actual lesson or activity. Although you cannot ensure that you will never fall into this predicament, what might you do to minimize this risk?

In *Case Study 6.12*, the plan for the group was linked to a book that was read by the students in the literature class, as well as to students' reported experiences in the previous group meeting. This learning map helped establish the relevancy of the discussion and provided a context for the direction that the leaders wanted to take in the group that day. Remember to keep the introductions and learning map clear and concrete, but also brief; spending too much time on the introduction means having less time for the task at hand.

Offering Instructions

Another important aspect of facilitating a group has to do with the way in which task instructions are communicated to students (Brophy, 1999). Something as simple as be-ing clear when delivering task instructions has a huge impact on the group process. When students are unclear about task requirements, they may become unengaged and disruptive as they scurry to figure out what to do.

When giving instructions, first minimize distractions. For example, "Okay, every-one stop what you're doing, please, and listen carefully to these very important direc-tions for what we will be doing today." Be sure to speak clearly and slowly, and whenever possible, offer information sequentially. Sequential cues offered one at a time, such as "First do this . . ." "Okay, now that you are done with that, the next step is . . ." are particularly helpful when presenting a task that requires many steps, when working in big groups, and when working with younger children.

It is important to adjust the way in which you provide instructions so that they are developmentally appropriate and sensitive to the variety of learning styles represented in the group. Asking a student to repeat back the instructions or inviting questions are ways to reveal misunderstandings; a question spoken by one student is often an unvoiced concern of another. Also, providing written task instructions is appropriate in some cases.

SCAFFOLDING

A scaffold is a kind of temporary platform that is constructed to support individuals who are working on a project. While typically used in the context of building, it is also a term used in the field of education; it refers to teacher behaviors that enable students to participate in classroom learning (Brophy, 1999). Two operative words in the definition of a scaffold are *temporary* and *support*. Temporary highlights the intent of a scaffold as providing assistance for as long as the assistance is needed, but not permanently. A scaffold model of instruction assumes that the kind of support that is needed by students to learn a task will change over time and according to the specific demands of the task. It is also assumed that once provided with support, students will develop the appropriate skills to continue a specific task on their own. Support refers to the ways in which teachers and group leaders help students in the learning process. They do not reduce challenging tasks so that students can do them easily, nor do they just leave students to fend for themselves. Support means to coach, prompt, offer cues, reminders, and instruction so the student will be successful in completing learning tasks.

The topics offered by school counselors in their counseling and classroom groups differ quite dramatically from other subjects that are taught in school. Therefore, many students will need scaffolding to construct meaning from these unique ideas and activities. Brophy's (1999) examples of scaffolding include asking students critical and thoughtful questions, giving them time to respond to those questions, and shaping student responses so they are clear and justified rather than random comments. Scaffolding may also include engaging students in the learning process by helping them stay on task, providing instruction so the material is understood, and helping students interact productively together around the topic or content of the group. Group leaders also provide scaffolds by giving explicit instructions for how to approach a particular task, directing interaction between students so they are speaking to each other, helping students name and express thoughts or feelings, managing member-to-member interactions, encouraging engagement from quieter members, and using rounds to encourage the voices of all. These are considered scaffolding behaviors because they are aimed at providing additional help to students for more active and meaningful participation in the group.

MANAGING PROCESS AND CONTENT

Group *process* typically refers to how members interact, how the group develops, and how things are done in the group. It refers to the relationships among group members and the ways in which learning occurs through dynamics in the group (Geroski & Kraus, 2002). Group *content*, on the other hand, typically refers to what the group is about. It is often reflected in the written goals or objectives of the group, the subject and topic, and the work plan or theme of the group (Geroski & Kraus, 2002). In short,

TABLE 6.1 Level and Type of Group Interventions

Type of Intervention	Level of Intervention	Intensity of Intervention
Conceptual	Intrapersonal	Low ↔ High
Experiential	Interpersonal	
Structural	Group	

Source: Cohen, A. M., & Smith, R. D. (1976). *The critical incident in growth groups: Theory and technique.* La Jolla, CA: University Associates.

process refers to the interpersonal dynamics among members and content is what group members talk about in the group. Together, group process and content are the *how* and *what* of the group.

Cohen and Smith's (1976) *Intervention Cube* model offers a conceptual way of thinking about a range of group leader intervention options for managing group process so the group can accomplish its intended goals. This is a conceptual model that allows group leaders to purposefully conceive and execute decisions in leadership to bring about specific and desired outcomes among the members. The concepts in the model are not simple, however, and we acknowledge this from the start. Nevertheless, we find Cohen and Smith's work so valuable for understanding complex phenomena that occurs in all groups that we ask readers to take their time and truly visualize this conceptual process. In the end, we believe that you will agree—this is a really fine model worthy of comprehension.

In the Intervention Cube, intervention options are organized into three dimensions: level, type, and intensity, as illustrated in Table 6.1.

Type of intervention refers to the ways in which members are asked to engage with material in the group (Cohen & Smith, 1976). A leader intervention type that focuses on helping members conceptualize or make meaning around a significant issue or idea is a *conceptual* intervention. An intervention type that focuses on a member's experience (feeling, thoughts, or behaviors) in the group is an *experiential* intervention. Intervention types that make use of planned activities, exercises, structured tasks or interventions that change the physical movement patterns of members in the group are *structural*. Very generally, conceptual interventions provide opportunities for meaning attribution or meaning making. Experiential type interventions invite members to be aware of their experience in the group, and tend to stimulate emotional awareness or arousal. Structural interventions typically introduce a change to the group functioning, and are often used to stimulate or change group member engagement patterns.

Level of intervention refers to who is addressed by a group leader intervention. An *intrapersonal* level intervention focuses on an individual, an *interpersonal* level intervention invites two or a few members to interact with each other, and a *group* level intervention addresses any or all of the individuals in the group (but no one in particular).

This brings us to the third dimension in this model: **intensity**. Group intensity refers to the impact of a particular group intervention in terms of stimulating group member sensitivity, emotion, or thought. This is presented as a continuous variable: low, medium, and high.

When the group leader is clear about what she wants to accomplish in the group, level, type, and intensity can then be manipulated in order to accomplish the intended objectives. The ways in which the group leader selects and combines the various intervention types, levels, and intensity allows for a wide range of intervention possibilities in the group.

Type and Level Interventions

Case Study 6.13 describes two groups: one classroom and one counseling group. We offer these illustrations as references for our discussion on the application of Cohen and Smith's Intervention Cube (Cohen & Smith, 1976). Looking at both groups concurrently offers the opportunity to compare and contrast how level and type interventions may be used by two different counselors, in two different circumstances, and in counseling and classroom groups.

CASE STUDY 6.13
Two Cases for Study—The Intervention Cube

Classroom Group

The goal for Mr. Jaramillo's fifth-grade classroom group is to expose students to work and career options. In the second session, Sebastian, a student in the group, disrupts the group by tapping his pen during a discussion. Shortly afterwards, Sebastian talks with two peers who are sitting near him, and they continue to whisper with each other while the counselor and other students are participating in the group discussion.

Counseling Group

Giana is in Mrs. McAllister's fourth- and fifth-grade counseling group for girls focusing on divorce. The goals of the group are for the members to develop strategies for managing the stress around the divorce, to support one another in their experiences, and to have the opportunity to grieve the change in their families that have resulted from the divorce. The six members of this group have recently experienced divorce in their families (within the last 6 months), they all elected to participate in the group, and they all have parental consent to be in the group. This particular session is the fourth of eight weekly sessions. In this session, Giana becomes very emotional when she tells the group about a fight she witnessed between her parents. As she talks about it, she also mentions she believes it was her fault that her parents were fighting.

Group Leader Intentions

Mr. Jaramillo will want to keep his classroom group engaged in the content, while also managing the disruptions from Sebastian. In the counseling group, Mrs. McAllister will want to manage the intensity so that Giana can get the support she needs from group members and so that all of the group members can benefit from the concern that she brings to the group (which they probably also share).

Reflection Questions

1. Reviewing the discussion that follows in the text, discuss how the suggested interventions serve their intended purposes.

2. Working in a group, use the Intervention Cube to develop other strategies to use in the group. Ideally, we suggest that you work in conjunction with one or more students—with the goal of establishing a number of purposeful, unique interventions that are potentially effective. Remember that the Intervention Cube affords school counselors a unique language to share successful strategies with others.

In response to the disruption in the classroom group, a *structural* **type** intervention might be used to shift the large group into smaller groups so that students are more personally engaged with the material and less likely to be distracted by others. For example, Mr. Jaramillo might ask students to pair up and read five items from their learning style inventory to their partner and have them guess about the style profile. This structural type intervention has an *interpersonal* **level** focus since it requires students to engage in pairs. Alternatively, Mr. Jaramillo could make a *structural* **type** *intrapersonal* **level** intervention by asking Sebastian to take out his learning inventory and complete the questions in the inventory. In this case, the intervention is focused solely on one student and specifically structures a task for him, which is why it is considered an intrapersonal level intervention.

In Ms. McAllister's counseling group, a *structural* **type** intervention might be used as the group begins to wind down towards the end of the session. In this case, she might ask group members to engage in deep breathing or a progressive relaxation exercise to help lower the intensity of the emotion and promote regrouping and self-regulation, generating an emotional level that is more appropriate for returning to the classroom. It is a *group* **level** intervention because it requests all of the group members to participate in the activity together.

Mr. Jaramillo and Ms. McAllister may opt to use *conceptual* interventions to manage their situations. *Conceptual* **type** interventions, you will recall, are aimed at focusing members to think about an idea or a concept. They may be delivered at the *intrapersonal*, *interpersonal*, or *group* **level**. Often, group leaders offer a series of directions in the group that shift from one type and one level of intervention to another, as illustrated below.

In Mr. Jaramillo's group, the students might be asked to take a minute to think (*conceptual*) by themselves (*intrapersonal*) about which style seems to fit them, based on the ranking they received after taking the learning style inventory. Afterwards, students could be assigned to work in small groups (*structural* **type** *interpersonal* **level** intervention) to share their profiles with one another and to provide feedback to each other regarding the characteristics they display that are illustrative of a concept in the profile. For example, if Jairo's profile indicated that he was artistic/creative, the students in his small group might offer Jairo an example of when they saw him being artistic or creative. As a way of summarizing at the end of the group, Mr. Jaramillo might ask the group, "What did we learn today?" Because this comment is not directed at anyone specific in the group, it would be a *group* **level** intervention. This kind of *conceptual* **type** *group* **level** intervention is often used at the close of groups to refocus the members on what they have learned as they leave.

In the counseling group, Ms. McAllister would probably be looking for interventions that would validate Giana's experience and feelings, provide her with the support of other group members, and also draw other students into the experience in a way that does not allow for the needs of one member to dominate the group. She would want to engage other students into the issue that Giana raised, since others in the group would also likely feel responsible for their parents' conflicts. Initially, Ms. McAllister might choose to use an *experiential* **type** *intrapersonal* **level** intervention to validate Giana's feelings and experiences. For example, she could ask Giana how it felt to think she was responsible for the fight or how it felt to overhear the fight between her parents. She would, of course, want to remind students in the group about confidentiality, and she would also want to remind Giana that she could share as much or as little as she wants. While this intervention would not focus on Giana's feeling *in* the group; it would be intended to elicit feelings, thus fitting with the *experiential* **type**. Ms. McAllister would probably use basic counseling skills such as empathy, reflection, and paraphrasing as a part of this intervention.

Ms. McAllister would also be thinking about how to help Giana express the sadness that she reports, and she might want to help Giana develop a cognitive understanding or framework to help her think about her assertion that she is responsible for her parent's anger at each other. Ms. McAllister might also consider how to bring other group members into the experience so they can both support Giana and also explore their own related experiences and feelings. To accomplish this, Ms. McAllister could use a combination of type and level interventions. First, she might use this *conceptual* **type** intervention: She could express wonder about Giana's statement of feeling responsible for her parent's fight. Notice that this type intervention is still focused on Giana (*intrapersonal*).

Moving a group member from a feeling to a cognitive state is likely to lower the intensity in the group. However, the leader must move slowly in shifting attention from member to group in order to avoid giving the impression that expressing emotions in the group is not safe and also so as not to abandon, a group member when she is emotional. Ms. McAllister could use an *interpersonal* or *group* **level** intervention to extend the learning potential from Giana's experience to benefit others in the group. This could be tricky, as she would need to be careful to do so in a way that does not raise the intensity too high—emotional intensity can be frightening for children and adolescents, especially when they are with peers. Ms. McAllister could ask if others in the group (*group* **level**) sometimes had thoughts (*conceptual* **type**) that they were responsible for their parent's anger at each other. To promote meaning-making, she could add a statement such as, "sometimes when we do not understand why things are happening, we assume that they are happening because of something we did, when that might not be the case at all." This intervention invites other group members into the discussion by sharing their thoughts or stories of similar experiences. It offers a conceptual framework for understanding their experiences, but it does not raise the intensity by singling out an individual student right away.

Because repeated storytelling can sometimes have the effect of lowering the intensity in a group, both counselors will probably need to intervene at times to raise the intensity in their groups stimulating intentional thought and examination or feeling (**type** interventions) responses or by directing interventions at individuals or pairs in the group (*intrapersonal* and *interpersonal* **level** interventions). The group leader is always aiming for a level of intensity that will stimulate meaningful engagement but also provides safety for students. That is, so the group is functioning in the Growth Zone.

Varying Intensity

It is important to point out that when group members feel that participating in the group is too risky (i.e., it is too intense, perhaps leaving them feeling uncomfortable or vulnerable), they are not likely to benefit from the group. For children and adolescents, feeling unsafe in the group often shows itself in passive nonparticipation or acting out behaviors.

Similarly, if groups do not have a high enough level of intensity, members may become uninterested, detached, and non-participatory. Sometimes, this results in passive or acting out behaviors. Therefore, it is important that the group leader carefully manage the intensity—both in classroom and counseling groups—in order to stimulate meaningful engagement, avoid boredom, and provide safety for group members. In this section we offer a general discussion on how type and level interventions can be used to alter the intensity in classroom and counseling groups.

Group **level** interventions, in general, tend to be rather low in intensity, and are often used to stimulate discussion without leaving members feeling singled out. Since these interventions do not call upon any one student directly, they afford students an opportunity for self-censuring—students have the power of deciding how and when to participate. *Conceptual* or *structural* **type** *group* **level** interventions invite group members to respond by thinking, noticing, listening, or by talking or answering a question. Notice how inviting the group (rather than a specific individual in the group) allows students to be self-reflective but to make their own choices about what, when, and how to verbally participate in the group. *Group* **level** interventions that *require* students to speak to the whole group will probably raise the intensity in the group. This is particularly true when the group is populated with students who tend to feel reluctant to speak, and particularly in classroom groups because of the larger number of students.

There are ways to encourage verbal participation at a group level without raising the intensity too high. Forced rounds sometimes mediate the anxiety that comes from having to speak in front of the group because they set the expectation that everyone will say something, relieving students of the decision of whether or not to contribute. In addition, they offer a predictable order for when they will have to respond, giving students time to prepare their thoughts. When using rounds, it is advisable to be selective in determining which group member talks first and to be mindful of the round direction. In fact, selecting where the round starts and in what direction it goes are two ways in which the leader can facilitate a round that will bring forth the best in all group members. The first to speak in the round will set the response or set the tone for others, so it is a good idea to initiate the round with a student who is likely to approximate your expectation for response or who can set a good response model. It is also helpful to set the direction of the round away from a student who may need more time to think about a response, and towards a student who has a difficulty waiting. Allowing students to pass (i.e., not say anything) in group rounds can lower the intensity level for some students who may be very reluctant to speak up in the group. These are in-the-moment group leader decisions that will have an impact on the intensity of the group.

Inviting students to speak in pairs or dyads (*conceptual* **type** *interpersonal* **level** intervention) is likely to be less intense for some students than speaking in the larger group. However, dyads may arouse anxiety for students who are concerned about who they are paired with and what they should or should not say. Social status hierarchies are set into motion when students are invited to select their own partners for paired participation. So, it is a good idea to be explicit about the instructions for dyad activities and for the leader to select dyad pairings rather than leave it to the students to pick partners. When appropriate, the leader should remind students of and enforce a standard for confidentiality before they begin speaking in pairs.

Experiential **type** group interventions facilitate the expression of feelings or emotionality. Due to the focus in schools on cognitive learning tasks, we find that *experiential* interventions tend to be used less frequently than other types of interventions, particularly in classroom groups. This is unfortunate. There is no reason for avoiding experiential interventions in schools, as they offer many rich and powerful learning opportunities for youth (see Luckner & Nadler, 1997, for an excellent account of the benefits of experiential learning).

Because the expression of emotionality in the group can provoke anxiety, *experiential* interventions should be used judiciously, especially if time limits students' ability to regain the composure needed to go back to their academic class. In groups where screening is not possible (i.e., in classroom groups), *experiential* **type** interventions should be used only after you are familiar with all of the members in the group so that you are in the position to anticipate the amount of arousal that may occur. It is the responsibility of the group leader to monitor and alter the intensity in the group so all members of the group are meaningfully and safely engaged in learning. However, do not let these cautions inhibit you from using appropriate experiential interventions. Remember that working in the Growth Zone requires that students be stimulated to work at a level that is within reach, but just beyond where they are currently functioning. Altering intensity and using experiential interventions judiciously are two excellent ways of stimulating risk within a context of safety.

In general, *conceptual* **type** responses are likely to feel a little less intense in a group than feeling or experiential responses. However, they may feel a little intense for students who are concerned that others will judge what they say. This is particularly true if students are asked to consider something that is difficult to understand or if the topic is presented as a competition. Asking students what they might have thought in the *past* (or how they might have felt in the past) rather than how they think (or feel) in the *present* provides a cushion of distance to mediate the anxiety around the possibility of saying something "stupid" or having an emotional reaction in the group.

Finally, *structural* **type** interventions typically have the effect of lowering the intensity in groups because they offer explicit parameters for engagement. This is probably why teachers and counselors like to use activities, exercises, and games when working with children and adolescents in groups—the rules for engagement are explicit. However, because of their potential for lowering the level of intensity in the group, an over-reliance on group activities—both in classroom and counseling groups—may dilute important curriculum and detract from the goals or objectives of the group. So, while it is nice when learning is fun, we emphasize that it is the responsibility of the group leader to assure activities are used as a means to specific learning objectives. Our discussion of planning group activities in Chapter 3 highlights the importance of using processing questions when using structural group interventions. Processing questions are designed to intentionally bring a meaning-making component into group activities.

Although *structural* interventions typically lower the intensity in the group, the idea of doing an activity can feel very threatening for some youth, as the anticipation of who they will be working with and what will be required of them can be very intense. Therefore, providing students with clear rules for engagement and structuring the ways in which students will be asked to interact in activities are important ways to consider intensity when using structural interventions in the group.

Using Process to Facilitate Content

Counselors working in schools are charged with providing services that focus on meeting or supporting the academic, career, personal, and social needs of students (The *ASCA National Model* [ASCA, 2005]), and much of this happens in classroom and counseling groups in schools. We maintain that the best way to teach a psychoeducational curriculum in a classroom and a counseling group is to use the group as a laboratory for learning. That is, to use the group as a time to learn and try out new behaviors. This is particularly true when the purpose of the group—the content—is for students to learn social, interpersonal, or communication skills. For example, if the goal for a middle school counseling group is to develop assertiveness skills, than it is probably not enough to talk about and study those skills; the students in the group should probably be directly engaged in using these skills with each other in the group. Focusing on the interaction among members—group process—is a powerful way to achieve these social curricular goals. In this way, group process facilitates the content goals.

In practice, this means that the group leader prepares specific plans outlining how students will engage with each other (i.e., a group process focus) in order to address content goals. We point this out because sometimes group implementation plans are not in sync with the intended learning goals for the group. For example, if the goal for students in a high school group is to be able to give each other appropriate feedback but they are not engaged in a process of giving each other feedback, then the group process is not consistent with the goal. The students may be studying feedback exchange, discussing feedback exchange, learning models for giving feedback, but if they are not actually giving each other feedback, the group process is not consistent with the group content.

In other groups, group process dynamics actually run parallel to the particular content objective or larger goals of the group. For example, students in an elementary school classroom group were learning about decision-making through a structured activity where they were working in small groups to implement a decision-making model. During that activity, a few students became engaged in a conflict and they were making poor decisions about how they were treating each other. In this case, it could be said that while the students were engaged in learning about decision-making and practicing what they were learning in a group activity, they were not being led to transfer these skills to their own group dynamics. So, the group process ran parallel to (never truly having impact on the students' experiences) and failed to support the content goals.

In addition to structuring group activities to advance content goals and objectives, you will want to be alert to opportunities to harvest critical incidents or spontaneous situations in the group for their learning or therapeutic potential. This is what is sometimes referred to in teacher language as using *teachable moments* in the group. In group work circles, we refer to similar phenomena as *working in the here-and-now* (for more on working in the here and now, see Carroll & Kraus, 2007). It is difficult to know if and when to shift the focus in the group from the content or activity to the group dynamics and processes, and it takes considerable skill to make these shifts.

WHEN TO SHIFT THE FOCUS   Opportunities for using process to facilitate content often show themselves serendipitously in the group. So, the group leader must always be on the lookout for spontaneous learning opportunities or teachable moments in the group.

Decisions about shifting the focus from content to process dynamics (and shifting back again) must be made judiciously, while always considering the purpose of the group (Hulse-Killacky, Killacky, & Donigian, 2001). Asking "What is the purpose of this group?" and "Is what's happening here in the group right now related to that purpose?" can guide this decision-making. Put simply: If what is happening in the group is related to the objectives or goals for the group, than it might be a good idea to shift the focus to the group process. When what is happening in the group is clearly not related to the intended tasks for the group (i.e., the content objective), then refocusing the group away from that issue should be the priority. Two examples in *Case Study 6.14* illustrate ways in which the group leader thinks about whether to shift from a focus on group content to a focus on group process.

CASE STUDY 6.14
Two Examples of Shifting Between Process and Content

Case One

The content focus of a high school counseling group with nine students was on learning anxiety reduction strategies in anticipation of final examinations that were scheduled in a few weeks. The leader's plan was to use a cognitive-behavioral model to teach specific anxiety reduction strategies. Members were selected from sophomore year honors classes. All members had elected to participate in the group and consent was obtained from their parents.

When asked to experiment with the anxiety reduction strategies in small groups, some of the students became off-task, entering into private nonrelated conversations. The counselor asked some of the students why they were off-task and they responded that it was because "talking relieved [their] anxiety." While it might be argued, as the students perhaps were trying to do, that talking amongst themselves might help the students feel less anxious, the counselor decided that her planned activity would be a more effective means for reaching the intended learning objective of anxiety reduction and she decided to redirect students back to the assigned task.

Reflection Questions

1. This counselor emphasized content while trying to honor the group's naturally occurring process. This can be seen as a value-added intervention. Select someone in your class and explain how?
2. Playing the devil's advocate, I can see that if talking with each other reduced the members' anxiety, then maybe the group was successful even without the cognitive-behavioral strategy instructions. However, why would such a here-and-now, stress-reducing experience not be entirely sufficient?

Case Two

Mr. Nyal is a school counselor working with a middle school health classroom group for 6 weeks to address the topic of harassment. His lesson plan for this week called for reviewing the school harassment policy. The topic that had been discussed in the classroom for the previous 4-week unit was bullying. During the first 4 weeks, students had defined bullying and role-played ways to respond when they saw bullying in the hallways.

Mr. Nyal started the group by asking students to subgroup into triads and review the written school policy on harassment. Realizing at once his mistake in not assigning the subgroups, Mr. Nyal watched helplessly as students scurried to form the small groups for the task. This task of forming small groups immediately revealed a number of exclusionary problems. One group insisted on taking in a fourth member, whispering to the extra member, "Come to our group, so you don't have to go over there with them. Mr. Nyal won't care," while one or two students appeared to be groupless.

Since the group had discussed (the previous week) how exclusion was one of the ways that bullying starts, Mr. Nyal thought that it would be important to use this teachable moment to help students see how quick and seemingly unintentionally, bullying can start. Mr. Nyal called attention to the issue in a nonjudgmental and exploratory way. He used a conceptual group level intervention: "Okay. Hold up. Let's stop for a minute." When students were listening, he continued, "I wonder if people sometimes feel left out even if others don't mean to leave them out. Like in here, when I asked you to group up in threes, I noticed that students called out who they wanted to be with and some students were left without a group."

He paused and then added, again keeping his interventions on a group level to avoid raising the intensity too much higher: "Let's take a minute to talk about how it feels to not be invited into a group—I know that all of us have had that experience."

After a few students talked about how it has felt for them in the past when they were left out of a group, Mr. Nyal asked, "How can something like a noninvitation lead to what we talked about last week: 'bullying climates'?" Again, his interventions were conceptual type interventions and remained on the group level. He was careful about making the students who experienced feeling left out not feel even more estranged from the group.

After students acknowledged that bully climates often started with exclusion, Mr. Nyal asked them to focus on what had just happened in this group.

David reported that exclusion happens very often without even realizing its larger effects, adding, "I wasn't trying to be mean. I didn't think I was bullying, but now I realize that Jen may have felt that way."

A few other students commented on how they did not mean to bully anyone but they could see how they did things that could make their peers feel left out. Mr. Nyal then asked the group to identify ways that they could try to be more inclusive in this group so that no one felt left out and avoid creating a bullying climate. Although this teachable moment was not scripted into his lesson plan, taking the time to process what was happening in the group was an excellent way for Mr. Nyal to facilitate a process of interpersonal learning that tied into the content objective that he had for the group.

Reflection Questions

1. Mr. Nyal beautifully demonstrated the skill of regulating intensity. What might have happened had he not kept the intervention at the group level?
2. Given the results reported in this case, one can see the benefit of Mr. Nyal's intervention. However, discuss with a partner an alternate ending.

3. What if the scenario found David becoming exceedingly defensive and actually added to Jennifer's sense of exclusion with his statement, "Mr. Nyal, you can't blame us for picking the best team members, can you?"

HOW TO SHIFT THE FOCUS   Basic counseling skills, such as paraphrasing, summarizing, questioning (focused open-ended probes), cutting off skills, and immediacy, can be used to make content-process shifts (for more complete descriptions of these and related skills, see Appendix D). Content is often talked about in abstract terms and the ability to think abstractly is a fairly sophisticated cognitive skill. So, be wary when using abstract conceptual interventions so you are not just talking to a select few children or adolescents and excluding others. Paraphrasing and summarizing can be helpful to assure that all of the students in the group understand more complex discussions.

It is important to keep in mind that using group process to facilitate content requires a certain degree of risk-taking on the part of the group members—it is risky to move from talking about something conceptually (which is often what a focus on content entails) to talking about one's own experience in the group (which is what a focus on process typically entails). The extent to which students will engage in this kind of risk-taking will depend on the level of safety and trust felt in the group. It should be mentioned that moving from a focus on content to group process dynamics may engender some anxiety for group leaders as well. Relinquishing tight hold on the agenda reins and purposely inviting spontaneity into the group can be very threatening for even the most seasoned group leader. It is simply hard to predict how such in-the-moment discussions will evolve if we are not holding on tightly to what we had planned in advance. However, we encourage group leaders to welcome such opportunities as they present themselves. Mr. Nyal and the counselor providing anxiety-managing strategies to high school juniors in Case Study 6.14 demonstrated that shifting the focus to process dynamics can yield huge dividends.

Finally, we point out that moving with teachable moments in the group does not mean that there is no agenda or plan for the group. Nor does it mean that the desired group process is leaderless. On the contrary, the agenda for the leader when working with group process dynamics *is* to skillfully manage the process and to keep it focused on the intended learning goal and objectives. The dimensions of Cohen and Smith's Intervention Cube (1976) offer a sound model for doing so.

TIPS FOR MANAGING DISTRACTIBLE GROUPS

There will be times in the group when distractions happen that are largely beyond your control. For example, interruptions from the school intercom, someone walking in the room, and students playing on the playground just outside the window, are common school distractions that are largely beyond the control of group leaders working in a school setting. However, there are many distractions in school groups that really can be avoided. Taking care of small details in advance to running the group goes a long way towards managing and avoiding distractions and keeping a group productive. For example, students often become distracted when they are transitioning between activities and when they are waiting too long. Also, group leaders sometimes unintentionally cause distractions by, for example, displaying interesting materials before introducing an activity or by having a private conversation with a student or teacher in the room while the whole group is waiting. We offer these general tips for avoiding distractions in the group:

- Be mindful of not creating distractions yourself.
- Be sure to provide instructions clearly and introduce materials at an appropriate time.
- Have a plan for how you will manage transitions and maintain a flow in the group.
- Be firm about not being drawn into individual and private conversations during group time. It is always appropriate to tell teachers, parents, students, administrators, that this is not a good time to talk and you will schedule a better time to talk as soon as possible. Do not answer your office telephone when facilitating a group.
- Be flexible. You will have to work with the group where it is at. If the students are antsy from sitting too long at a prior task, you may need to adjust your plans to allow them an opportunity to move around. Sometimes you will need to directly attend to an incident that happened in the group in order to help students quickly shift away from the distraction. For example, if a critical incident occurred and still seems to be affecting students, you will probably want to acknowledge what has happened by entering into a short discussion about the incident, as appropriate. However, be careful to keep your own learning objective in mind and be prepared to shift the focus back to your task as soon as possible. Good judgment should guide your decision-making about when to stick with the lesson plans and when to shift and address the here-and-now in the group. A bottom line of student safety, issues of confidentiality, and a focus on the intended goals of the group should drive all of your decisions around shifting the focus in the group.
- Be "withit." Brophy (1999) used the term *withitness* to describe a kind of teacher presence in the classroom that is key to effective classroom management. Withitness refers to an aware and monitoring presence in the group; a kind of group surveillance that provides the leader with feedback about how things are going in the group. Specific withit group leader behaviors include regular scanning to monitor attention, interest, progress on a task; intervening promptly and appropriately when students are disengaged; and attending to multiple activities and events simultaneously. Good group management cannot happen without group leader withitness—the group leader must always be aware of what is happening in the center and at the perimeters of the group.

CHAPTER 7

Responding to Problems in the Group

"The least intrusive and most natural behavior management strategies are, of course, good teaching practices" (Kerr & Nelson, 1998, p. 158). In fact, research suggests that almost 90% of all students in classrooms never need any kind of disciplinary action when they are engaged in learning (Queen, Blackwelder, & Mallen, 1997). We agree: The most effective way to manage groups with youth is to create a group environment in which everyone is meaningfully engaged. Having said this, challenges seem to find their way into even the best planned and most carefully managed classroom and counseling groups.

Challenges in groups typically make everyone a little uncomfortable and they often leave even the most experienced group leaders with some questions on how best to proceed. Groups are complicated systems, and the range of potential challenges that may arise in the group is a function of a number of variables including group topic, dynamics, membership, history, and context. However, experienced group leaders know that the ways in which they respond to these challenges will have a significant impact on the further functioning of the group, as well as the well-being of individual group members. So, it is critical for all classroom and group counseling leaders to have a strong repertoire of response strategies for responding to problems in the group.

THINKING ABOUT PROBLEMS

We have struggled with the term "problem" when writing this chapter. By offering suggestions for how to deal with problems in groups we do not want to convey that we see individual group members as problems, even when their behaviors are problematic. Labeling a child as problematic, intentionally or unintentionally, risks creating an undesirable uni-dimensional identity conclusion for that child—that is, when children are identified as problems they tend to see *themselves* as problematic and others tend to see them as problematic as well. The results of problem identities are fairly predictable: The problem behaviors continue and the responses by others further story the problem identity; these youth become known as "problems" and tend to become isolated, particularly from children who are not in the problem-category; opportunities to see themselves in other ways (i.e., not problematic) diminish; and their potential for benefitting from instruction becomes severely constricted. Clearly, this is not a recipe for healthy human development.

We want to acknowledge that all individuals have multiple ways of being. So, while a particular behavior may be problematic, calling attention to it does not imply that there is something wrong with that child. Identifying a behavior as problematic does not—and should not—endorse the idea that all of the behaviors displayed by that child are problematic. We recommend that group leaders refrain from engaging in what often amounts to reductionist diagnoses for the multiple and complex challenges that may present themselves in groups, and instead focus response efforts toward making appropriate and healthy responses that continue to steer the group in the direction of learning goals and objectives.

Alternatively, we like to encourage group leaders to view problems as they arise in groups as opportunities. This requires a keen sense of immediacy. Both of us authors recognize in hindsight how many opportunities have availed themselves in this way, only to be missed by us altogether. When something occurs in the group, in the moment, that exemplifies some aspect of the group's objectives—use it. Too often counseling group leaders feel they must contrive examples or activities in order for students to really talk about something pertinent to the objectives of the group.

For example, twenty minutes into a counseling group session with sixth-grade students who were exploring their accruing multiple disciplinary referrals, one student, Lemar, blurts out, "Phew, what is that smell, somebody's so gross in here! That's disgusting . . ." In the moment, perhaps to save another group member embarrassment or risk that the group may devolve into a raucous mess, the counselor quickly but gently admonished Lemar by encouraging him to stick to the discussion and not be so disruptive. She said, "Lemar, that is really what gets you in trouble—please." Lemar complied, amidst some giggles and smirks. Later, during a peer supervision group, the counselor insightfully commented that she had really missed a chance to use Lemar's spontaneous uproar to help the group make growth-oriented meaning. She could have pointed out during group how so many of their disciplinary referrals are "sort of like Lemar's outburst." The counselor went on to share that the problem—Lemar's inappropriate comment—was a perfect opportunity to bring a very real event into the group rather than merely speaking abstractly in the group about inappropriate behavior. She concluded that this was the perfect problem opportunity and she hoped not to miss similar ones in the future. Although we do not advocate that all problems should be seen as opportunities, there are often times when great learning in the group can be driven by such keen intervention.

It is important to mention the use of theory to guide the ways we conceptualize students' strengths and challenges. We have purposefully attempted to remain atheoretical while writing this text; that is, we have purposely not emphasized one theoretical position over another. We believe our book will help counselors lead successful classroom and counseling groups with youth, but we are not naïve. Group leaders will have their own preferred theoretical orientation and those theories will influence how they understand problems. Theoretical orientation also influences ideas regarding

personality development, identity development, cognitive development, how people learn, how they change, the influence of culture in society, resiliency, etc. It is imperative as we begin this part of the book to openly acknowledge and welcome
school counselors, counselor educators, supervisors, and counselors-in-training to
integrate our structure of group leadership with their own theoretical underpinnings.
To leave either out, we believe, would not be conducive to effective and successful
groups in schools.

THINKING ABOUT RESPONSES

One of the most critical skills for the group leader working with youth is to be able to
determine which behaviors should be tolerated in the group and which ones require
leader intervention. Our position is that it is the responsibility of the group leader to
intervene in response to problematic behaviors when it is clear that those behaviors
are interfering with members' abilities to benefit from the group. As Charles and
Senter (2002) point out, "the teacher [group leader] is responsible for communicating
the sort of psychosocial environment desired, initiating the conditions that lead to it,
and maintaining a good environment once it is achieved" (p. 56, bracketed text
added). When students are interfering with the learning that is happening in the
group and when they are disrespectful or dangerous to others, prompt intervention
is required.

   This leads us to our second point: Selecting a response that is most appropriate for
a particular problem in the group is critical. Jones and Jones (2001) warn that "the disruptive influence of the teacher's intervention [to misbehavior] should not be greater
than the disruption it is intended to reduce" (p. 301, bracketed text added). Too much
leader intervention can inhibit student participation in the group; too little can have the
same effect. We agree with Jones and Jones that the intensity of the disruption should
inform the intensity of the response needed.

   We believe that the group leader should always endeavor to respond to problems
in the least invasive way possible, as appropriate to the situation, of course. Our selection of the term *least invasive* is intentional. The term *invasive* sometimes refers to an aggressive act of stepping in, often without permission or invitation. Being the leader of a
group implies permission—in fact, it compels the leader to step into the group. However, the concept of *least* invasive suggests an authoritative leadership positioning
where the role of the leader is to provide parameters and structures to invade, when
needed, and otherwise to allow group members to do the work *of* and *in* the group. As
mentioned in Chapter 6, *intensity* refers to the experience of the members of the group
in response to a particular leader intervention. A higher level of intensity in the group
generally refers to members' experiences of discomfort or reactivity. However, high levels of intensity are not bad in the group. What is critical is the leader's ability to manage
her interventions so that the level of intensity for group members is one that is conducive to learning and growth.

   When the students are not able to manage themselves in the group, leader intervention is required. In these cases, interventions should serve to move the individual
and the group through the problem and to help the group regain appropriate and semi-
autonomous functioning. On a continuum of responses, the less invasive responses to

problems tend to be nonverbal, instructional, and re-directive responses. Slightly more invasive strategies are ones that call specific attention to the student and the problematic behavior. These responses bring about a little more intensity and they may generate some reactivity in the group. When the midlevel responses are not powerful enough to affect the desired change in the group, more invasive responses will be needed. Obviously, some problems in the group will immediately require the most invasive interventions. These higher intensity interventions, outlined in Chapter 8, should be used immediately when behaviors are out of control and/or dangerous to the student, the counselor, or other students in the room.

DIVERSITY-WISE DECISIONS

A review of textbooks on behavior management for insights on working with students from diverse socioeconomic conditions, race, disability, sexual orientation, gender identity, as well as other group membership identities, confirms Zirpoli and Melloy's (1997) observation that most texts on behavior management largely ignore the topic of cultural influences on behavior. Could it be that all cultural groups have similar norms regarding appropriate participation in the group? We doubt it. Could it be true that behavior management techniques have universal applicability? We think not.

We did find that many of the more recent texts do outline some effects of the conditions of poverty and/or student's special needs (including disabilities, emotional challenges, and limited English proficiency) on student behavior and performance in the classroom (see Charles & Senter, 2002; Charles, 2005; Emmer & Evertson, 2009; Hardin, 2008). However, we agree with Zirpoli and Melloy's (1997) position that myths associated with individual ethnic groups and "a lack of appreciation for different cultural norms, contribute to a frequent misunderstanding and misinterpretation of children's behaviors" (p. 456). Zirpoli and Melloy call for us, as educators, to "examine the effects of their [our] own racism and stereotypes on children's behaviors" (1997, p. 456, bracketed text added). This need for attention is underscored. The deficiency model of conceptualizing individuals within the framework of their identity characteristics (i.e., children in this group will probably have difficulties with X . . .), arguably based on misunderstandings about other cultures and, likely, unintentionally practiced by well-meaning individuals, underlies biased behavior management techniques that have some very real and damaging effects on individuals, as well as schools and school communities (Zirpoli & Melloy, 1997). Although sometimes unintentional, we cannot condone this type of practice in group work in schools—school counselors must be sensitive to these important diversity issues in all that they do; ethical and successful group work certainly demands it. We remind school counselors to refer back to all applicable codes of ethics to reinforce our emphasis (see *Ethical Standards for School Counselors* [ASCA, 2004] Preamble & E.2.a–d; *ASGW Best Practice Guidelines* [ASGW, 2007] B.8 & 9).

Becoming familiar with the norms and expectations that different groups bring to the school community is an important starting point for thinking about culturally appropriate responses to behavioral challenges. This requires establishing rapport with the families that are represented in the school community (Zirpoli & Melloy, 1997). It also requires working with those families in creating norms and expectations that are appropriate to a school setting (keeping in mind that some norms may be appropriate for the home, others for the neighborhood, and others for the school setting). Many schools create advisory boards with diverse membership as a venue for this type of collaborative process.

School-related norms should support a focus on learning and a respect for the multitude of perspectives that come to the learning process. When the school community works together in articulating norms and expectations, the result should be a set of rules that are articulated in explicit language, and outlining (as much as possible) culturally appropriate responses for serious rule breaches. Also note that this ideal reflects our position of responding rather than reacting to misbehavior. In our experience, although reacting is easier, it almost always contributes to escalating behaviors, which is ultimately the opposite of our intention. Clarity can be extremely valuable in creating school practices that are respectful, responsive, and reflective of a diverse student body, and can go a long way in preempting misunderstandings and inappropriate actions. Soliciting input and encouraging dialogue will not eliminate all bias in schools, but collaborative conversations on how to manage student behavior in schools communicate an openness to valuing multiple perspectives and provide an opportunity for counselors and educators to learn from the students and families with whom they work. We suggest that these processes should be a matter of practice in all schools, not simply something that happens after a problem occurs.

Leader responses to behavior problems in the group should always be based on shared understandings regarding behavioral expectations and responses to behavioral infractions in school community. The specific techniques that we offer in these chapters are specific response strategies that can be used within these understandings. However, we caution that the ways in which these strategies are used—with whom, by whom, in front of whom, and after what behavioral infractions—are what makes them both effective and appropriate. Determining appropriate response to behavior problems in groups requires sensitivity to issues of home culture norms, school norms, and an awareness that these decisions are often influenced by bias and oversight. Unfortunately (and fortunately), there is not one simple formula for responding to problems that are intertwined with issues of disenfranchised group status. Careful thinking, appropriate sensitivity, and managing bias are required for appropriate implementation (for guidelines on this, see *Ethical Standards for School Counselors* [ASCA, 2004] Preamble, E.2).

In addition to Zirpoli and Melloy's (1997) attention to the importance of understanding students' ethnic and cultural background when responding to behavioral infractions, we would add that conceptualizations of misbehavior must also include the understanding that student behavior always exists in a social context, and that social context in schools and communities is not equally fair or just for all students. It usually is not the differences among students that create problems in school; it is the ways in which difference is not tolerated in school communities that is problematic.

This means that responses to student misbehavior must also take into account the different social experiences that students have at school. Being a member of a minority group in a school community does have an impact on how students are seen by others, on interpersonal interactions among students, and it shapes how students come to see themselves. The social perceptions that surround membership identity also affect how students behave in the school community (Tatum, 1997). We know that some students will be silent to hide their differences (Williams, Nielsen, & Bystrom, 1998), others will adopt a sense of humor or some other suit of armor (Pang, 1998), and still others may act out (Tatum, 1997). As Tatum points out, the anger and resentment that some students of color feel as they come to experience and understand institutional racism protects them from the "psychological assault of racism and keeps the dominant group at a distance" (p. 60). Clearly, sometimes circumstances do require different responses. We realize that this statement will likely make group leaders, teachers, school administrators, and even parents a little uneasy. This uneasiness, we think, may be due to a misinterpretation of what we are saying, as well as a discomfort with the lack of uniformity it implies.

Our position is clear: Students and school communities cannot afford a one-size-fits-all response to the unique needs and circumstances of different students, *and* we also assert that all behavioral infractions *do* require appropriate responses. For example, students are not allowed to hit others in school. Never. And there is a consequence in most schools for hitting behavior. However, when Ahmed's hitting is in response to a racist comment by a peer in the hallway, does that not temper the way in which we will proceed? Of course is does. Applying even the most cut-and-dry rules requires sensitivity, as well as justice and fairness. All students need to learn to be accountable for their behavior and school communities also need to be accountable for being fair, respectful, and keeping a focus on learning. In this case, there should be a consequence for Ahmed's violent behavior in school. No school should tolerate physical aggression between students. However, there also should be consequences for racist and bullying behavior. No students should have to experience racial slurs in their school community. The result of the intervention in response to this incident must not only communicate zero tolerance towards physical aggression, but it must also communicate zero tolerance for racial disrespect. Therefore, this behavioral infraction warrants different conversations and different responses.

Finally, we refer to the concept of windows and mirrors. As you will recall from earlier discussions, Style (1998) uses this metaphor to describe the ways in which classrooms can be structured to help students be exposed to the realities in the lives of others, as well as to see their own reality reflected back and validated. It is important that you, as a group leader, endeavor to create the kind of learning environment that offers both windows and mirrors for all students present in the group. Such an environment only thrives when there is no tolerance for hate, no tolerance for hurt, and no tolerance for a lack of respect. It is an environment that does not—and does not *appear to*—reward and punish students according to group affiliation. It is critical for group leaders, as with all members of the school community, to act assertively and quickly in response to any behaviors that infringe on these important learning community principles. This also requires all group leaders to be under constant self-scrutiny regarding their own levels of comfort, preferences, and biases.

GENERAL PRINCIPLES FOR RESPONDING

Before moving into specific intervention strategies, we point out that it is wise to establish a clear and relatively unwavering position on responding to problem behaviors in groups, and this should be done prior to their inevitable occurrence. Although establishing such principles might be an individual task for some counselors in schools, it may be a system-wide endeavor for others. Our advocacy around responding is based upon predictability. If you have established principles that are known by others, surprises will be minimized and this benefits students, parents, and guardians, as well as teachers and administrators. Here we offer a few general principles for responding to problems in groups:

- As a general rule of thumb, responses to problems in the group should follow this model: stop misbehavior, maintain leadership, be respectful to all in the room, and then get back on task as soon as possible (Mendler, 2005).
- Inappropriate anger and reactivity increases tension, disobedience, and disruption; calmness breeds calmness.
- Ignore behavior that is ignorable; respond to behavior that warrants response.
- Speak clearly, authoritatively, and always with respect.
- Be as consistent as possible; yet, realize that not all students will or should elicit the same kind of intervention from the group leader. Some students will respond best to one kind of intervention whereas other students may require other kinds of interventions.
- Almost all contact with students regarding undesirable behavior should be individual and private; and all contact must be respectful. Avoid situations where the student loses face in front of his or her peers.
- In most cases, interventions should focus on behavior in the present rather than past behavior.
- Speak *to* rather than *about* students.
- Accept no excuses: When sensible rules and expectations exist, no excuses are necessary.
- Refrain from interpreting the meaning of a given behavior, especially in the moment when the behavior is problematic. Instead, focus on concrete observable actions. (If an intervention that focuses on making interpretations is indicated, these discussions should happen after the difficulty has been curtailed, when everyone is calm, and preferably in an individual meeting outside of the group.)
- Whenever possible, use I-messages. An I-message offers a direct communication about the problem and the effect that the problem has on others (Emmer & Evertson, 2009). The I-message format is:
  I feel _____.
  when you _____.
  Please _(offer correction, instruction, or re-direction)_.
- Whenever possible, try to provide options and choices. Also remind students that choices come with consequences. Positive consequences should be associated with pro-social behavior. (Consequences are discussed in more detail later in this chapter.)

SPECIFIC IN-GROUP STRATEGIES

Here we offer a number of problem response strategies that can be implemented in the group. For this reason, we call them *in-group* strategies. These strategies do not require long conversations with an individual student, they do not need advance planning, and they typically can be implemented in front of the group without causing undue disruption. As you will notice, however, even though they are considered to be in-group strategies, we frequently suggest that you take a student aside while responding to the problem in these ways. These suggestions to intervene privately are offered in the vein of being vigilant with regard to respecting and honoring students when intervening to correct their behaviors. In the next chapter, the focus is on interventions that typically require advance planning or some type of out-of-group interaction with the student.

Planned Ignoring

Ignoring misbehavior can be an effective response as it limits the power that is given to a student through misbehavior. As Larrivee (2005) writes, "Student misbehavior carries its own limited power and will soon exhaust itself if it is not fueled, especially if the behavior is done primarily to annoy the teacher" (p. 52). So, ignoring slight infractions and minor misbehavior may effectively avoid giving a misbehaving student power to control the group in a negative way, and it is likely to cut off the reinforcement of undesired behaviors that can come from more intensive responses. Ignoring misbehavior also offers an opportunity for the student to self-correct and save face after a small mistake.

We all know that it can be very difficult, sometimes, to ignore and not take misbehavior personally (Kauffman, Mostert, Trent, & Hallahan, 2002). It also can be exceedingly frustrating for the leader and other group members when the best laid group plans are disrupted by one student in the group. Ignoring student misbehavior, then, really requires monitoring one's own responses, avoiding blame, and not making interpretations about student intent (because these interpretations typically entail placing blame). Ignoring requires letting go.

While ignoring can be a very effective, we also caution that some misbehaviors will escalate when they are ignored. So, the after-effect of intentional ignoring needs to be monitored carefully and you will need to move into more invasive responses quickly if ignoring does not produce the desired result. The bottom line for considering whether to ignore misbehavior rests on the issue of safety: If a student behavior is interfering with his or her emotional or physical safety or that of others, it must be stopped immediately. It cannot be ignored.

Quiet Attention

It is sometimes advantageous to call attention to a minor disruption in a way that does not interfere with the group process and does not change the focus of the group (from the group to the problem). For example, a simple glance, finger to the lips, or indication that you will be there shortly can help diffuse a problem before it becomes large and noticeable (Emmer & Evertson, 2009). Jones and Jones (2001) suggest placing a sticky note on the corner of a student's desk to remind student of expected behavior and they suggest cueing a student by reinforcing other students who are acting appropriately. Similarly, calling on a student to answer a question when problematic behavior is beginning can redirect problematic behavior into engagement. Larrivee (2005) calls this strategy *interest boosting*.

Proximity control is another intervention that can interrupt a problem before it gets too big (Zirpoli & Melloy, 1997). Proximity control refers to having an adult nonverbal physical presence near a potential problem to keep it from escalating. This is a way of managing the problem by physical presence without interrupting the flow of the group (Emmer & Evertson, 2009). This is most easily accomplished by moving near the student who is off task, remaining calm, and if necessary, scaffolding that student's participation in the group (e.g., asking the student a content related question or asking for the student's opinion on the topic at hand). The adult presence serves as a cue to the student to get back on task or change her behavior and the scaffolding participation offers an entry into more appropriate engagement in the group.

Another form of proximity control is to rearrange the physical placement of students in the group in response to student misbehavior. For example, a student who is displaying some difficulties can be moved closer to the leader or can be directed (directed, not asked) to sit with specific students who will not encourage or who will not tolerate the misbehavior. When using proximity control, it is important to use minimal verbal and matter-of-fact statements that do not publicly shame the student and to limit the degree to which the misbehavior becomes a focus in the group.

Dealing with Objects and Other Distractions

Sometimes misbehavior happens as a result of over-stimulation or multiple demands on the student's attention. Some students are more easily able to attend to multiple stimuli than others. When the distraction is caused by an object, simply asking a student to put the object away is the simplest way to respond. This response invites the student to take responsibility to curtail the problem. Alternatively, you can request that the problematic object be handed to you with the commitment that it will be returned at the end of the group time. First offenders should probably be invited to take responsibility for removing the object on their own, however, as this gesture communicates confidence in the student's ability to handle the situation. Keep in mind that it is much easier to remove an object from a student when there is already a rule in the group about distracting objects. Therefore, we highlight the importance of having clear and specific rules, as they can help prevent power struggles in the group when problems arise.

When the distraction is caused by something that is beyond your control, like a noise in the hallway or an exciting soccer game outside the window, it is probably best to use immediacy by acknowledging the distraction and your inability to stop it. After recognizing the distraction, the group leader can elicit group member assistance in keeping focused on the task and offering periodic reminders about attention. In times when it feels near impossible to wrestle control of the group, flexibility is usually the best strategy, even if it means changing your plans for the group.

Humor

Humor has a way of putting people at ease, and for this reason, it can be a very useful way of interrupting disruptive behavior or defusing tension before it escalates in the group (Larrivee, 2005; Zirpoli & Melloy, 1997). It can be especially effective when working with older students (Sprick, 2006). Some examples of using humor to diffuse problems include telling a funny story, retelling of a funny incident, making a joke, making a play on words, or using a funny nonverbal behavior or expression. For example, a classroom group leader recalled this funny story when she noticed Ian becoming a little upset in the group: "Did I tell you (to the group) about the time when I was in fifth grade and I was so frustrated, I told the teacher 'I can't stand in here anymore.'? So, the teacher offered me a seat. I meant to say, 'I can't stand it in here any more' but everyone was laughing so hard, all I could do was laugh too!" Another example of using humor to diffuse tension was Larrivee's (2005) example of offering a student the "High Flyer Award" when her kite flew off into space during a kiting activity.

Using humor as a behavioral intervention can be very powerful. However, it also has the potential to be extremely problematic if the (unintended) result is confusing, insulting, or causes discomfort to group members. We offer these guidelines for using humor in response to problems in the group:

- While it is sometimes appropriate to respond to minor disruptions with humor; it is not an appropriate response to major disruptions.
- Humor can be effective in distracting a problem-in-the-making or in helping a person "lighten up," but there may be an incendiary effect of using humor if it is used in response to an individual who feels unheard, unacknowledged, or disrespected. Therefore, think carefully prior to responding humorously to an incident in the group. It is always a good idea to check in with the involved individuals after using humor to be sure that the intent of the humor was not misunderstood (Sprick, 2006).
- Humor should **never** be used at the expense of anyone in the group. Even when it is unintentional, collusion with one student against another is always inappropriate and can be very damaging. Always be aware of group dynamics prior to joining with a student in humor.
- Humor must **never** be used in response to a situation in which one student is being disrespectful to another student. That is, never make light of a situation in which one student is putting down another student. For example, it would be inappropriate to make a comment about a "bad hair day" in the group if a student was being teased about her haircut.
- It is a good idea to return to the problem or situation that was problematic (sometimes this is best done individually rather than in the larger group), once it has been diffused (Sprick, 2006). This helps assure that misunderstandings did not unintentionally result from the humorous remark.
- It is important to remember that humor is situated in cultural and social contexts that are available to some groups of people and not to others. That is, there is no universal standard for what is funny. Therefore, humor must be used with care. For example, a joke about a current TV show will not have meaning to students who have not watched that show. A comment about a material object may be lost on individuals who are not familiar with that object (e.g., a dream catcher or a worry stone). Mention of a particular snowboarding maneuver, for example, will not have meaning to those individuals who have never snowboarded. These comments may unintentionally leave out some individuals and inadvertently underscore social and cultural capital and status hierarchies that are probably already operating in the school or group. Be careful.
- Do not mistake cynicism or sarcasm for humor—they are not. Cynical and sarcastic comments do not contribute positively to a group in any way (Sprick, 2006). Although sometimes considered witty, cynical remarks often feel like put-downs and because they are typically ambiguous, sarcastic remarks can be confusing and misinterpreted by students. Sarcasm and cynicism can have the unintentional effects of making individuals feel excluded and create or reinforce divisions in the group. Group leaders should be on the lookout for attacks that are cloaked as

humor and to establish a norm that these comments are not welcome in the group. Of course, this means that the group leader, too, should also resist being sarcastic and cynical in the group.

In summary, while humor can be a helpful way to diffuse small potential problems in the group, it is a deceptively challenging intervention and should only be used only after careful consideration.

Hurdle Help

All students at some time or another need a little assistance to get through challenges. Larrivee (2005) uses the term *hurdle help* for teacher actions that help students move through minor challenges and get back on task. Examples of hurdle help include asking a key question to shift the student's thinking and help him understand a concept, reminding a student to stay on task, or offering encouragement. Hurdle help can be very effective in response to minor or mounting misbehavior without drawing too much attention to the problem. When using this intervention, it is important to remember to shift the focus back to the group after hurdling a student back on task. This will prevent the individual and the challenge from becoming the dominant focus of the group. *Case Study 7.15* offers an example of how hurdle help can be used to re-direct a student in a classroom group.

CASE STUDY 7.15

Hurdle Help

In an elementary classroom group, Kevin was challenged to draw a picture of himself. He complained out loud that he did not know how to draw and even threw the crayon on the desk in frustration. The counselor saw that Kevin's behavior was escalating and decided to intervene by using hurdle help. He approached Kevin and asked if he could help him start his picture. Kevin responded with a "yes" and handed a green crayon to the counselor. The counselor then asked what shape he should draw to start off the picture. When Kevin said "a circle," the counselor asked him to point to where it should go on the paper and then, quickly, asked Kevin how big the circle should be. With the instructions from Kevin, the counselor drew the circle. He then asked Kevin, "What's next?" Taking instructions from Kevin again, the counselor drew the neck in blue and then stood up. Shortly, the counselor said, "Why don't you take over for a minute. I'll be back in a few minutes. I just want to check to see who else may want help." In this way, the counselor dismissed himself from Kevin with the knowledge that he would come back and would help again if needed.

Reflection Questions

1. Hurdle help proved successful for Kevin. What are the counseling elements that appear in this intervention?
2. As you reflect on how this particular intervention might be effective in other problem scenarios—what skills are crucial for its success?

Unhooking from Power Struggles

The need for power—for both children and adults—is not an inherently bad thing. In fact, most educators and counselors would agree that a sense of empowerment is critical for child development—that it enables one to developing a sense of mastery in one's environment (Larrivee, 2005). Indeed, Glasser (1998a) identifies gaining power to be a basic human need. However, he points out that "our needs [e.g., gaining power] push for fulfillment; whether in our attempt to satisfy them we do right or wrong is up to each of us to decide" (Glasser, 1998a, p. 29). So, a need to feel powerful is not a bad thing; but sometimes the ways in which individuals seek to fulfill their power-need can cause problems.

Charney (1991) describes a *power struggle* as a "deliberate desire to challenge the teacher with defiance and insurgence, rather than an unwitting provocation or imperfect impulse controls" (p. 111). As she points out, a power struggle is less about one not having self-control than it is about struggling with someone to gain power and control; it is a statement of defiance not a show of deficit. Implicit in Charney's description of a power struggle is that two or more individuals are always implicated in a power struggle—it is not an individual behavior. In school groups, power struggles happen among students and they also happen between adults and students. It is that latter combination that we will be focusing on here in this discussion. However, the strategies discussed can also be used (with some alteration) in coaching students through peer-peer power struggles as well.

Student-adult power struggles in groups typically transpire in some variation of this scenario: a student refuses to follow a group rule. This disrupts the group and the leader responds in a way that asserts power. This furthers the disruption. This action, then, is typically followed by a leader response that asserts power. This assertion is then countered by the student's assertion of power. A struggle ensues. Working with power struggles requires that both the leader and the student unhook from the struggle over power. Ironically, often the best way for the leader to unhook from the power struggle is to offer the student power. Here are some ways to avoid power struggles:

- Provide opportunities for all of the students in the group to feel a sense of power.
- Let the "hooks" pass by. For example, if a student says "this is stupid" when you are passing out papers for a particular exercise, it might be best to ignore the statement. As Mendler (1992) suggests, do not take offensive behavior personally.
- Deal with the student individually, not in the group.
- Manage yourself well. If you are beginning to feel frustrated or angry, you are probably already hooked into a struggle for power. When you notice these feelings, take a breath, step away, ask a colleague to intervene, or acknowledge your feelings to the student and suggest that the issue be resolved at another time. For example, Ted comes into your classroom group late every week. When you confronted him about this behavior last week, he commented "I'm never late when where I have to be is worth being my time." Since he is late again, you assume that his behavior is intended to insult you by suggesting that your group is a waste of time. You begin to feel tense and catch yourself from making a snide remark after he walks into the room, smiles, says "oh, sorry . . . again" and takes his seat. Since you are having a personal reaction to Ted's comment, it might be good to just

ignore his behavior at the moment and continue with what you were doing. You can deal with his lateness at a later time.

Sometimes we are already in a power struggle before we even realize it! The following steps (although they do not necessarily need to be followed in this order) provide a guide for how to deal with power struggles:

1. When a student is casting a power hook, listen to her words, feelings, and experiences *without* agreeing or disagreeing.

2. Validate the student's concerns—understanding that they are real concerns for that student. For example, if Marissa complains that she should get another turn in an activity because she had less time than the others, you can listen carefully to her concern and validate it. You might say, "You really feel that it wasn't fair for you and that you should have an extra turn."

3. Be sure not to accuse the student of anything. We recommend discussing the event as an external event between the two of you (i.e., a conflict between you rather than a student's problem).

4. Tentatively identify what is happening as a power struggle or conflict and suggest the issue be dealt with at another time when tensions are not high. For example, Junior was not able to meet his goal in a ropes challenge and refused to return to the group for the processing activity. This is a pattern that has occurred in the past; when Junior was not successful, he refused to join the group. When he was successful, he bragged to his peers and joined the group, engaged in discussion. In an effort to avoid being hooked into a power struggle about participation again, the counselor said to him privately, "I hear that you think this is unfair, Junior. It seems that it is difficult for you to join the group right now and it seems that we may even be in a bit of a power struggle. Since we're both a bit hot-headed right now, I suggest that we rejoin the group now and spend some time afterwards talking about what happened. Okay?"

5. Whenever possible, respond to power requests by granting power. Choices allow for power. Offering the student a choice invites her to step out of a power-needing and into a decision-making role. However, be careful to structure the choices and the power they grant in ways that are also consistent with the needs of the situation. In the above example, if Junior continues to refuse to join the group, you might say, "Junior, at this point you have two choices: You can join the group now and we can talk about this later, or if you decide to remain apart from the group, you will not be allowed to join the group later when we get to decide on our final incentive activity and field trip." Choice-option responses are discussed in more detail later in this chapter.

6. It is probably a good idea to step away from the group to deal with the power struggle, especially if it appears that an audience is reinforcing the problem. This typically means stepping into a private space to deal with the conflict together. Time-out (discussed in Chapter 8) can also be used to calm a power-struggle situation. However, time-out is sometimes contraindicated in response to power struggles (Charney, 1991) because it is difficult to enforce time-out when the student is not cooperating or is highly agitated. Therefore, time out should not be offered unless it is an option that will give the student a chance to gain composure or save face rather than a punishment.

7. Remind the student that there are consequences for inappropriate behavior.

8. Sometimes having a specific known language for behaviors that have a history of being problematic allows you to avoid prolonged and public conversations about an individual's behavior in the group. Speaking in this kind of code-language about a behavior pattern positions the behavior as the problem, rather than the individual. In the example mentioned above, you may remind Junior "It looks like we're on the verge of a 'blowout' here, Junior. We've worked hard not to let 'blowouts' happen in group anymore and that has been working very well for you. So I was hoping that you could rejoin the group without that happening. Remember there are consequences to 'blowouts.' I hope you are able to make an appropriate choice." This language may, in effect, conjure up a partnership with a shared language.

9. Accusations, interpretations, and judgments are inflammatory to power struggles; these tend to distance people from available constructive solutions. Discussing the situation that *caused* the power struggle is something that should happen, if appropriate, when both parties are calm and respectful and when the power struggle is over. In our earlier example, Junior was invited to discuss the problem, if he chose to, but at a later time. This avoids arguments and disagreements about the details and helps avoid blame-placing conversations that have a way of attracting power struggles when individuals are angry. Keep in mind that, in the end, no one can force a student into a meaningful conversation about a problem. For some students, attempts to do so will have the effect of extending the life of the power struggle. In our example with Junior, allowing him the choice of whether to have a conversation about the problem gives power back to him. There will be times when you, as the adult, will decide that it is important to have a discussion about the power struggle, even if the student does not want to. But again, these conversations are rarely constructive when the power struggle is in full effect. The best option is to offer choices and alternatives whenever possible and attempt to deal with the problem at a time when both parties are calm and not engaged in struggling for power and control.

10. Always communicate your belief in the student's ability to handle difficulties. In the example above, the counselor pointed out her confidence in Junior's ability to handle the potential blowout, since he had worked hard to keep blowouts from happening in the past. This statement communicated confidence and offered evidence of past successes. When and if the current power struggle is resolved without a blowout, it would be a good idea for the counselor to highlight this additional success. Students should get credit and be appreciated for their hard work in solving problems and avoiding power struggles.

Feedback Exchange and Group Problem Solving

Sometimes the best way to respond to a problem in the group is to actually have the problem—and its solution—become a focus in the group. This type of intervention is used when it would be helpful to elicit multiple perspectives in the resolution of the problem, to shift the focus of the intervention from leader-student to student-student, and when the leader wants to harvest the problem for its learning potential for everyone in the group. In this section, we offer two interventions to this end: *feedback exchange* and *group problem solving*.

FEEDBACK EXCHANGE   Feedback exchange refers to the process of telling another person in the group how you have experienced and/or how you are affected by her. For example, Clara told Abraham that she noticed he rolled his eyes when she spoke and that she was offended because it seemed like he did not care about what she had to say. Feedback allows individuals to learn how they are perceived by others in the group and offers an opportunity for self-evaluation (Gladding, 2003; Klein, 2003). Klein asserts that feedback is one of the most important learning processes that can be used in groups.

Feedback exchange works best to stimulate learning when it occurs in a context of safety and care. That is, feedback is not likely to be productive if it is given in a hurtful or evaluative way. For example, if Clara blurted out, "You're a jerk" to Abraham in response to his eye rolling, it is unlikely that further interaction between the two of them would be productive.

Another important aspect of feedback is that it is not particularly effective in eliciting change if the receiver is not ready to hear it. The group leader plays an important role in structuring feedback exchange in the group so that members can give and receive feedback as part of a meaningful learning process. The group leader's attention to such interpersonal dynamics is not only good leadership form, it represents ethical leadership as well (see ASGW, 2007, B.4). To this end, we recommend structuring feedback exchange as outlined below:

1. *Begin by asking the recipient if he is open to hearing feedback.*
   - If he says yes, it may be appropriate to remind him that it is important to listen to the feedback and not respond until he has had a chance to think about what he has heard.
   - If the individual indicates that he is not open or ready for feedback, that option must be respected. The counselor can let the recipient and the feedback giver know that she will check in later to see if the recipient is ready.
2. *Feedback should be delivered in a clear statement of what was observed.* Invite the feedback giver to offer her comments as concrete observations. The feedback should be about something that was directly experienced or observed. Avoid accusations about intent, feelings, thoughts, and conversations based on hearsay.
3. *Invite the feedback giver to tell the recipient how she was specifically affected by the behavior.* Here the counselor may need to intervene to keep the feedback focused on what was observed and what was felt, and to cut off any hurtful or interpretative statements or reactions that may be stated in anger.
4. *After the feedback has been given, the counselor can thank the giver for giving the feedback (for being courageous enough to give the feedback) and then invite the recipient to think for "one whole minute" before responding.* Sometimes gentle support is needed by the recipient on how to respond in an appropriate fashion. Be willing to offer what the recipient may need in that formative moment (see # 6 below).
5. *If the recipient is planning to respond to the feedback, the counselor should remind the original feedback giver to listen quietly and respectfully to what the recipient has to say.* If the recipient chooses not to respond to the feedback giver, the counselor may need to help him acknowledge that the feedback was heard, and to follow up with him at a later and more private time. Follow up with the recipient is important in case he needs help making meaning of what has been said or choosing an appropriate response.
6. *Keep in mind that many youth are likely to take in feedback and make appropriate changes to their behavior without verbal exchange.* That is, for many

individuals, just pointing out that a mistake has been made is all that is needed to affect change. This is especially important when working with youth because receiving feedback can be very embarrassing and saving face in front of peers is always important. So, avoid requiring a recipient to verbally respond to feedback if she is not inclined to do so. While you may expect that an individual who has received feedback will change her behavior, it probably is not necessary that she also be required to offer a verbal account (in such a public setting) of how she will change. In fact, forcing this kind of response may actually initiate defiance or a power struggle, and short-change the opportunity for learning and change. In short, it is very important to be attuned to the needs and emotional safety of the giver and the recipient when facilitating feedback exchange. An example of structuring feedback exchange is provided in *Case Study 7.16*.

CASE STUDY 7.16

Feedback Exchange

In a classroom group, led by the school counselor, Adout blurted out, "No way I'm going to be a partner with her" as she pointed to her once-friend, Maria.

The counselor, Mr. Leidy, responded by saying, "Okay, let's take a quick time out. Sounds like you're giving some feedback to Maria, but it's hard to know exactly what that feedback is, Adout."

"Should we talk about this?" he asked both of them. Both Maria and Adout agreed.

Mr. Leidy structured the conversation by reminding students about using feedback rules and indicating that he was going to start with Adout. "Okay, are you ready to hear some feedback, Maria?" he asked.

"I guess," she responded.

Adout said "Maria, you told me you'd save me a seat in the lunchroom but you didn't save me one. I had to sit with the other group and they weren't nice to me."

Mr. Leidy said "Adout can you tell Maria how it felt for you to get to the lunch room and find that there was no seat at the table for you?"

After Adout told Maria how she felt, Mr. Leidy asked Maria, "Do you want to say anything to Adout, Maria?"

When Maria responded that she did have something to say, Mr. Leidy said, "Okay, Adout, can you be in a listening place now?" When Adout agreed that she was ready to listen, the counselor invited Maria to comment back, being careful to shape the comments in specific terms that were not accusatory. She was encouraged to speak about her own experience.

Reflection Questions

1. Divide this example of a feedback exchange into its critical parts. Look back at the steps previously outlined and see if all elements of effective feedback are present.
2. Thinking from a very personal place, is there anything that you might be inclined to do differently although aiming for a similar outcome?

It is helpful to think about feedback exchange being a process rather than a statement. As such, it can sometimes lead to an extended conversation—sometimes taking over the focus of the group. When feedback exchange threatens to co-opt the group (long after the learning potential has been harvested), the leader may need to intervene and suggest that the conversation continue at another time and, perhaps privately rather than in the group.

Uncoached feedback exchange happens daily in school halls, playgrounds, cafeterias, and classrooms. However, these are not always constructive experiences for the students. When feedback is given in ways that are evaluative and judgmental or when it is vague and non-specific, hurt, shame, and/or anger are likely to result. By structuring feedback exchange, all of the students in the group have the benefit of learning how to engage in difficult conversations constructively. They learn that clear and direct communication can help create solutions to interpersonal difficulties, and they have the opportunity to learn and practice these important communication skills in other settings.

GROUP PROBLEM SOLVING   When a difficulty in the group affects many members or has an impact on the functioning of the group, it becomes a group problem. Typically, group problems warrant group solutions. While feedback exchange typically happens between two individuals in or out of the presence of others in the group, the *group problem solving process* engages all of the members of the group. Group problem solving is premised on the idea that all members of the group have a role to play in working on a solution to the problem. Working through problems in the group extends learning from the individuals most directly involved in the problem to all members of the group due to the teaching and modeling of a conflict resolution process. It can also foster group cohesion and genuineness among members, and can help the group move into the working stage (Corey & Corey, 2006; Gladding, 2003).

The process of group problem solving typically follows a conflict mediation model whereby the leader directs members of the group in identifying the problem and brainstorming solutions. In some groups, students can actually facilitate the problem solving process with their peers by being coached and under close supervision of the leader. We have adapted Luckner and Nadler's (1997) problem solving/conflict mediation steps and Popkin's (1994) Active Problem Solving models in these suggested steps for group problem solving:

1. *Identify the problem.*   Using I-messages is most effective to this end. Be sure to listen to and respect each member's perspective and insist that all individuals respect each other.
2. *Attempt to reach consensus on the identification of the problem.*   It can be helpful to point out that there may be conflicting perspectives and needs that play into problem situations, and that there are likely to be competing solutions to the problem as well. Emphasize that right versus wrong and good versus bad dichotomies work against win-win solutions.
3. *Generate alternative solutions.*   Attempt to generate a list of many possible solutions from all members of the group. Include all suggestions, even if you do not agree with all of them, as this stimulates further thought and communicates openness and respect for all members in the group.
4. *Evaluate the suggestions.*   Engage members to use critical thinking skills to evaluate the various solutions, identifying the potential benefits and drawbacks of all of the options.

5. *Make a "best fit" decision regarding the solution to the problem.*   It is best to generate a consensus regarding the solution; however, doing so may not always be possible. Keep in mind that participants who do not have *buy in* to a solution are not likely to honor it. You will probably need to help students focus on finding a solution that works best for the individuals most directly affected by the problem. It sometimes helps to remind students that although a potential solution may not be the best solution, it should be one that they can live with. This is a time to teach and model flexibility.

6. *Implement the solution by identifying how and by whom action will be carried out.*   Again, use group members—those who are and those who are not affected by the problem—to help generate suggestions for the action plan. When students are generating solutions, remember that it is sometimes easier to identify actions than it is to carry them out. You will probably need to intervene to help students commit only to actions that are realistic and you may also need to coach students later in carrying out the plans they have made.

7. *If no solution has been attained, discussion should focus on how the group can move on.*   Sometimes, group members may decide that the conflict cannot be resolved, but that they can continue to work together in the group, despite the disagreement. If this is the case, consensus should be reached on this decision, as it then becomes a solution to the problem.

8. *Follow up with an evaluation of the solution at a later date.*   Help individuals or the group revise a decision if it is not working as intended. Remind students of how well the group worked to reach a solution.

Keep in mind that when social skills are the focus of the group—whether it is a counseling or classroom group—a group problem solving intervention is likely to be consistent with the overarching goals and objectives for that group. Therefore, even if it is an unplanned activity in the group that day, group problem solving is likely to be an appropriate educational process in most school groups.

Returning to Rules

We have referred to rules as parameters of behavioral expectations for group members, serving as a guardrail to shape and contain the group. The importance of establishing rules that are appropriate and that are reflective of a diverse larger school community has already been thoroughly discussed. We now turn your attention to responding to problematic behavior by using group rules. We recommend this mater-of-fact approach: (a) *Restate the rule*. When restating a rule, always do so in clear, simple, nonpunitive language. (b) *Offer a simple instruction* to the student that you expect that she will comply with the rule. (c) *Shift the focus* immediately back to the task that (or individual who) was interrupted. For example, "Griffin, in here we have a rule of listening when others are speaking. Let's remember to not talk when others are speaking so we can hear what others are saying. Okay, go ahead now, Curtis." If the rule is broken again or the infraction presents a significant distraction or danger to the group, the rule may need to be stated along with consequences for what will happen if the rule is not followed.

This matter-of-fact response is a simple approach to addressing many problems in the group. However, as Kline (2003) points out, it does not allow for any exploration of the underlying problem that may have caused the misbehavior or rule infraction. In some cases, particularly when rule infractions occur with frequency in the group, it may be more appropriate to engage the group in a discussion about the situation in order to facilitate deeper understanding of why a particular behavior is problematic. When the problematic behavior is related to intolerance or bullying behaviors, a simple "restatement of the rules and move on" approach can silence important issues and send the wrong message to group members. Therefore, when and how to respond with rule restatement must be considered in light of the learning needs of the group and student safety.

Consider the relative benefits using this type of intervention publicly versus privately. Bringing group attention to an individual who is breaking a rule has the potential of gathering an audience for misbehavior. Or, conversely, it may also arouse shame and/or engage the student in a power struggle. However, it should be pointed out that offering student feedback is a natural part of the teaching process, and it is respectful to offer students an opportunity to take responsibility for adjusting their behavior. Decisions regarding public versus private intervention will depend on a number of factors, including the specific individual, the dynamics in the group, the purpose of the group, the level of seriousness of the behavior problem, and the extent to which others in the group can benefit from the public restatement of the rules.

Remember the *Intervention Cube* (Cohen & Smith, 1976) discussion in Chapter 6 when considering how to respond to rule infractions, both publicly and privately. A lower intensity group level intervention may sound like this: "I just wanted to remind everyone that in here we do not talk when others are talking. We'll let you continue, Melika, just as soon as people are in the listening position." Here, the intervention does not singularly name any one offender but clearly delivers the message. Alternatively, you could privately offer feedback to the individual who is breaking the rule (intrapersonal level intervention), probably evoking some intensity. This can be delivered as a quick whisper or a nonverbal cue. Calling the student outside the room to discuss a behavioral infraction, which is another option, raises the intensity and delivers a strong message of expectation to the offending student. Sometimes this level of intensity is appropriate to elicit a change in student behavior.

Sometimes disruptions happen in the group that do not constitute a breach of stated group rules, per say, but which are problematic and may warrant an intervention that focuses on rules. For example, the ground rules in a seventh-grade group did not explicitly address respecting property or materials. Students were involved in an activity that used clay and three students began to throw the clay at each other. The counselor intervened by stating a new rule of no throwing clay: "Sorry folks. We can't throw clay in here." While this rule was never explicitly stated in the group, it was clearly an appropriate request.

Finally, it is important to point out that most students have a good general sense of school norms and expectations and they also know when rules are being broken. However, not all students have an equal status position in the school and in school groups. Many students do not feel empowered to stop inappropriate peer behavior when it occurs in the group. So it is important to remember that it is ultimately up to the group leader to enforce rules and to create an appropriate group climate for all members of the group.

Choice-Options

Working with choice-options refers to offering students a limited number of options from which they can select a more appropriate or constructive behavior. For example, in a third-grade classroom group, Juana began to wander around the room and was disruptive to other students. The counselor said, "Juana, you have two choices: You can join your group and continue on your art work or you can decide you are finished, put your materials away, and sit quietly until the rest of us are done." This response offered Juana two clearly articulated options for her continued participation in the group.

Responding to student misbehavior by offering choice-options communicates student responsibility for her behavior, particularly when the choices and their consequences are clearly articulated to the student (Emmer & Evertson, 2009), and can help the student feel less controlled by others (Jones & Jones, 2001). Offering *limited* choice-options (offering just a few options) gives more structure than offering *open* choice-options (inviting the student to identify the options), thus streamlining the decision-making process. The structure of limited-choice options is particularly helpful when working with students who cannot locate appropriate behavioral options in the moment of confrontation or in situations where you want to respond quickly to the misbehavior and shift back to the task at hand. In situations where few options are available or when the leader wants to give the student the opportunity to choose but also wants to encourage a specific course of action, *weighted* choice-options can be offered. Weighted choice-option interventions offer a range of options, but in this offering, some of the options are more appealing than others. A classroom example of a weighted option is when a teacher proposes that a student finish his work by the end of the class time or to make it up after school. When intervening in classroom and counseling groups, it certainly is appropriate to shape choice-options so that the most appropriate or constructive options are likely to be selected.

When offering choice-options, it is important to do so in a calm and non-punitive way. Also, be careful to offer students real and appropriate choices. In the above example, the options offered to Juana assume that Juana is fully capable of sitting quietly and waiting for others. If Juana really was not able to follow through on sitting and waiting, the leader would find herself needing to intervene again. So, that option may not have been realistic or appropriate in that situation. There are subtle differences between appropriate and realistic, so you must think carefully when offering options. Sometimes, options might be *possible* for a particular student, but not *appropriate*. For example, Meaghan is a student who prefers to work on her own, who often isolates herself, and who has few friends. Inviting her to choose whether or not to participate in a group activity may not be in a choice that is in her best interest. In this case, better options might be for Meaghan to participate in a particular activity with or without assistance rather than not at all.

Options that invite students to work in the hallways or afterschool also warrant caution. These kinds of options are not appropriate if they require supervision that is not available. Keep in mind that when impossible or inappropriate options are offered to students, they are not *real* choices. Offering such options (and then later recanting them) is likely to lead to a compromised situation for the group leader and may leave students feeling manipulated. Also, not following through on the selected option sends the wrong message to students and endangers the effectiveness of this intervention in the future. Finally, we point out that choice-option interventions are not particularly effective when used in response to misbehavior that occurs repeatedly, when the misbehavior seriously compromises learning opportunities for others in the group, or when misbehavior puts individuals in danger. In those cases, a clearer articulation of what is expected—with no options—is most appropriate.

The manner in which you engage students in choice-option discussions deserves important consideration. As with all disciplinary actions, having a private choice-option conversation with the individual can help avoid public embarrassment and may also serve to side-step a power seeking response. Also, it is important to remember that some students may be reluctant to actually *verbalize* to the leader what option they have decided on, but they respond behaviorally instead. For example, Meaghan may not *say* that she has decided to join the group, but her *action* of moving her desk back into the group with her peers and raising her hand in response to the next question signals the option she has selected. We suggest that group leaders recognize and be respectful of the student's manner of selecting an option, however it is communicated. If you feel strongly that a verbal acknowledgement has to be made in response to a nonverbal choice that has been made, you can verbalize what you see the student doing and validate that the student has followed through on the conditions of that choice. For example, "I see, Juana, that you have decided to put your papers away. Remember that making this choice was also agreeing to sit quietly until everyone else is done." It is also sometimes helpful to follow this by communicating your belief that the student will make good on his or her decision: "I know that you will be able to follow through on your decision, Juana. Keep in mind some of the ways that you know about how to sit quietly when you start to get bored so you don't interrupt others who are still working." In this way, your response also cues the student to follow through on the behaviors that are needed to comply with choice that she has made.

Consequences

A consequence is something that happens after a particular event or behavior. In behavioral terminology, consequences are defined as the "events or changes in the environment following a target behavior" (Zirpoli & Melloy, 1997, p. 8). Consequences can either reinforce or punish the behavior they follow. While *reinforcement* has the effect of increasing the occurrence of the behavior that precedes it, a *punishment* is intended to reduce the occurrence of a particular behavior (Kerr & Nelson, 1998). In groups, consequences (both reinforcements and punishments) are used to enforce limits; shape behaviors; and provide, illustrate, and/or enforce boundaries or parameters. For example, the consequence of not coming to group is missing out on the fun activity that happened in the group that day. Although perhaps unintentional, if this consequence has the effect of decreasing the undesired behavior of skipping group, then it could be considered a punishment. An example of a reinforcement is when students come to group, they have fun.

It is also important to remember that consequences are not just actions imposed by teachers or counselors in response to desirable or undesirable behaviors. Consequences also happen in classrooms and groups unintentionally. In the above example, when the group is fun, it reinforces the desired behavior of attending the group. Similarly, when a student makes a funny comment in a classroom and other students laugh, the consequence of making a joke is peer attention and laughter. Both intentional and unintentional consequences have the similar impact of shaping a behavior. Also, consequences are considered not only for their reinforcement value in the here-and-now, but also for how they will influence future behaviors. Therefore, the consequence of a given behavior also has a precedent-setting effect.

Before going further, we want to point out that in the lay public, as well as many professional communities, the term *punishment* is often saddled with negative connotations. However, in its purist sense, punishment does not imply the use of aversive or punitive actions (Zirpoli & Melloy, 1997). That is, when used appropriately, the purpose of punishment is to reduce the occurrence of a particular behavior; it is not designed to hurt, damage, or shame. This being said, it is also the case that the use of punishment is sometimes problematic. This is true for a number of reasons, not the least of which is because its perception of being coercive makes people wary of using it as a behavioral strategy. Another reason to be wary of using punishment is that even when it is used appropriately, punishment does not easily discriminate between appropriate and inappropriate behavior. That is, you may unintentionally punish appropriate behaviors when they occur at or around the same time that the inappropriate behaviors occur (Zirpoli & Melloy, 1997).

Another concern with the use of punishment is that it may be more effective in achieving temporary behavioral changes instead of teaching responsibility and promoting long-term changes (Queen, Blackwelder, & Mallen, 1997) largely because it does not teach appropriate behavior (Larrivee, 2005). For example, while a punishment may be given to a student for speaking out in class, it may also diminish the likelihood that this student will contribute to class discussions in the future. Finally, punishments sometimes elicit undesirable consequences (Larrivee, 2005; Zirpoli & Melloy, 1997), such as shame or anger, even when they are delivered in an appropriate way. Students may act out in response to punishment by revenge, asserting power, or by becoming disengaged. So, using positive reinforcement, even in response to the most challenging or inappropriate behaviors, is usually far more effective than using punishment (Zirpoli & Melloy, 1997).

NATURAL CONSEQUENCES   *Natural consequences* refer to events that occur naturally in the environment that have the effect of reinforcing or punishing a particular behavior (Larrivee, 2005). Burning one's finger after touching a hot stovetop is an example of a natural consequence. In this case, the burn would be a *natural punishment* because it would (hopefully) decrease the stove-touching behavior. Natural consequences are powerful reinforcers and punishers because they typically happen without any adult intervention and often occur outside of the control of the individual. Of course, it is important to monitor the potential impact of using natural consequences for behavior control, as it is your responsibility as the group leader to be sure that students are always safe from potential physical and emotional harm. For example, while getting hit by a car is a natural consequence of running into the road, it is the group leader's responsibility to make sure that the children in the group do not run into the road.

More specifically to a school setting, praise, recognition, and positive teacher attention are generally considered to be natural consequences that reinforce appropriate behavior (Kauffman, Mostert, Trent, & Hallahan, 2002; Zirpoli & Melloy, 1997). These teacher behaviors occur naturally in classroom environments when good behavior is abundant (although we would also consider praise to be a logical consequence when it is used intentionally to reinforce a specific behavior). Similarly, student popularity is a natural consequence of being nice to others in many social circles (although popularity is based on numerous other factors as well). Natural consequences are generally preferred over artificial or contrived consequences for reinforcing a behavior because they are likely to maintain desired behaviors after artificial incentives or reinforcers are withdrawn (Zirpoli & Melloy, 1997).

As noted, natural consequences can also reinforce undesired behavior. For example, the natural consequence for a student who is truant for English class might be that she misses a test that was given on a day that she was truant. However, if that student is permitted to take the test the next day (with the benefit of knowing what questions were on the test after talking to peers who already took the test), the truant behavior would be reinforced. Therefore, it is important to think carefully about how consequences for behaviors can unintentionally reinforce undesirable student behavior.

LOGICAL CONSEQUENCES   Unlike natural consequences, *logical consequences* are imposed consequences. They are called logical because they closely and logically relate to the behavior that they are intended to shape (Larrivee, 2005). Logical consequences, too, are intended to increase (i.e., reinforce) or diminish (i.e., punish) a particular behavior. For example, parents sometimes give their children free time to play as reinforcement for completing their chores. In a high school setting, an example of a logical reinforcement might be to give students of good standing permission to leave the school grounds during a free block. An example of a logical punishment might be that a student misses basketball practice (and thus, a chance to start in the next game) because she has to stay after school to complete a math assignment when she was off-task in class. Not allowing a student who was physically pushing others to participate in a desirable group activity may be a logical consequence for aggressive behavior. The latter two examples are punishments because they are intended to decrease undesired behaviors (e.g., the off-task behavior in math, the aggressive behavior). The use of logical consequences in schools is popular because this behavior management approach puts consequence distribution in the control of the teacher (or counselor, in our case) rather than at the disposal of natural forces.

Logical consequences should always be related to the behavior they are intended to reinforce or punish and they should be instituted from a position of appropriate ethical behavior and care, and with a focus on teaching appropriate behavior and self-regulation (Larrivee, 2005). With this in mind, we advocate using Larrivee's "Four Rs of Consequences" (p. 203): Consequences should be *related* (to the event that is being shaped), *reasonable, respectful*, and *reliably* enforced. Logical consequences are most effective when they immediately follow the target behavior, when they are combined with verbal praise, and when they are applied consistently or according to an appropriate schedule of reinforcement (Zirpoli & Melloy, 1997).

Queen, Blackwelder, and Mallen (1997) offer a number of suggestions for imposing logical consequences. These include never arguing, raising your voice, or becoming emotional with students when imposing consequences. Instead, they recommend being simple and matter of fact, and to always use respectful language. They also caution not to offer undeserved praise (because it can feel disingenuous) and to be vigilant about being fair to all students in the room when using logical consequences. Again, the use of reinforcement to shape desired behaviors is favored over the use of punishments largely because of the many unintended and undesirable side effects of punishments (Zirpoli & Melloy, 1997).

REASONABLE CONSEQUENCES   The term *reasonable consequence* (Hoover & Kindsvatter, 1997) is used by some to highlight the importance of imposing consequences that (a) make sense, (b) are developmentally appropriate, (c) are related to a personal learning outcome that is student specific, and (d) are focused more on instruction than on punishment. Reasonable consequences are based on the premise that most students can be persuaded by reason and fairness to behave in an appropriate way. Therefore, a reasonable consequence for a misbehavior would be imposed with a focus on helping the student understand the infraction and the expectation. For example, Kayla was distracting the school counselor and other students in a classroom group by incessantly tapping her pencil when they should have been working quietly. The school counselor asked Kayla to stop tapping her pencil. In response, Kayla broke the pencil and sauntered to the garbage container in the front of the room and threw the pencil away. The school counselor was outraged and immediately told the student that she could not go on her class field trip on Friday. In this example, the school counselor's response was obviously unreasonable. Had the school counselor taken time to assess the purpose of Kayla's distracting behavior or help Kayla understand why the pencil-tapping was inappropriate before asking her to put the pencil away, then Kayla and other group members may have learned a valuable lesson.

STEPS FOR IMPLEMENTING CONSEQUENCES   We offer guidelines below for imposing consequences with youth in schools. You will notice when reading these guidelines that they are in some ways similar to the processes we outlined for intervening in response to power struggles. Consequence discussions should be facilitated in a way that diffuses mounting conflict and struggles over power and that scaffold student reengagement in the work of the group.

- *Always intervene privately (and use a soft, calm tone).*   Keep in mind that consequence conversations sometimes take longer than a quick redirection. So, you will probably need to provide direction to the group to stay on task and move with the individual student out of hearing distance so that the other students are not distracted and so that they do not provide an audience for misbehavior. For example, "We will take a few more minutes to work on these pictures. Please continue to work in your small groups for 5 more minutes. Aaron, can you please come here for a minute?"
- *Name the problem.*   Begin the consequence discussion with a clear statement identifying the problem or behavior of concern. This should be clearly stated and understandable, using concrete observations whenever possible. For example, "Zoey, I see that you broke three colored pencils and threw them on the ground."
- *Provide feedback regarding the effect of the behavior on you or on the group.*   Use I-statements. "I feel a little angry that you're breaking my materials and I can see that your group members are spending a lot of their work time trying to talk you into not breaking pencils. That does not seem fair."

- *Identify the rule that was broken (if one was broken).*   This should be stated simply and directly. "In this group we have all agreed that we would respect others and school property."
- *Identify the consequence of the behavior.*   If appropriate, offer the student the consequence choice-options. "Zoey, you have a choice: You can pick up the pencils you have broken and put them in the garbage and then get back on task or you can sit outside of the group and finish your work on your own during the after-school study hall period." Mendler (1992) recommends that students not be permitted to remain in the classroom if they are unable to accept the consequences of their behaviors or if they are unable to come up with respectful or responsible alternative behaviors.
- *Do not require that a student verbalize that a choice has been made: Accept action as a response.*   The adage "actions speak louder than words" is helpful here. For example, if Zoey begins to pick up the pencils without saying anything, accept that this is her way of indicating that she has made a choice about her behavior. She may also need prompting to rejoin the group after the pencils are thrown away, but do not insist that she verbalize to you what action she has chosen (if her actions obviously indicate her decision).
- *Stay focused on the problem and the solution. Implement solutions respectfully.* Do not shame students. Consequences should never insult a student's dignity nor should they impede student's engagement or motivation to learn. Avoid moralizing, do not use put-downs, and be sure that the particular consequence is in proportion (in intensity) to the behavior that it is intended to correct (Albert, 1996). Also, it is best to avoid offering interpretations of the reasons for the misbehavior and avoid predictions of the long-term consequences for the student if the behavior continues. Be consistent and fair, and do not allow whining, bargaining, etc.
- *You may need to impose a timeframe by when the choice needs to be made and indicate that a non-response is a choice which also has a consequence.*   For example, "Zoey, I see that you have not decided which option you will take. I will give you one more minute to make a choice and then I will have to make the choice for you. My choice will be for you to sit out now and join me after school. You can make a different choice, but you need to make it now."
- *Always follow through on implementation of the consequences.*   Everything that happens in schools seems to happen in a fishbowl—students are always watching how adults behave. If you do not implement the consequences that you have committed to, the message to students is that you are unreliable. This message can erode trust and invite future behavior infractions.
- *Return to the group as quickly as possible.*   The purpose of the group should always be the focus of the group. Do not let a problem hijack your agenda.
- *Communicate confidence that the student will be able to get back on track and self-correct the misbehavior.*   For example, "I know that this is not a great situation for you right now, but I have confidence that you will be able to pull it together and finish this activity. I would be happy to talk with you about what happened that caused all of this, but we'll have to do that at another time. Right now it's important to get back on track. I think that you can do it."
- *Catch student "being good" as soon as possible after his or her behavior has been corrected.*   For example, the counselor offered Zoey a thumbs up signal immediately after the pencils were thrown away and she rejoined the group.

A BOTTOM LINE

In conclusion, we want to highlight some important points on leader positioning for responding to problems in the group. First, some of the suggestions in this chapter will not work with some students, in some situations, and under some circumstances. Second, some of the suggestions here will conflict with some of the theoretical positions that you hold regarding personality, identity, social, cognitive development, and how to motivate change. For example, Adlerians may be particularly cautious of offering praise. Behaviorists will likely disagree with suggestions about discussions. Our intent here is to offer a broad spectrum of options for responding to problems in the group and your job is to find the ones that fit (at a particular time and in a particular situation). What we do argue for, however, is that all of us who intervene with youth in groups in schools do so from a position of fairness, with an eye towards developing potential, and with a firm grounding in respectful and ethical behavior. We believe that all of the interventions mentioned here have the potential to hold true to these principles—and all of them can also illusively escape these principles. The bottom line is that it is up to the group leader to assure that all that happens in the group, happens from these basic premises.

CHAPTER 8

Addressing Problems Outside of the Group

We continue our discussion of strategies that can be used in response to problems in the group. The strategies listed in this chapter require the group leader to take individual remedial action with a group member outside of the group. That is, these interventions require individual discussions and planning with students when others are not present. They are recommended for times when it simply is not appropriate to solve the particular problem in the group. Most often, this is when a student refuses to participate in the group; in cases of extreme defiance, theft, property damage, and when the disruption is related to a student's health or other personal issues (Charles & Senter, 2002). These interventions typically occur before, after, or between group meetings. Later in the chapter, we will present a case study about Jake, an eighth grader with enormous anger and very little control expressing it. This case study gives readers a view of between-group de-escalation. In extreme circumstances, when immediate private intervention is required, the group may need to be dismissed in order for these strategies to be implemented without delay. This may be the case, for example, if a student displays violent or dangerous behavior in the group.

In general, the strategies outlined in this chapter would be implemented only after other planning, management, and response strategies have failed. Issues of safety, supervision, and adhering to policy regulations, must inform the parameters of our interventions at all times and school counselors must ground their decisions securely to uphold their obligation to pertinent ethical code and standards. Once again, we direct your attention to the *Ethical Standards for School Counselors* (ASCA, 2004) and the *ASGW Best Practice Guidelines* (ASGW, 2007), as well as the *American Counseling Association Code of Ethics and Standards of Practice* (ACA, 2005).

CONTRACTS

Contracts are verbal and/or written agreements regarding behavioral expectations that are negotiated between a student and the group leader. They often serve as the medium for individual goal-setting and rely on intrinsic motivation, reasonable consequences, and/or punishments for shaping desired behaviors. Contracts are typically used when there have been repeated problematic behaviors that impede group functioning or when a problem is so severe that immediate intervention is required (Emmer & Evertson, 2009). For example, if a student in the group has had difficulty regulating her anger when certain topics are raised, the counselor and student may draft a contract outlining specific expectations for the student and conditions for management of the problem. Expectations for the student in this example may include strategies for the student to use to gain control, such as deep breaths, elective time-outs, and counting exercises. It may also identify some actions that the counselor or group leader may take to help the student maintain self-control such as cueing and reminders. Sometimes contracts contain stipulations or contingencies, such as stating that the student will be asked to go directly to the time-out room in the school if the anger continues to escalate. Contracts may also identify consequences for noncompliance.

Drafting the Contract

It is important to meet privately with the student to initiate the contract in order to avoid giving public attention to personal issues, to avoid triggering shame, and to avoid giving an audience to a student who misbehaves. However, while the contract process is initiated outside of the group, the implementation of the contract, once drafted, often does happen in the group. Below are specific steps for drafting a contract along with the example of Ismael and Mr. Weaver. Their story will serve as a running case study illustrating the process of contracting while providing suggestions for each step along the way.

Step 1   Initiating the Contract   Approach the initial contracting meeting from a problem-solving position. We suggest that you position yourself as someone who is on the student's side trying to eliminate the problem. Begin with a clear articulation of the problem. This conversation should not be side-railed by lectures, hypotheses regarding the intent behind the behavior, nor suggestions about etiology. *Clear*, *concise*, and *specific* are the words to keep in mind when working a contract with a student.

Contracting Example: Initiating the Contract   After Ismael repeatedly disrupted the counseling group by running into the hallway, and once, outside of the school building, the counselor, Mr. Weaver, set up an appointment to meet privately with Ismael. He started the meeting by saying, "Ismael, the reason we are here is that I am concerned about your running out of the room during group."

Step 2   Identifying the Problem   To help the student understand the problem, offer a clear description of the behavior you observed and a nonblaming account of how you are affected by the behavior. You can invite the student to comment on your observation or perspective.

Contracting Example: Identifying the Problem   Mr. Weaver continued, "I want you to know, Ismael, that I worry when you run out of the classroom because I don't know where you are going. I also worry because I sometimes don't understand why you have left the room. Also, it is very disruptive when you run out of the group."

"What do you think, Ismael, as you hear me say this?" Mr. Weaver asked.

Step 3   Goal-Setting   Once the problem has been identified, move into goal-setting. The purpose of goal-setting is to create a plan for how to manage the problem in a more constructive way. A good way to set goals, particularly when the student is unable to identify constructive goals himself, is to talk about what would be different in the future if the problem behavior did not exist. This helps identify a target pro-social behavior.

Once identified, the next task is to brainstorm how to accomplish this target behavior or goal. It is sometimes tempting to write a contract about what the student will not do in the future, but basing the contract on expectations for desired behaviors is far more constructive towards developing win-win goals and generating student buy-in for the contract to work. Two good rules of thumb here are to offer suggestions only as often as you elicit suggestions from the student and to hold off on articulating consequences until pro-social participation is outlined.

Contracting Example: Goal-Setting   Mr. Weaver worked with Ismael to clarify the behavioral expectations and goals for future participation in the group: "You say that you won't run tomorrow. Can you describe what you will be doing in the group if you are not running?" "How will you stick to this goal when you are in the group?" "What can we do to help you keep from running when things get bad?"

After Ismael offered that taking time-out to calm himself when he was upset and wanted to leave the room might be a good idea, Mr. Weaver said, "Okay, good. That sounds like a good idea to take a time-out in the room as a strategy for when you begin to get tense and want to leave the room. I know that it's sometimes hard to notice that things are getting difficult until they're at a point when you can't stand it anymore. Any thoughts about how I or your teacher can help you notice when you seem to be getting stressed and help you remember to give yourself a time out?"

Step 4   Articulate Expectations and Outline Contingencies   As you are discussing with the student how you will be involved in helping her reach the identified goals, also be clear about the expectations for group behavior and articulate how these expectations will be enforced. In addition, list the consequences (punishments) of continued problematic behaviors if there will be consequences. While some use contingencies such as tangible rewards or consequences as a way of motivating compliance in contracts, we suggest avoiding external reinforcements or nonlogical consequences when possible.

Contracting Example: Articulate Expectations and Outline Contingencies   After the behavior expectations were fully discussed, Mr. Weaver told Ismael that he wanted to talk about what he would be doing to help Ismael stick to the contract— the specifics. First, he asked for input from Ismael: "I hear you saying that you won't run out of the room, Ismael, but it sounds like you don't have many strategies for staying when things are tough in group. I wonder if we could try to identify one or two specific strategies that you could try that might help you stay in the room when things are not working for you."

After Ismael indicated that he didn't have any ideas, Mr. Weaver offered some: "How about if I help you, Ismael, by pointing out when I notice you starting to get wound up. I will use the phrase 'it's time to get centered' to help you remember. I will also remind you to use the time-out chair if you need to when I notice that things are still difficult."

"Okay," Ismael agreed, getting antsy to go back to his class.

"But," Mr. Weaver added emphatically, "because it is so very disruptive to the group when you run, Ismael, I also need to let you know that I will be asking you to make up any group time you miss after school—that is only if you do end up leaving. This make-up time will happen after school in my office, where I will ask you to sit silently for the total amount of time you missed."

Mr. Weaver clarified that Ismael understood the contingency he was adding to the contract, explaining how serious the situation was and why it warranted this consequence. Ismael nodded that he understood the seriousness of the situation, as he began to doodle on a piece of paper. Mr. Weaver understood this as a sign of understanding and did not push him to articulate that he did understand.

When contracting with students, it is important to listen carefully to the student and to determine the student's motivational level. This will help you be clear about what, specifically, the student is willing to commit to. Students are more likely to commit to working on goals that seem appropriate and attainable to them. So, addressing the issues that engender the most investment on the part of the student first, even if they are not what you perceive to be the most pressing issues, can be a good starting point. If you spend time exploring the student's perceptions, you may even find that there is overlap in what you and the student want to have happen. For example, if the student has a goal to make friends and the group leader has a goal that the student will use respectful language to others, there probably is considerable overlap in these goals. So, developing a contract that focuses on working on friendships and using respectful language would meet both goals well. The contract just makes the link between these goals more explicit.

Step 5 Documenting the Contract While contracting *discussions* are important, contracts tend to be more effective when they are drafted in writing. This allows everyone to be clear about the expectations and contingencies and the process of documentation adds an air of formality to the process. Written contracts should include these components:

- the desired goals that the student is working towards and/or the behaviors that will be eliminated;
- the specific ways in which the leader or teacher will support the student (this may include offering cues and prompts, reinforcement, and identifying locations and conditions for time-out);
- the consequences for noncompliant behaviors, as well as any reinforcements for desired behavioral changes, if identified;
- the plan for reassessing the terms of the contract; and
- signatures from all parties involved.

Some students will be marginally engaged in the contracting process and may refuse to sign anything. It is sometimes appropriate to set consequences for students who are not willing to engage in the contracting process. However, we recommend that if you opt to go in this direction, select consequences (for nonparticipation) that are logically connected to the problem. Also, be sure to inform the student in advance if a consequence will be instituted for noncompliance. Consequences for nonparticipation should not be punitive; they should reflect logical consequences and decisions based on safety.

Contracting Example: Documenting the Contract   Because the school administrator decided that Ismael's running away behavior was dangerous, Ismael was not permitted to go on a walking field trip in school unless he committed to a contract regarding his running away behavior. Also, the administrator decided that Ismael would not be permitted to go on any field trips until he was able to remain in group without running for three subsequent sessions. The contract that was drafted and signed by Ismael and Mr. Weaver is seen in Figure 8.1.

Agreement
Ismael R. and Mr. Weaver

9/24/08

I, *Ismael R* , agree that I will participate in group by:
- Doing all of the activities,
- Working with my friends in group,
- Dealing with anger and nervousness by centering myself by taking a breath, counting to 10, or asking Mr. Weaver for if I can sit in the time-out chair.

I, *Mr. Weaver* , agree to help Ismael in the group, especially when he seems to be having a hard time with anger and nervousness by offering to help and reminding him that "it's time to get centered."

We both understand that if Ismael runs from the group, he will make up all missed group time after school in Mr. Weaver's office. He will have to sit silently for the total amount of time and Mr. Weaver will not talk to him during any of the make up time.

Also, we both understand that Ismael will not be allowed to go on any school field trips until he can show that he is able to be safe. This means that he will need to participate in three groups without running away before going on a field trip.

Signatures:

| _____*Ismael*_____ | _____*Weaver*_____ | _____*Mr. R*_____ |
| Ismael | Mr. Weaver | Mr. R (Ismael's dad) |

FIGURE 8.1   Contract

Working with the Contract in the Group

Once the contract is drafted, the group leader should always follow the terms of the contract. Typically, this includes offering reminders, reinforcements, and punishments. We recommend using a Reality Theory WDEP (Wubbolding, 1988; Wubbolding & Brickell, 1999) approach when implementing the contract in the group. Reality Therapy is the therapeutic application of Glasser's Choice Theory (Glasser, 1998b); WDEP is a specific method of applying the principles of Reality Therapy. WDEP is an acronym for a fairly straight forward process that can be implemented in the group. WDEP stands for: *Wants, Doing/Direction, Evaluation,* and *Plan.* The premise of this approach is that all behavior is purposeful and directed towards satisfying basic fundamental needs and it stresses responsibility and action (Glasser, 1998a; Wubbolding, 1988; Wubbolding & Brickell, 1999).

- The *W* stands for *wants,* needs, and perceptions (Backler, Eakin, & Harris, 1994). When the contract is based on what the student wants to achieve, then responding with a W question can serve to redirect the student to focus on her contract goals. For example, "Selina, what were your goals for this week?"
- The next step of the process is *D: Doing.* In this step, the group leader asks the student what she is doing in the moment or invites her to examine the direction of her life and/or how she is spending her time (Backler, Eakin, & Harris, 1994). This line of inquiry asks the student to be aware of the problematic behavior and is typically asked as a fairly straightforward question: "What are you doing?"
- Next, the *E: Evaluate.* Here the student is asked to evaluate her behavior with regard to her wants and goals (Backler, Eakin, & Harris, 1994). That is, the student is asked whether her particular behavior is consistent with her contract/goals and/or with her wants and needs. For example, "Selina, is talking to Carlos going to help you get your work done so you don't have to miss field hockey practice after school?"
- Finally, the *P: Plan.* When the student identifies that the particular behavior being demonstrated is probably not meeting her needs or goals, she is invited to think about a plan for getting refocused on what needs to happen to meet those goals. In this example, the counselor might ask, "What do you need to do next, Selina?"

A variation in this process can be used when students have not even formalized any contract goals: Simply ask the student to name the particular problem that is happening in the group. After the problem has been identified and/or named, ask the student to evaluate whether what he is doing is helping the group. Next, ask the student what he will do next to get back on task.

TIME-OUT

Time-out is a behavior reduction strategy that is designed to remove a student from an environment that reinforces undesirable behavior (Zirpoli & Melloy, 1997). Time-out might be thought of as time-out from positive reinforcement. Typically, time-out is implemented when a student chooses not to follow the rules or when a student makes poor choices and it is clear that an adult needs to intervene to help the student regain control or make another decision (Charney, 1991). Time-out also provides an additional benefit of providing students with a time and space to get away from a situation in or-der to cool down, reflect, and/or to get composure (Jones & Jones, 2001).

Time-out is typically used in the context of extremely disruptive behaviors. Be-cause it has sometimes been used in schools inappropriately (e.g., inappropriate dura-tion of time-out, used as a break for teachers rather than a discipline method for correcting student misbehavior) and because it effectively removes students from edu-cational opportunities, time-out is a fairly controversial procedure in most school dis-tricts (Kerr & Nelson, 1998; Zirpoli & Melloy, 1997). However, time-out can be a very effective way to respond to problematic behavior when used appropriately. It is helpful for school personnel to have a good understanding of the types and appropriate uses of this behavior management strategy.

Types of Time-Out

As mentioned, the primary purpose of time-out is to remove student from a situation that reinforces inappropriate or undesirable behavior. There are two categories of time-out: exclusionary and nonexclusionary time-out (Zirpoli & Melloy, 1997). Basically, both types entail removing students from a problematic situation, but they differ in the ex-tent to which the student is secluded from the group activity.

Exclusionary time-out refers to the removal of an individual from an activity or a stimulating environment for a specified period of time (Zirpoli & Melloy, 1997). A range of exclusionary time-out options, in order of restrictiveness, are as follows:

- *Contingent observation time-out* is an exclusionary time-out procedure where the student is removed to the sideline of an activity, but not required to leave the room altogether. He is able to participate by watching the activity or group.
- In *isolation time-out*, the student is totally removed from the reinforcing environ-ment and is prevented from observing the ongoing group activity because he is re-quired to turn away from the group. For example, classrooms often have a designated corner or space (e.g., thinking chair) for these types of time-out.
- *Seclusion time-out*, the more extreme version of time-out, involves a physical removal from the room. In this case, the student is required to be in a secure but secluded space for a specified period of time.

In all of these types of exclusionary time-out, the student is returned to the activity after a predetermined period of time has passed and after the undesirable behavior has stopped.

Nonexclusionary time-out procedures are those whereby the student is not removed from the reinforcing environment, but instead, attention and other forms of reinforce-ment are withdrawn (Zirpoli & Melloy, 1997). These may include planned ignoring (ig-noring for no more than about 30–60 seconds) or removal of specific reinforcers (e.g., toys, papers, pencils) for a short period of time. Again, these procedures are always en-forced within a specified and reasonable time frame.

Implementation of Time-Out

The effectiveness of using time-out as a response to behavior problems rests on how well the procedure is implemented. We emphasize that the time-out experience is intended to remove the student from stimulation. It is a procedure that must be implemented in a way that is fair, respectful, appropriate, and safe for everyone in the school—especially the student involved. It is important to remember that the time-out area should not be reinforcing to the student, that time-out be carefully supervised by an adult, and that the expectations for time-out behavior should be articulated explicitly. Once the time-out is completed, the teacher or group leader should try to reinforce the students' new compliant or appropriate behavior as soon as he has rejoined the group and displayed appropriate behavior. We offer the following principles for implementing time-out:

- Time-out is not effective unless the group is desirable and reinforcing in the first place. That is, students must want to be in the group (e.g., they are engaged, happy, safe) if removal from the group is used to shape their behavior.
- There should be an established, predictable, and consistent rule and behavior system in place in the group prior to using time-out (Charney, 1991).
- Time-out should be considered only after less restrictive behavior management measures have been attempted.
- The time-out situation must *not* be reinforcing (Emmer & Evertson, 2009). No toys, papers, assignments, games, conversations with counselors, or attention of any kind should be permitted while the student is in time-out. These reinforcements can be returned to the student after time-out has ended (preferably after the student has demonstrated a positive behavior).
- A verbal warning should always precede time-out placement. The warning should be brief and nonreactive.
- Time-out should be presented as a directive, not a negotiation (Charney, 1991) and should immediately follow the misbehavior. Time-out should be enforced consistently, calmly, and with no discussion. We suggest imposing time-out in this way:
  1. Identify misbehavior.
  2. Identify consequence (time-out).
  3. Identify conditions (time limits or desired behavior) that will terminate time-out.
- The conditions of time-out must be appropriate to the student and the situation (i.e., 1–5 minutes maximum) and they should be clearly articulated so the student is aware of what is happening. For example, a specific time can be set on a timer or clock and specific conditions such as "You need to be quiet for 1 full minute" must be identified and enforced. Vague conditions (e.g., "When you're ready . . .") detract from the intent of time-out and can lead to misuses, yielding the intervention ineffective.
- Time-out should occur in a physically and emotionally safe space for the student. Students should be monitored continuously while in time-out, especially when they are in seclusion. At the risk of being overly obvious, never lock a student in a room and never use a space in a dark basement for time out.
- Do not release student from time-out as a result of inappropriate time-out behaviors (e.g., cursing while in time-out does not release child from time-out). Inappropriate behaviors should be ignored or the student should be given one option for a choice to remain in time-out and stop the undesired behavior or to move into a more restrictive time-out situation.
- After time-out, the student should return to an environment that offers immediate access to reinforcers. This should occur without fanfare and as soon as possible.

Appropriate behaviors should be promptly reinforced and efforts should be made to reengage or redirect the student to a more appropriate behavior.

- Finally, remember that time-out does not work for every student and it is not appropriate in every situation. It is a procedure that needs to be used for a specific reason, with purposefulness and intentionality, and with respect and care.

DE-ESCALATION

Fortunately, most student behavior in classroom groups can be managed through proper planning, good group management, and appropriate implementation of the response strategies covered in Chapters 7 and 8. However, when student behavior spirals out-of-control, a more immediate and directive response is required. The goal of intervention with individuals who are unable to regulate themselves—who are out-of-control—always is to respond in ways that ensure safety, provide support, and that help restore their personal equilibrium and self-regulation.

According to Cavaiola and Colford (2006), individuals typically move into an out-of-control state gradually, beginning with a period of anxiety or agitation, then losing control more and more to the point of becoming irrational and defensive. Some individuals resort to physical force when they have lost their ability to manage themselves verbally. De-escalation begins with paying attention to the warning signs and acting early (Charney, 1991). This awareness requires what we referred to in Chapter 6 as leader "withitness." Warning signs that may suggest that a student is moving into disregulation include a refusal to participate in the activity or discussion; rude, loud or inappropriate comments; apparent anger, anxiety, agitation or distraction; and verbal threats to others.

When you notice that a student may be moving toward being out-of-control, and particularly when there has been a serious behavioral incident in the group, the appropriate response is to (a) de-escalate the student in order to help her return to a more self-regulated presence and (b) to thwart possible danger to that student and/or others in the group. The six de-escalation steps outlined below are adapted from Robert's (2005) *Seven Stage Crisis Intervention Model*. The steps include: assessment, developing rapport and relationship, identifying the problem, attending to the student's affective needs, moving through resolve, and follow-up. Before our detailed explanation of these six steps, we suggest that you review *Case Study 8.17* where we observe middle school counselor, Ms. Grover, intervene with Jake at the very closing moments of their fifth counseling group session.

CASE STUDY 8.17

De-escalation

As the other group members are leaving group for the day to return to their next class, Ms. Grover notices that Jake, who has been uncharacteristically quiet and quite unwilling to participate fully in group for the last 50 minutes, does not get up to leave. He seems to be stewing about something. While others are gathering their book bags and are preparing to walk out of the office, Ms. Grover approaches Jake. "Jake it's time for class, come on—I doubt that you want to be late."

Jake responds, "Shut the f—up, I'm not going anywhere—this group pisses me off. It is a waste of my time—whole bunch of stupid-assed wimps sitting around for an hour wasting my time." With this outburst he stands abruptly, his chair flips back and several of the remaining students look alarmed and unsure of what to do, where to go. Jake appears startled by the chair, and perhaps even by his uproar and language. He likes Ms. Grover and they have had a positive relationship since sixth grade.

Ms. Grover, speaking to the other students: "Kids, please give Jake some space, you can head to class. Jake will be okay." Then, to Jake, she says, "Jake, I can see how frustrated and angry you are and I want you to help me know what is going on for you right now. But, first, I need to be sure we'll be okay; can you show me this will turn out okay, and that you will be able to sit down and talk with me?"

Jake says, "I didn't mean to throw that f—ing chair! I don't want to go to class—I hate this g—damn place—I'm too wound-up. And now I'm screwed—getting' up in your face."

Ms. Grover responds, "I understand that you didn't mean to tip over the chair and that you didn't mean to say what you said. But Jake, for us to talk about what is going on, I want you to take a seat. Could you take a few deep relaxing breaths, open and relax your fists? I see how tight and clenched your whole body appears right now."

"I should just leave," Jake says. "I'll be suspended anyway what the hell difference does it make if I'm in this much trouble?"

"Jake, we are not talking about consequences now," Ms. Grover responds. "I want to talk with you about what is happening. I want to know what has triggered all this, and I want to support you in making the best decisions that you can now. Leaving, we both know, is not going to benefit you. Can you sit down, breathe, calm yourself?"

At this moment two teachers who have been alerted to the problem in Ms. Grover's room appear at the door. For an instant, it looks like their presence will further escalate Jake. "Thank you for checking on us," Ms. Grover says to both teachers. "Jake, I'm hopeful that you will make the decision to sit down so that Ms. Rodrigues and Mr. Spruill can leave us knowing you and I will be okay. It is clear that you are really upset right now, and we want you to be okay."

Jake walks to another upright chair, sits, and puts both hands up in front of his face to hide tears. He says, "This is so messed-up. I can't do anything right. I didn't mean to throw that chair."

Ms. Grover again speaks to the two teachers standing near the door, purposefully out loud so that Jake can hear that she is not talking about him: "Thanks, would you please stay nearby in the hall, just to be sure we are going to be alright here?"

She turns her attention to Jake. "Jake, thank you for sitting down and beginning to relax—I can see how powerful these feelings are for you right now, and you have begun to do a good job of dealing with them—big feelings require a lot of control and skill. You're taking much better care of your feelings now than a few moments ago." She asks, "Is it okay for me to pull a chair near and sit next to you so that we can begin to talk about what is happening now?"

Jake replies, "I guess so." He appears absolutely exhausted and his breathing has returned to normal. By now, perhaps no more than 2 minutes later, Jake has regained his composure and focus. It feels like a crisis is diverted, but there is still a lot of work to be done. Ms. Grover pulls up a chair keeping sufficient distance, sits down, and begins the next steps of de-escalation.

Reflection Questions

1. This final case is one filled with red flags, potential danger, and certainly with many decisions that the counselor must make in the moment. What are you feeling when you read about Jake? What would your gut, initial, reflexive reaction have been had Jake been your student?
2. What decisions do you envision yourself making in the urgency of this moment?
3. Do you think you are ready to encounter such an experience that arises from classroom or counseling groups in schools? What skills do you have that would be strengths in this situation? What skills do you possess that will enable you to implement a de-escalation and what do you believe you will need to develop?

Case Study 8.17 demonstrates the first four steps of our de-escalation plan, and although no two student "melt downs" look or sound alike, we are certain that there are similarities you will be able to recognize. As we look now at that skills and steps of de-escalation, please keep in mind that safety—yours, students, and the entire school community—is paramount. In balance to this, it is also helpful to remember that even the worst, scariest interactions in or resulting from group have powerful potential for student development and growth.

Step 1: Assessment

De-escalation begins with conducting a brief, rapid assessment of the individual and the situation (James & Gilliland, 2001). This assessment begins with a review the student's *affective*, *behavioral*, and *cognitive* states. The intent is to make a quick determination of the extent to which the student is able to self-regulate in these areas. This assessment also requires assessment of the group—that is, how the whole group is responding to the problem or incident.

When assessing the student's affective state you will want to pay attention to over-emotionality or, on the other end of the spectrum, severe withdrawal or detachment. Extremes in these areas are likely to indicate a lack of self-regulation and an inability for the student to participate appropriately in the group. However, if the student is able to begin to express feelings appropriately with your coaching, she may be able to quickly regain control and equilibrium.

Assessment of the student's behavioral functioning focuses on what the student is doing. If the student does not seem to be able to control his body, is fidgety, or unable to sit still, this may be a sign that he is becoming agitated. Having the student do something concrete and functional, such as put a book away or take a deep breath, may help him be more in control of his behavior and body, and will help you assess the extent to which the student actually can regulate himself.

Assessing the student's cognitive state refers to determining the extent to which the student is thinking rationally about a situation. Irrational thinking typically leads to irrational behavior. Assessing the quality of the student's thinking requires attending carefully to the content of what he is saying. You can elicit this information by asking concrete questions about the triggering event (e.g., "Can you tell me what happened?"). Gaining an understanding of how the student is thinking about the situation will be helpful in determining how to move towards resolution. In the more severe cases, this assessment might entail a mental status exam—determining whether the student is able to locate himself in current time and space (e.g., Is he aware of who he is and where he is?).

As mentioned, conducting a brief assessment also involves having a good sense of the group and how the group is responding to the potential problem. Group variables to consider include (a) determining if others in the group feel sympathetic to or align with the student who is the focus of the problem, (b) assessing if the other students have an adequate level of maturity and self-regulation in order to manage themselves when a peer is acting out, (c) determining if peers actually have the skills needed to participate in resolution or to be able to witness a potential out-of-control peer, and (d) thinking about the extent to which witnessing the incident benefits or is a detriment to others in the group. The purpose of this assessment is to determine what to do with other students in the group when one student is having a high level of difficulty.

If members are sympathetic to an individual who is escalating out of control, they may be able to help defuse the situation by offering support or assistance to their peer. For example, a student who appears agitated because she does not understand a group task can be paired with another student in the group who is sympathetic to the need for help. Of course, you should never rely on group members to defuse an out-of-control student. You should only enlist peer support if you have assessed that there is no danger in doing so and if your clinical judgment suggests that this intervention would be beneficial. On the other hand, if group members are bothered or angry in response to the situation or the individual, their reactivity may imperil successful resolution of the problem in the group.

Again, the extent to which students in the group can be—and should be—asked to help is clearly related to the level of disruption or danger posed by the situation. You should always end the group immediately when one individual is out-of-control and poses a danger to others. This can be done by inviting or requiring the individual to move out into the hallway or insisting that the other students in the group leave the room immediately. You should always seek assistance if the level of danger is high enough to warrant removal in these ways—never work alone with a student who is dangerous and out-of-control. Physical restraint should never be used by school personnel who have not been trained in using proper restraint procedures and should only be used in situations where restraint is appropriate and deemed a necessity.

Step 2: Rapport and Relationship

Establishing an immediate connection with a student who is becoming out-of-control is critical. Calling on your relationship to support the student will help establish the important sense of trust you will need to help the student gain control. Be sure to shift the group to work independently for a few minutes while you intervene privately with the individual. This is particularly critical when the group is having a reinforcing effect on the student behavior. Intervening privately also helps the student save face, helps avert a concern about being reprimanded in front of the group, and it helps the student avoid a display of lack of self-control in the group. Options and consequences for student misbehavior is a personal and private manner, so, this level of intervention should not be a public group event.

Use open-ended questions to invite the student to explore the problem or to evaluate her condition or the situation. Ask, "What happened?" This elicits the student's perspective on the problem and, as mentioned earlier, this question also helps you determine the extent of the student's cognition and affective functioning.

It is important to position yourself as standing in relationship with the student against the problem—externalize the problem as something that has happened rather than something that is wrong with the student. Doing so will enable you to take a less-threatening, problem-solving approach. Also, be sure to attend directly to the student, maintain eye contact, and listen to what he is saying. Be calm, genuine, accepting of the student's perspective, and empathic. Position yourself physically to communicate that you are open and that you are listening to the student. It is also a good idea to repeat or paraphrase the words the student uses in order to communicate that you hear and empathize. When working with individuals who are out of control, be careful to move slowly and telegraph your movements (i.e., tell the individual what you are doing and why), do not use threats or ultimatums, be aware of any potential throwable objects in the room near the individual, avoid being cornered, and always have assistance nearby (Cavaiola & Colford, 2006).

Step 3: Identify the Problem

As you listen to the student articulate her perception, your work will focus on trying to identify what exactly caused the disruption. It is rare that one isolated event will cause a big disruption, so identifying the problem likely entails uncovering a progression of events that have led to the current outburst or disruption. A number of basic counseling skills are typically used to separate out and recreate the story-line of the problem. These include reflection of content, paraphrasing, and summarizing as a way of communicating your understanding of what has been said, asking open questions to elicit more information and closed questions to determine facts or details, and exploring the student's feelings in response to the events or situation that occurred.

As you work to sort out the details and get an understanding of the problem, you will also want to contribute your understandings and experiences into the discussion. In doing so, limit your comments to concrete observations that are free of interpretations, and deliver them with respect and sincerity. Be careful to offer your ideas with an appropriate level of tentativeness, indicating that you are not *imposing,* but merely *offering* your perspective. For example, comments such as: "this might be very frustrating," "you have stopped working," "I notice your silence," signal to the student that he has been heard, he is noticed, and that you are attentive to his cues. Be sure to offer to help the student as you notice the cues that seem to be leading towards loss of control. For example, after a student tells you that she is very frustrated when completing a task, a comment such as "let me know if you want me to step in and help you keep the frustration from getting in your way" stands in support of the student against the frustration and may even invite the student to recognize that you have picked up a cue that she is escalating. Always be sure to validate the student's experience.

Once you have begun to grasp the situation and after you have listened to the student, it is helpful to offer a clear articulation of your understanding of the problem. This presentation of the problem should be delivered with appropriate tentativeness and an invitation for the student to clarify or add to what you have presented.

If the student is not able to articulate that there is a problem or is having difficulty expressing his perspective, you may need to be more directive in naming the problem.

You can do this by offering your observations and informing the student why the behavior or the situation is problematic. I-messages work well to this end (recall the I-message format in Chapter 7). For example, "Robbie, I heard you use threatening language towards Seth. I am worried that since you feel so strongly about this, you may follow through on your threat. I guess that I'm also feeling a little frustrated because for weeks we have been talking about the use and abuse of power that happens through threatening language, and I believe—I might be wrong, but I believe that you understand the implications of what you have said. You know that you can't participate in the group today if you threaten others. Also, we need to resolve this issue that has come up between you and Seth."

Step 4: Attend to Affective Needs

De-escalation work is not psychotherapy—at least not in the long-term self-exploration sense of therapy. However, it does require a therapeutic response. In most cases, this entails slowing things down and responding to the emotional needs of the individual. In attending to the student's emotional needs, invite the student into a safe place where you are in control, and offer empathy as the student expresses emotion.

Of course, cautions are appropriate here. You must be careful not to invite the student into a therapeutic space that is beyond what you can attend to in the school setting or that is beyond the kind of therapeutic relationship that is appropriate at that time. For example, if a student begins to disclose details of past abuse while expressing emotion, you should be emotionally available to contain the student in a safe place and also be careful to safeguard the child's confidentiality (i.e., assure that other students or adults are not hearing personal disclosures). When students are highly emotional, you always want to be cautious about eliciting too much detail or too much information until you are sure that they have adequate self-control. This is especially true when you have an idea that the expression of emotion will reveal trauma. Once the student is back to a self-regulated state, you will need to locate appropriate therapeutic resources and, if abuse has been revealed, you will need to notify legal authorities to follow-up.

Attending to the affective needs of the student is accomplished by using basic reflection, focusing, and paraphrasing skills. It is appropriate to agree with the student when you do, particularly around facts and reasonable responses, and it is also appropriate to apologize for any wrongs, mistakes, and miscommunications you may have committed. You should always acknowledge injustices when they exist. For example, "As I listen to you, Ryan, I hear your perspective that the principal was not fair to you when she accused you of taking the money from the classroom last week. You think that you have been singled out because you are a student of color." It is also always important to acknowledge the client's perspective, even if you do not agree with the conclusions that the student draws. Attending to the student is not about debating facts and perceptions.

Sometimes when students become aware of how their behavior is affecting others, they feel badly and become self-conscious and/or defensive. This response can trigger an out-of-control response. Therefore, responding with an offer of assistance (rather than a demand or a punishment) can help de-escalate the situation. For example, "Camille, I am hoping that I or someone in the group can help you find a way to rejoin us" or "I am willing to help you with whatever is going on, if you want."

This is also a good time to help the student recognize or remember his strengths and past successes—particularly those successes or abilities that have enabled him to overcome similar challenges in the past. You may also want to normalize feelings (without trivializing them) and to provide information or education, if appropriate. For example, "I know that it is your first day back, Loung. Sometimes it can be hard to get back into things when you have been away for so long. Things have changed and it looks like all of us will need to adjust a bit. Huh?"

Step 5: Moving Through Resolve

The next step in de-escalation is helping the student slowly move through the situation and also all that was created in the wake of the incident. This entails addressing the immediate issues or problem and also attending to the fall-out. By this we mean that in addition to moving into more self-regulated state, the student will also need help in assessing the impact of what has happened and making things right again. For example, if she said some things to people when angry, those individuals will need attention. If the physical space of the room has been altered, restoring the room to its previous condition may be part of reaching resolution. Most importantly, if the student's peers were affected by the problem, the student will need to think about how to regain face and reenter into appropriate and mutually satisfying relationships with them again. It is important that this step of resolution not be omitted, in the hope that a "forget and forgive" strategy will make everything work out okay. Restoring is an important part of resolution, and most youth need adult support to help them attain resolution.

Moving into this stage of intervention is indicated when the student has returned to a more self-regulated and less emotional state, when his thinking has become more rational, and when his behavior is appropriate to the setting. Begin by identifying just a small number of outstanding issues to be resolved. It is important not to overwhelm the student with a long list of what he has done wrong and how it has impacted large numbers of people. Keep it simple, realizing this is an opportunity for the student to experience success. To this end, you can ask the student what he thinks still needs to be resolved. Do not be afraid to offer suggestions, particularly if you are able to see some areas that are in particular need of resolution that the student has not mentioned. For example, if a student insulted a peer when he was yelling, it will be critical for the student to attend to that peer.

Most students will need help in developing a plan for resolving these issues. This plan will probably entail an outline of specific steps or actions, and, in some cases, the counselor may actually need to help the student rehearse what to say or how to carry out the plan. For example, Sheri broke another student's iPod when in a rage about something the student said to her. In the resolution, Sheri felt badly about breaking the iPod and said that she really wanted to replace it, or at least make a good faith effort to do so. To this end, the counselor and student needed to create a plan for talking to the student about the desire to replace the iPod, determining the cost of the replacement, and outlining how that money would be secured. When it came to the part of the plan where Sheri was to propose replacing the iPod to both the student and her parents, she rehearsed the words she would use with the counselor first.

As the student moves into this action step, it is helpful to reaffirm the student's ability to make good choices and to communicate confidence in the student's ability to follow an appropriate course of action. For example, "I bet you can handle this situation well" goes a long way in encouraging the student to take action and is important. Of course, helping the student outline specifically what she will do in handling it will help even more. As mentioned, you may need to monitor that the student has handled the situation and be prepared to coach or cue her to do so. Articulating encouragement and confidence in the student does not absolve the counselor from the responsibility of scaffolding and monitoring appropriate action.

Step 6: Follow-Up

De-escalation follow-up entails monitoring the consequences that have occurred as a result of the incident and monitoring the student in order to avoid future outbursts, including working with teachers and administrators to assure that appropriate supports are in place. Follow-up also includes working more directly with the student to enable the development of adequate coping strategies that can be used to prevent similar problems in the future.

An incident in a group that is serious enough to warrant de-escalation will almost always result in some consequences for the individual student involved. Some of the consequences will be natural consequences. That is, there will be consequences that occur naturally in response to the incident and are largely out of the control of the counselor (at least initially). In most cases, however, incidents that warrant a de-escalation level of response will probably also have additional imposed consequences for the student.

In cases when rules have been broken during the incident, or the student has caused serious harm or destruction, it is appropriate that logical consequences—likely punishments—will be instituted. These may be imposed by the leader of the group, by the teacher of the class, by a school administrator, by parents, or legal or law enforcement authorities. However, it is important that you discuss this eventuality with the student *after* she is self-regulated and calm. When the time is appropriate, be sure to use matter-of-fact clear language to clearly articulate the offense and the consequence that will result. If you are not sure what the consequence of the student's actions will be, it is helpful to inform the student that there will be consequences for the actions and to prepare her by informing her about who and how decisions will be made.

In cases where the student has not been able to fully calm himself and/or when issues of harm to self or others remain, even remotely, you must follow appropriate duty-to-warn protocols (James & Gilliland, 2001) as per the code of ethics in the counseling profession (in particular *ACA Code of Ethics and Standards of Practice* [ACA, 2005] B.2.a; *Ethical Standards for School Counselors* [ASCA, 2004] A.7.a & b; and *ASGW Best Practice Guidelines* [ASGW, 2007], A.7.d). Cobia and Henderson (2007) point out that most schools have policies regarding reporting threats of harm. They recommend taking every threat seriously and for school counselors to consult and document all actions involving protection from harm.

Even if questions of harm to self or others do not surface, the issue of informing others—administrators and parents—about the incident in the group warrants careful consideration. School counselors are required to operate under the policies of the school in which they work (Linde, 2007) and most schools have policies regarding disciplinary action responses. The professional codes of ethics mentioned above indicate that professional consultation does not breach a client's confidentiality. This means that informing administrators about incidents that require de-escalation, as well as seeking their input on appropriate consequences, is very appropriate. In many schools, these kinds of incidents warrant immediate referral to instructional support teams or services. At the very least, an incident serious enough to warrant de-escalation should prompt coordinated action plans among teachers, administrators, and counselors in order to determine a plan of support and prevention against further incidents.

It is important to point out that parents and legal guardians have the right to be informed of what is happening in their child's life. The *Ethical Standards for School Counselors* (ASCA, 2004) indicates that school counselors have a duty to provide parents with "accurate, comprehensive and relevant information in an objective and caring and manner" (Code B.2.c). We would agree that causing or being part of a major disruption in a school warrants some form of parental notification. In cases of ambiguity, the best legal and ethical practice is to inform the building administrator about the incident and for the two of you to make thoughtful decisions regarding information provided to parents. Cobia and Henderson's (2007) point out that school counselors should work to involve families in their work because parents are valuable allies in working with children in schools (we would argue that it is the school personnel that are valuable allies for parents in raising their children), we recommend informing parents in all cases of concern and actively eliciting a collaborative effort with parents in all follow-up planning.

Finally, it is important to address the other two critical aspects of follow-up—that appropriate supports are in place for the student and helping the student acquire adequate coping strategies. Providing adequate concrete support and helping the student develop a sound repertoire of coping skills are, perhaps, the most important follow-up measures that you can offer. Coordinated efforts with school personnel and parents assure that consistent and adequate supports in these areas will be developed. Working as a team composed of multiple players increases the likelihood for implementation and success.

RESPONDING WITH AN AWARENESS OF WINDOWS AND MIRRORS

Tatum (1997) powerfully points out that many of us have early memories of race relations that are shrouded by emotions such as anger, confusion, sadness, surprise, and embarrassment. These memories are typically rooted in our observations of the world around us, beginning in early childhood. Little discussion or meaning-making about these observations sends a loud and powerful message: This is unspeakable. In Tatum's words, "Children who have been silenced often enough learn not to talk about race publicly. Their questions don't go away, they just go unasked" (Tatum, 1997, p. 36, bracket added). When observations and curiosities about race are not silenced, Tatum argues, possibilities for learning how to spot and resist racism, strategies for responding to injustice, and opportunities for critical thinking are possible.

We call attention to Tatum's point about children's observations and the learning that is gleaned from these observations because it has relevance here in our final chapter on responding to problems in groups. We want to raise awareness to the issue of what others see and subsequently learn when a peer is being disciplined in the group. The group experience is a public experience—all of the members of the group are watching and they are learning something when we intervene in response to problems in the group. So, we must ask: Who are the children who "get in trouble" in group (and at school)? Are intervention practices distributed widely among children in our groups (and also in our schools)? What messages about race (and nondominant group membership) are unintentionally promoted and what subtle social practices are reinforced through our discipline practices in our groups (and in the larger school community)? What do others see when they look at what is happening our group? In our school?

A new paragraph here is intended to give pause to our above comments and then to follow-up with some quick clarifying points in this discussion. First is for us to clarify that our intent is not to advocate for not intervening with children who have created problems in the group because they fall in one of the under-represented minority identity characteristics that we have mentioned throughout this book. Let us be clear: If there is a problem behavior in the group it must be addressed—no matter who has exhibited the problematic behavior. What we do want to point out, however, is that if peers notice that some children in group always seem to be the ones in trouble, the messages to all students in the school is powerful and damaging.

More to the point: if it is the children who are in nondominant groups who always seem to be getting in trouble, then perhaps the individual discipline problem is more symptomatic of a larger issue that is institutional or community-based. And so, while intervention must address the individual, it must also be part of an effort to combat the larger issue that has caused manifestation at the individual level. For example, Shella, a fifth-grade student who moved to a suburban elementary school a year ago, was initially popular but over the last year appears to have few friends. With her popularity in decline, teachers notice an increase in her disruptive classroom behavior that they characterize as "attention-getting behavior." You worry as you notice an edge of anger in her behavior in your classroom group, and you also are aware, after talking to Shella's mothers, that their family has been maligned by a small number of individuals in the community because Shella's mothers are in a same-sex relationship. So, while Shella's disruptive and angry behavior is of concern and needs to be addressed, the context of that behavior is of equal concern. Another example: A number of parents have come to you, the school counselor, because a popular young man on the school football team (whose parents are, by the way, very active in the school athletic boosters club) was caught at an underage drinking party and yet was not penalized by being prohibited to play in the next game. These concerned parents were outraged because only a year before a similar incident happened with a student on the team whose parents were not involved at the school, and he was suspended for the next 2 weeks of practices and games.

We would be naïve to believe that such inequities do not exist in our educational system at large. Just as we have asked that school counselors be tuned-in to such inequities within our classroom and counseling groups, we ask you here, at the close of our book, to pay attention to them in a far larger group—the school, our community, and our society. Simply put, our points are these: context does matter; intervention sometimes needs to extend beyond the individual.

EPILOGUE

Several hundred pages ago, when you first settled in to begin studying this book, you read: "Our reason for writing this textbook is to share with graduate students and practicing school counselors alike, clear, concise and well-exampled directions for leading large and small groups–both psychoeducational and counseling groups—in school settings. We have written this text with the ultimate goal of helping school counselors adapt, expand, and strengthen their personal and professional command of group leadership skills." Now, in closing, we ask you, "Did we accomplish our task?" Such a reflective loop is more rhetorical than practical—we know. But, we have thoroughly enjoyed our personal journeys and our writing partnership while creating this text and we truly wish we could know what you, the readers, will take away from it! The two of us, Anne and Kurt, over the years, before, during, and since our graduate school experiences together, have led many groups and we have taught many counselors who we hope have left our workshops, classes, and our mentorship ready and excited to lead groups in schools. Writing this textbook enabled us to look back, investigate how we initially learned to lead groups, and what we have learned as a result of our leading them. Our task was to share those lessons with you. We hope we have done this in a way that has both enhanced and inspired your work as a group leader.

As we come to the end of the book, we actually have several hopes: (a) We hope that you will develop a love of leading groups in schools, as we have. As a result of our work in groups in schools, we have seen the power and promise of group work with children. We wish for you similar opportunities throughout your career. (b) We hope that you will communicate clearly and convincingly with students, parents, teachers, and administrators the value of classroom and counseling groups in schools. We have had numerous chances to visit schools where groups seem to be always running and a wide variety of student needs are met as a result. However, we have also seen many schools where groups never take place, which is a most unfortunate loss for the students in those schools. And finally, (c) we hope that this book—and whatever additional learning experiences you have undertaken while reading it—really gives you the courage and the resolve to lead groups in your schools. As you read in the assessment chapter, knowing how to do something (in this case, how to lead classroom and counseling groups) doesn't mean you will. This book, we trust, will give you a solid foundation from which you may step into the world of group work—promoting that courage and the resolve to lead many and varied groups in your school. We hope that you will take that first and hundreds of subsequent steps to strengthen your group skills and by so doing, really maximize your abilities as a school counselor. We most sincerely wish you the very best of success.

APPENDIX A

Elementary Level Sample Plans

- Sample Classroom Group Unit Plan
- Sample Classroom Lesson Plan—Lesson 1
- Sample Counseling Group (Overall) Plan
- Sample Counseling Session Plan—Session 2

ELEMENTARY LEVEL CLASSROOM GROUP *UNIT* PLAN

Topic: You and Me: Bully-Free

Grade/Class: Third Grade (Teachers: E. Nichols, R. Graveline, M. Rodgers)

Approximate Number of Students: 18–21 per class

Rationale:

The State Harassment Prevention Bill (Sec 1. 16; 11 [a]) requires all public schools in the State to have an intervention plan for handling harassment complaints and to implement a bully prevention program, K–8.

District Developmental Guidance Plan Standards addressed in lesson:

1.13 Listening Skills
1.14 Speaking Skills
2.13 Respect for Self/Others
2.14 Communication Skills
2.2   Problem Solving
3.1   Conflict Resolution
3.3   Harassment/Bullying
3.7   Decision-Making
3.10 Teamwork

ASCA National Standards addressed in lesson:

PS: A1.5 Identify/Express Feelings
PS: A1.6 Distinguish Between Appropriate and Inappropriate Behavior
PS: A1.7 Personal Boundaries
PS: A1.8 Self-Control
PS: A1.9 Cooperative Behavior
PS: A2.3 Differences
PS: A2.4 Diversity
PS: A2.6 Communication
PS: A2.7 Communication
PS: A2.8 Friendships

Goals for Unit:

1. Students will understand the ways in which students bully others and the implications of bullying behavior.

   Objectives:
   - Students will learn the three types of bullying.
   - Students will learn the three roles in bullying behavior.
   - Students will understand that bullying is an action for power and is very hurtful.

Source: Adapted from Mercer, K. (2006, May). *Developmental Guidance Bullying Curriculum.* Class assignment for EDCO 340 Developmental Guidance in the Schools class. University of Vermont.

2. Students will learn and use strategies and skills for responding to bullying.
 Objectives:
   • Students will learn Stamping Out Bullying Strategies.
   • Students use Stamping Out Bullying Strategies in role-plays.

3. Classroom will be "bully-free."
 Objectives:
   • Students will name bullying when they see it in the classroom.
   • Students will use Stamping Out Bullying strategies in the classroom.
   • Students will use Classroom Climate behaviors discussed in classroom morning meetings to make classrooms safe and fun.

Number of Lessons in Unit: 6
   • *Lesson 1:* The Ways of Bullies (pt 1)
   • *Lesson 2:* The Ways of Bullies (pt 2)
   • *Lesson 3:* Perspective-Taking
   • *Lesson 4:* Feeling the Bully Shoes
   • *Lesson 5:* Stamping Out Bullying
   • *Lesson 6:* Stamping Out Bullying

Assessment Plan:
   1. Students will understand the ways in which students bully others and the implications of bullying behavior.
      • The Ways of Bullies True/False Assessment in Lessons (Pre):1 & (Post):6
      • Question round in Lessons 2 & 3.
      • Round question: Name one effect of bullying.
   2. Students will learn and use strategies for responding to bullying.
      • Things I Can Do Peer-Administered Short Answer Assessment in Lesson 4.
      • Role-Play exercises in Lessons 5 & 6.
   3. Classroom will be "bully-free."
      • Review of "We need to talk about . . ." reports in Morning Meeting (introduced in Lesson 2).
      • Bully Contract (introduced in Lesson 6).
      • Teacher/counselor observation (give teachers Bully-Free Classroom Indicators as a guideline for assessment). Follow-up reports in person.

ELEMENTARY LEVEL CLASSROOM GROUP LESSON PLAN

You and Me: Bully-Free

Week 1: The Ways of Bullies (Pt 1)

Grade/Class: Third Grade (Teachers: E. Nichols, R. Graveline, and M. Rodgers)

Time: 35 minutes

Lesson Objectives:
- Students will learn the three types of bullying.
- Students will identify/express their feelings.

Materials:
- Movie Forrest Gump,[1] cued at minute 18
- VCR
- Pictures of bully scenes (see Bully folder)
- Three laminated sets of shoe prints (see Bully folder)
- Ways of Bullies assessment (20 copies)

Plan:
- Introduce learning topic: Bullying.
- Give The Ways of Bullies assessment (pre-test).
  o Students write name on top.
  o Explain that they may not know the answers to these questions—and that's okay. I'm just curious to hear what you have to say on this topic of bullying.
  o Counselor will read each (6) questions out loud.
  o Students circle yes/no on own assessment form.
  o Collect.
- Play 5-minute clip of bullying incident in Forrest Gump.
- Process film clip:
  o What happened?
  o Why?
  o Was that fair?
  o How do you think that Forrest felt? His friend? The bully?
- Define "bullying." Write key words (bold) on the board.

  Bullying happens when someone **hurts or scares** another person. It often happens **repeatedly**. The person being bullied often has a **hard time defending him/herself.**

  Bullying is about being **mean and aggressive** and **trying to have power over someone else.**

- Bully behaviors include:
  o punching, shoving, hitting;
  o spreading rumors;

---

[1]Finerman, W., Tisch, S., & Starkey, S. (Producers), & Zemeckis, R. (Director). (1995). *Forrest Gump* [motion picture]. United States: Paramount Pictures.

o keeping people out of the group;

o teasing in a mean way;

o getting some people to gang up on others.

- Introduce three types of bullying:

  o Verbal—an attack with words: shouting at someone, saying something mean to someone;

  o Physical—attacking someone's body: hitting, kicking, punching;

  o Relational—hard to see, covert: rumors, teasing, refusing to play.

- After discussion of these types, show Forrest Gump clip again.

- Process with these questions:

  o Which of those types of bullying happened to Forrest Gump in the clip?

  o Do these sometimes happen together? Alone? In sequence?

  o Closing round: Now that we're talking about bullying, what are you thinking as we finish for today?

Name: _____

The Ways of Bullies

1. People use bullying to feel strong and powerful ....   T   F
2. Teasing is a form of bullying......................................   T   F
3. Words don't hurt people ....   T   F
4. Bullies never bully people when others are around ....   T   F
5. Targets and witnesses can stop bullies................................   T   F
6. I know what to do if I witness or am the target of a bully   T   F

Comments:

_____ I need to talk about a bully problem that I am having.

ELEMENTARY LEVEL COUNSELING GROUP (OVERALL) PLAN

Topic: Friendship Group

Grade/Class: First Grade

Approximate Number of Students: 4-5

Rationale:

Through peer groups, children develop many personal, social, and academic skills, such as leadership, empathy and teamwork. Children who struggle to form friendships sometimes become passive, aggressive, isolated, disengaged, and non-participatory in their academic learning. This group is designed to help students develop social skills that are facilitative of healthy friendship development.

- ASCA National Model Standards addressed in this group: A:C1, C:A1.3–10, C:A2.1, C:C2.2, & PS:A–C.
- District Plan competencies addressed in group: Elementary Level Social Competencies 2, 3, 5, 8; Elementary Level Personal Competencies 5 & 8.

Goals for Group (Overall):

- Students will learn and identify characteristics of a good friend.
- Students will learn strategies for and practice cooperation, turn-taking, and working with peers.
- Students will learn strategies for and practice assertiveness.

Number of Sessions: 6 weeks—35 minutes per session

Group Assessment Plan:

> **Goal:** Students will learn and identify characteristics of a good friend:
> - List generated in friendship brainstorm (Session 2)
> - Content of friendship collage (Session 5)
>
> **Goal:** Students will learn strategies for and practice cooperation, turn-taking, and working with peers:
> - Counselor observation of student behaviors:
>   - Name Game (Session 1)
>   - Friendship Song (Session 2)
>   - Pick and Tell Game* (Session 2)
>   - Friendship Group Activities (Sessions 4 & 5)
> - Student report in final check out (Session 6—see session plan).
> - Teacher report (use Teacher Feedback Form).
>
> **Goal:** Students will learn strategies for and practice assertiveness:
> - Student participation (observation by counselor) in:
>   - friendship collage (Session 5)
>   - friendship bracelets activity (Session 6).
> - Student report in final check out (Session 6—see session plans).
> - Teacher report (use Teacher Feedback Form).

---

*Pick and Tell Game: Gardner, R. A. (1992). Dr Gardner's pick-and-tell games. Cresskill, NJ: Creative Therapeutics.

Source: Adapted from Mercer, K. (2006, May). *Developmental Guidance Bullying Curriculum.* Class assignment for EDCO 340 Developmental Guidance in the Schools class. University of Vermont.

Friendship Group

Teacher Feedback Form

(First Grade version)

Teacher Name: _____

Students in Group: _____

One of the goals for this group was for students to learn strategies for turn-taking, working with peers, and appropriate assertiveness. Please comment on any changes you have noticed that this student has made in these areas.

One of the goals for this group was for students to learn about friendships. Do you notice any changes in how this student is approaching peers or in how this student is making or acting with friends? If so, please explain.

Comments, suggestions, additional needs for this student:

Thanks for taking the time to respond to this survey!!!!!

ELEMENTARY LEVEL COUNSELING GROUP SESSION PLAN

Friendship Group: First Grade

Group Session 2

Session Objectives:

- Students will identify the characteristics of a good friend.
- Students will work cooperatively.

Plan:

1. Welcome students back and review last session topics/activities:
   - Quick review of group rules.
   - Quick review of last three sessions:
     o Worked on listening to each other as we got to know each other.
     o Worked on taking turns: Why it is important and how it sometimes is hard to take turns.
     o We talked about what is a friend (characteristics). Take out poster created last week.
2. Today we are going to work on a friend collage. We're going to talk about what being a friend looks like.
   - Take out two sample pictures and put picture up on document reader:
     o Does it look like that these two people are friends in this picture?
     o What do you see that says so? Not?
   - Display sample pictures that illustrate "friendship."
     o Ask students what they see that says "friendship."
3. Now we are going to work on creating a friendship collage—explain what a collage is if students don't know—about friendship. Here are the rules:
   - You must create one collage for the group. This means that you will need to work together to select which pictures to put into the collage.
   - You must decide who gets to cut out which pictures.
   - You must decide how to arrange the pictures on the posterboard and how to use the markers to create a message on the board about the pictures (show example).
   - After they are decided, let me know and I will pass out the glue so you can glue them in the spots.
   - Questions?
4. Place magazines on table with scissors.
5. While students work, structure their group behavior in order to highlight friendship skills they are using. Scaffold inappropriate behaviors, if necessary. If students are not acting appropriately, process in the group, reviewing the rules for the group and the friendship characteristics mentioned last week.
6. At 10 minutes remaining: Give time warning and start to pick up.

Source: Adapted from Nicole Lewis. (2007, May). *Developmental Guidance Small Group Counseling Plan: Friendship Group.* Class assignment for EDCO 340 Developmental Guidance in the Schools class. University of Vermont.

7. At 5 minutes remaining: Ending round/processing question:
  • What actions in the group did you notice that your classmates were using that were good friendship skills? (add observations)
  • What did you have to do yourself in order to be a friend to others? Was this hard sometimes? How did you manage to be a friend and to share when you really didn't want to?

Materials:

  • Group rules list
  • Sample pictures and example poster
  • Friendship characteristics list from last week
  • Magazines
  • Scissors
  • Glue
  • Posterboard
  • Markers

Source: Adapted from Nicole Lewis. (2007, May). *Developmental Guidance Small Group Counseling Plan: Friendship Group.* Class assignment for EDCO 340 Developmental Guidance in the Schools class. University of Vermont.

APPENDIX B

Middle Level Sample Plans

- Sample Classroom Group Unit Plan
- Sample Classroom Lesson Plan—Lesson 2
- Sample Counseling Group (Overall) Plan
- Sample Counseling Session Plan—Session 4

MIDDLE LEVEL CLASSROOM GROUP UNIT PLAN

Topic: Media Influences on Body Image

Grade/Class: Sixth Grade (Health Classes; Teacher: C. Rodgers)

Approximate Number of Students: 18–25 per class

Rationale:

Unhealthy eating and dieting behaviors often lead to eating problems, which are increasingly prevalent in preadolescence. While there are many causes of eating disorders, research suggests that one of the major influences is negative body image. Research indicates that one of the most effective ways to confront problems in body image is to have students critically examine the link between body image and media. This unit is designed to help students develop "media literacy" or to critically examine the ways in which media influences our ideas about body and body image.

District Developmental Guidance Plan Standards addressed in lesson:

2.14 Critical Thinking Skills
3.4   Healthy Choices
3.7   Decision-Making
3.1   Personal Health

ASCA National Standards addressed in lesson:

PS: A1.1   (Positive Self Attitudes)
PS: A1.2   Beliefs and Values
PS: A1.5   Feeling Expression
PS: A1.6   Distinguish Behavior
PS: A1.8   Self Control
PS: A1.10   Personal Strengths
PS: A2.2   Respect Points of View
PS: A2.4   Respect Individual Differences
PS: A2.4   Respect Diversity
PS: A2.6   Communication Skills
PS: B1.1   Decision-Making
PS: B1.2   Consequences
PS: B1.3   Alternatives
PS: B1.4   Coping
PS: B1.7   Respect/Differences
PS: B1.8   Peer Pressure

Goals for Unit:

1. Students will critically examine the ways in which men and women's bodies are portrayed in the media and in society, in general.
2. Students will understand the ways in which ideas about body image are socially and culturally constructed.
3. Students will distinguish between healthy and unhealthy body images.

4. Students will determine an appropriate "body type" for themselves. (This is also a Health Class goal.)
5. Students will develop "refraining from comment" skills for not engaging in body image comments and self-perceptions.

Number of Lessons in Unit: 6

- **Lesson 1:** Let's Get Real Part 1
- **Lesson 2:** Let's Get Real Part 2
- **Lesson 3:** Body Mass Indicators Part 1 (Health Teacher)
- **Lesson 4:** Body Mass Indicators Part 2 (Health Teacher)
- **Lesson 5:** Refraining from Comment (Self)
- **Lesson 6:** Refraining from Comment (Others)

Assessment Plan:

1. Students will critically examine the ways in which men and women's bodies are portrayed in the media and in society, in general.
   - Student participation in "Let's Get Real" and "Refraining from Comment" discussion/activities (see processing questions in lesson plans).
   - Reflection question written at end of each week (as per weekly reflection prompt).
   - Body Image Questionnaire Pre (Lesson 1)/Post (Lesson 6).
2. Students will understand the ways in which ideas about body image are socially and culturally constructed.
   - Student participation in "Let's Get Real" discussion questions (see processing questions in Lessons 1 & 2).
   - Reflection question at end of Lessons 1 & 2 (see prompts in lesson plans).
   - Body Image Questionnaire Pre (Lesson 1)/Post (Lesson 6).
3. Students will distinguish between healthy and unhealthy body images.
   - Student participation in "Let's Get Real" discussion questions (see processing questions in Lesson 1: Let's Get Real).
   - Reflection question written at end of each week (as per weekly reflection prompt).
   - Body Image Questionnaire Pre (Lesson 1)/Post (Lesson 6).
4. Students will determine an appropriate "body type" for themselves (Sessions 4 and 5 conducted by Health Teacher).
   - Body Image Questionnaire Pre (Lesson 1)/Post (Lesson 6).
   - Body Mass Assessment (see Health Class assignment/assessment for Lessons 4 & 5).
   - Participation in Body Mass Assessment and discussion (see processing questions).
5. Students will develop "refraining from comment" skills for not engaging in body image comments and self-perceptions.
   - Participation in discussion of cognitive reframing: Unhelpful Self Talk.
   - Participation in discussions/class list of "no comments."
   - Reflection question written at end of Lessons 5 & 6 (see reflection questions).
   - Body Image Questionnaire—Post (final lesson).

MIDDLE LEVEL CLASSROOM GROUP *LESSON* PLAN

Media Influences on Body Image—Week 2: Let's Get Real (Part 2)

Grade/Class: Sixth Grade (Health Classes; Teacher: C. Rodgers)

Time: 45 minutes

Learning Objectives:

1. Students will distinguish between healthy/unhealthy media images.
2. Students will become aware of how body image is socially and commercially constructed.

Materials:

- 48 Hours Extremely Perfect 03/05/2004[1] (In Counselor office) (Original available from http://www.cbsnews.com/stories/2000/02/18/48hours/main162351.shtml)
- DVD player
- Reflection Question #2 (handouts—attached MAKE COPIES!!)

Plan:

1. (5 minutes) Review last week's lesson (video/TV/magazine extravaganza . . . clips of men/women/children) and discussion points.
2. (20 minutes) Present video clip from Extremely Perfect[2] (CBS 48 Hours news documentation about how media makes celebrities perfect).
3. (15 minutes) Discussion. Let's Get Real Lesson 2 Processing Questions:
   - Why do you think advertisers change the way people look?
   - How do standards of beauty become determined?
   - Do media and social images/words affect how people feel about their bodies? Do they affect you, personally?
   - What are some ways in which teens can have healthy bodies and health body images?
4. Closing Round: What stands out for you from today's discussions?
5. Reflection Question (prepared on handout for anonymous responses).

Let's Get Real Reflection Question #2:

What kinds of thoughts and feelings do you have about your body that may be influenced by others? Are these thoughts/feelings helpful/healthy?

---

[1]Zirinsky, S. (Executive Producer). (2003, Aug. 2). Extremely Perfect [Television series episode]. In *48 Hours*. New York: CBS News. (Available from: http://www.cbsnews.com/stories/2000/02/18/48hours/main162351.shtml. Program description: http://www.cbsnews.com/stories/2003/04/28/48hours/main551362.shtml

[2]Ibid.

Source: Adapted from Dickerson, K. (2006, May). *Individual Project: Developmental Guidance Unit Plan and Small Group Counseling Session Outline.* Class assignment for EDCO 340 Developmental Guidance in the Schools class. University of Vermont.

MIDDLE LEVEL COUNSELING GROUP (OVERALL) PLAN

Topic: Stress Management

Grade/Class: Seventh & Eighth Grade

Approximate Number of Students: Approx 6

Rationale:

Middle school is a time of great social and academic stress for many students—compounded by physical and hormonal changes in their bodies. An inability to manage stress appropriately can lead to inappropriate behavior, with effects on students' social, personal, and academic lives. The focus of this group is to help students who have been identified as having difficulties managing stress acquire helpful stress management strategies.

- ASCA National Model Standards addressed in this group: A:A3.1, PS: A1.5–9, PS: A2.6–7, PS: B1 (all), PS: C1.9–11.
- District Plan competencies addressed in group: Middle Level Competencies: Self Awareness, Coping, Decision-Making, Social Skills.

Goals for Group:

- Students will recognize signs of stress.
- Students will gain an understanding of how individuals are affected by stress.
- Students will develop skills for managing stress.
- Students will identify support systems in school that can help them with stress.

Number of Sessions in Unit: 6 weeks—30 minutes per session

Group Assessment Plan:

1. Students will recognize signs of stress.
   - Student participation in discussion (all sessions)
   - Student participation in Where is the Stress? activity (Session 1)
   - Student responses in What I Learned . . . questionnaire (Session 6)
2. Students will gain an understanding of how individuals are affected by stress.
   - Student participation in group discussion (all sessions)
   - Student responses in What I Learned . . . questionnaire (Session 6)
3. Students will develop skills for managing stress.
   - Student participation in Healthy/Unhealthy Expression Worksheet activity.
   - Student responses in What I Learned . . . questionnaire (Session 6)
   - Referral teacher report at follow up
4. Students will identify support systems in school that can help them with stress.
   - Participation in discussion (Session 6)
   - Student responses in What I Learned . . . questionnaire (Session 6)

Source: Adapted from Kearns, L. (2007, May). *Six Week Small Group Counseling Lesson Plan.* Class assignment for EDCO 340 Developmental Guidance in the Schools class. University of Vermont.

MIDDLE LEVEL COUNSELING GROUP *SESSION* PLAN

Topic: Stress Management

Grade/Class: Seventh & Eighth Grade

Session: Week 4 (of 6)

Session Objective:

- Students will develop strategies for managing stress (Part 1).

Plan:

Check in questions (whip rounds):

- Where did you notice your stress this past week (referring back to week 2 exercise)?
- Did the stress you feel correspond to a particular event (referring to last week) or was it general stress?
- Did you have a "blowout"?
- Did anyone notice the thoughts they had that might have increased their stress level (reflecting back on last week's discussion on "unhelpful thoughts")?

Introduce agenda:

- Ways to get a handle on stress. Today we will talk generally about some helpful tips. Next week we will talk about using your thoughts to control your stress feelings.

Anything to add to the agenda?

- Do students have any particular stress-related incidents that they need the group to help them with? Etc.

Getting a Handle on Stress sheet (see attached):

- Read through each item . . . have students comment or give examples and discuss how it might help.
- Have students check in blue the items they feel that they're pretty good at already. Check in red those that they would like to use more.
- If discussion is fluid, allow group to discuss.

Commit to trying one of these suggestions this week:

- Circle item on Getting a Handle Stress sheet to try.
- Discuss: What might get in the way of you being able to use this strategy?
- Discuss: How will you push through the resistance?

Closing:

- What are you taking from group today that will help you with stress this week?

Backup plan (or do before closing if there is time):

- Move directly to progressive relaxation exercise that is planned for Group 4.

Materials:

- Getting a Handle on Stress sheet (copies for all).
- Red and blue fine-point markers.
- Progressive relaxation script. (Just in case!)

Source: Adapted from Kearns, L. (2007, May). *Six Week Small Group Counseling Lesson Plan*. Class assignment for EDCO 340 Developmental Guidance in the Schools class. University of Vermont.

GETTING A HANDLE ON STRESS!!!!

1. **Work off stress.**   Blow off steam in a constructive way—through physical activity.
2. **Talk out stress.**   Find someone to talk to who will listen, support, and help you. Don't worry about burdening this person—the person to talk to is someone who really cares. Be clear with the person on whether you just want a sounding board or if you want help. Be open to help if you ask for it.
3. **Learn to accept what can't be changed.**   If the problem is out of your control, recognize this. Always look for aspects of the problem that are within your control. Problems rarely are all or nothing.
4. **Get enough sleep.**   Not having enough sleep can make it harder to deal with stress. If you're having trouble sleeping, try to increase your exercise routine and be sure to eat well.
5. **Take it easy and have fun . . . and also get your work done.**   Balance work and play. You will get stressed if you haven't done your work . . . and playing will help you relax. Schedule time for work and schedule time for fun. Both are important.
6. **Do something for others.**   Sometimes when we are stressed we get too focused on ourselves and our problems. Reaching out to help someone else can help us too!
7. **Take one thing at a time.**   Doing too many things at once is a setup for stress . . . and for failure. If you're stressed, take something off your "to do" list, figure out what needs to be done first (prioritize) and do one thing at a time.
8. **Take a stand.**   Sometimes stress is about not asserting yourself. If that's the case, think clearly (sometimes it helps to talk it through with someone else) and then assert what you need or assert your preference. Others will cope . . . and they'll probably also appreciate your clarity and your honesty. Be careful to assert yourself with respect and appropriate self-restraint, of course!
9. **Know your abilities . . . and your limitations.**   When you can't: Don't. When you can: Do.
10. **Get organized.**   Come up with a plan and follow it.
11. **Avoid perfectionism.**   Allow yourself to make a mistake. Attend to those things that shouldn't be done erroneously and let the others go.

APPENDIX C

High School Level Sample Plans

- Sample Classroom Group Unit Plan
- Sample Classroom Lesson Plan—Lesson 3
- Sample Counseling Group (Overall) Plan
- Sample Counseling Session Plan—Session 4

HIGH SCHOOL LEVEL CLASSROOM GROUP UNIT PLAN

Topic: Career Life Planning

Grade/Class:

- Tenth Grade (mostly) (co-taught/part of curriculum with Careers class teachers: D. Rose, L.Yuol)
- Class time: Sessions 1, 2, 4, 5: 55 minutes; Session 3: 90 minutes

Approximate Number of Students: 15–20 per class

Resources Required: Computer lab; access to Internet for several sessions; Assessments (self-scoring) as listed (as available).

Rationale:

One of the major developmental tasks of adolescents is to explore career interests and options in order to inform their decisions about courses to take and to determine post-high school direction. This process typically includes: (1) an inventory of student's interests, values, and skills, (2) information about the world of work, and (3) information about how to prepare for specific careers. This process is particularly important to students in the tenth grade as they finalize their high school curriculum choices in accordance to future life planning.

District Developmental Guidance Plan Standards addressed in lesson:

1.18 Research (Information Technology)
1.19 Using Resources
2.13 Critical Thinking Skills
2.14 Planning/Organization
2.2 Reasoning Strategies
3.1 Goal Setting
3.7 Decision-Making

ASCA National Standards:

C: A Career Awareness; A1.1–A1.10
C: B Career Goals; B1.1–B1.8 B2.1–B2.5
C: C Personal Application; C1.1–C1.3 C2.1–C2.4

Goals for Unit:

1. Students will become aware of their own career-related interests, values, and skills.

   Two of the following materials will be used:
   - Strong Interest Inventory (SII) (Consulting Psychologists—Press, Palo Alto, CA)
   - Campbell Interest and Skill Survey (CISS)(NCS Assessments, Minneapolis, MN)
   - Work Values Inventory (WVI)(Houghton Mifflin Co, Boston)

2. Students will develop an awareness of the broad variety of options in the "world of work."

Materials:
- America's Job Bank http://www.ajb.dni.us
- America's Labor Market Information System (ALMIS) http://www.ecu.edu/-lmi.html
- Resources for Minorities http://www.vjf.com/pub/docs/jobsearch.html

3. Students will learn about the specific preparation criteria for the jobs and careers that are of interest to them.

One of the following materials will be used:
- DISCOVER (American College Testing Program)
- Self Directed Search (SDS)(Holland, 1992)
- SIGI Plus (Katz, 1993)

4. Students will understand the relationship between school performance, personal qualities, training requirements and options, and future career choices.

5. Students will engage in dialogues regarding career aspirations, directions, process, and goals with other students in pairs and small groups.

6. Students will initiate discussions with parents/guardians regarding career-related interests, inventories and assessment results, resources for education and training, and individual career planning.

Number of Lessons in Unit: 5

Lesson 1: Introduction to Career and Life Planning
Lesson 2: Exploring Interests
Lesson 3: What Do All These Surveys Mean? (90-minute class)
Lesson 4: Access to Training/Education Information
Lesson 5: Individual Planning

Assessment Plan:

1. Students will become aware of their own career-related interests, values, and skills. Two of the following materials will be used:
   - Strong Interest Inventory (SII) (Consulting Psychologists Press, Palo Alto, CA)
   - Campbell Interest and Skill Survey (CISS)(NCS Assessments, Minneapolis, MN)
   - Work Values Inventory (WVI)(Houghton Mifflin Co, Boston)
2. Students will develop an awareness of the broad variety of options in the "world of work."
   - *Career and Life Planning Unit Assessment (Student version—final week)*
   - *Career and Life Planning Unit Assessment (Parent version—send home week 4)*
3. Students will learn about the specific preparation criteria for the jobs and careers that are of interest to them.
   - *Career and Life Planning Unit Assessment (Student version—final week)*
   - *Career and Life Planning Unit Assessment (Parent version—send home week 4)*

4. Students will understand the relationship between school performance, personal qualities, training requirements and options, and future career choices.
   • Career and Life Planning Unit Assessment (Student version—final week)
   • Career and Life Planning Unit Assessment (Parent version—send home week 4)
5. Students will engage in dialogues regarding career aspirations, directions, process, and goals with other students in pairs and small groups.
   • Career and Life Planning Unit Assessment (Student version—final week)
   • Counselor/teacher observation of student participation in group work
6. Students will initiate discussions with parents/guardians regarding career-related interests, inventories and assessment results, resources for education and training, and individual career planning.
   • Career and Life Planning Unit Assessment (Parent version—send home week 4)

HIGH SCHOOL LEVEL *LESSON* PLAN

Career and Life Planning Unit—Week 3: What do All These Surveys Mean?

Grade/Class: Tenth Grade (Career Classes; Teacher: D. Rose, L. Yuol)

Time: 90 minutes

Learning Objectives:

1. Students will identify key values and/or interests that are important to themselves and to their own career goal planning.
2. Students will understand the importance of selecting career goals that fit with their own values and interests.
3. Students will access information and resources that will help them match their interests to jobs and careers.
4. Students will communicate with others insights about themselves and others resulting from this lesson and unit.

Materials:

- America's Job Bank http://www.ajb.dni.us
- America's Labor Market Information System (ALMIS) http://www.ecu.edu/-lmi.html
- Resources for Minorities http://www.vjf.com/pub/docs/jobsearch.html
- DISCOVER (American College Testing Program)
- Self Directed Search (SDS)(Holland, 1992)
- SIGI Plus (Katz, 1993)

Plan:

1. (15 minutes) Counselor will offer a general review interest profiles—how to read them/make sense of them.
2. (5 minutes) Counselor will distribute the scored interest inventories that were taken the week before.
3. (15 minutes) Counselor invites students to review their results individually, circulating to help. Ask students to jot down three comments or questions they have.
4. (20 minutes) Small Group Discussion: "What does all this information mean to me?"
   - Students will discuss their results in small groups of four.
   - In each small group, discussions will be prompted by the questions below that they will ask each other and through feedback exchange (see below).
   - Student to peers in small group:
     o What have you learned about yourself from these instruments?
     o Does anything surprise you?
     o Do you feel the instruments missed anything?
   - Peers will take turns offering feedback to each member about how well the information they shared about themselves "fits" with your perceptions of them.
   - The counselor and teacher will circulate among groups offering feedback on their process, answer questions, offer feedback, structure feedback, keep groups on task, etc.

5. (20 minutes) Large Group Processing—End in Round
   - What was it like today sharing what you learned about yourself with your peers?
   - What did you learn about yourself? Any surprises?
   - How was it to tell your peers what you noticed about their interests, values, and skills?
   - What interpersonal communication skills that you have learned about in previous "guidance lessons" did you practice today?
6. (15 minutes) Survey.
   - Complete question 1 on Career and Life Planning Unit Assessment (COLLECT THESE FROM STUDENTS BEFORE THEY LEAVE—OTHER SECTIONS TO BE COMPLETED LATER!!)

Name:_____

Career and Life Planning Unit Assessment

1. Please rate the Strong Interest Inventory, Campbell Interest and Skill Survey, and/or Work Values Inventory. (Select only the assessment utilized.)

1	2	3	4	5	6
Poor				Excellent	

   a. Please explain the above rating.

   b. What did you learn about your interests and skills?

2. Please rate our use of DISCOVER, SIGI Plus, and/or Self Directed Search. (Select only the Instrument used.)

1	2	3	4	5	6
Poor				Excellent	

   a. Please explain the above rating.

   b. What really interested you through this experience?

3. Name three things that you learned about your own future through this career unit.

4. What is something specific that you learned about the kind of preparation you will need for the career interests you have?

5. Please rate the value of these exercises:

1	2	3	4	5	6
Poor				Excellent	

   a. Please explain the above rating.

6. Please give us feedback about what helped and what didn't help and what you liked/didn't like in the Career/Life Planning Unit.

7. Do you want your counselor to check in with you about your career thoughts and plans? (Circle below). Of course, you may always contact your counselor for more help with career and life planning ☺.

       Yes, please contact me.   No, I'm good for now.

LHS Tenth Grade Parent(s)/Guardian(s):

As you know your son/daughter has studied Career and Life Planning in his/her Career Class this year. We are hoping to receive feedback from you about how this unit was or was not helpful to you and your child as your son or daughter and you discuss high school and post-high school planning. Thanks for taking the time to complete this survey.

Lake High School
Counseling Office staff

1. Did your son/daughter mention what he/she was doing in the career and life planning class?
   a. Did he/she mention an interest inventory?

   b. Did he/she mention a world of work study?

   c. Did he/she mention a review of training requirements for specific jobs/careers?

2. Have you and your son/daughter had any conversations recently about his/her future career plans? If so, please tell us a little about those conversations.

3. What has your son/daughter learned with regard to career and life planning?

4. In your opinion, how did this unit benefit your child?

5. What questions or information do you need to help you talk with your child about post-high school career and life planning?

HIGH SCHOOL LEVEL COUNSELING GROUP (OVERALL) PLAN

Topic: What, Me Worry? (Anxiety Reduction Strategies)

Grade/Class: Sophomores and Juniors

Approximate Number of Students: 4-8

Rationale:

The purpose of this group is to help students acquire anxiety reduction strategies. This group was requested by teachers in the Math and English departments, based on observations of their Honor's students who were anxious about midterm exams and upcoming standardized SAT exam, which would be taken later in the year. Member selection will be based on teacher referral and self-referral. The group will implement a cognitive-behavioral model for reducing test anxiety.

- ASCA National Model Standards addressed in this group: A:A1.1, 4, 5., A:A2 (all), A:B1.4-5., A:B2.3, 2.5, A:C1-2, PS: A1.5-8, PS:B1 (all).
- District Plan competencies addressed in group: no district/school plans

Goals for Group:

- Students will recognize their personal signs of stress.
- Students will gain an understanding of how their feelings of stress are triggered by thoughts—many of which are unrealistic and distorted.
- Students will identify distorted thoughts and apply strategies for restructuring their thoughts.
- Students will acquire additional relaxation and anti-anxiety strategies—lifestyle and in-the-moment strategies.

Number of Sessions in Unit: 4 weeks—30 minutes per session

Group Assessment Plan:

1. Students will recognize their personal signs of stress.
    - Participating in signs of stress discussion (Session 1)
    - What I Learned . . . Questionnaire (Session 4)
2. Students will gain an understanding of how their feelings of stress are triggered by thoughts—many of which are unrealistic and distorted.
    - Participation in discussion, prompted by CBT strategies worksheets/instruction (Sessions 2, 3)
    - What I Learned . . . Questionnaire (Session 4)
3. Students will identify distorted thoughts and apply strategies for re-structuring their thoughts.
    - Participation in discussion, prompted by CBT strategies worksheets/instruction (Sessions 2, 3)
    - What I Learned . . . Questionnaire (Session 4)
4. Students will acquire additional relaxation and anti-anxiety strategies—lifestyle and in-the-moment strategies.
    - Participation in discussion after relaxation training (Session 4)
    - What I Learned . . . Questionnaire (Session 4)

HIGH SCHOOL LEVEL COUNSELING GROUP SESSION PLAN
WHAT, ME WORRY? GROUP SESSION 4

Session Objective:

- Students will acquire additional relaxation and anti-anxiety strategies. These will be life-style and in-the-moment strategies.

Plan:

- Begin with review of last week discussion on distorted thoughts and restructuring strategies. Round:
  - Did anyone use any of the strategies we discussed last week?
  - What distorted thought did you notice?
  - What was the distortion (refer to list . . . have student point it out)?
  - What did you do to correct the distortion?
  - What was the result?
- We have focused a lot on changing your thoughts to manage your stress reactions in here. Today we are going to focus on some other things you can do to manage stress. These are more of the life-style kinds of things that you learned in Health class (if you took that class); they are healthy lifestyle actions that help manage stress.
  - In general, what are good action strategies you can do to manage stress. (Prompt students to think about exercise, recreation and quiet time, and diet.)
  - Teach students progressive relaxation exercises (see book) . . . building on Session 1—where we feel stress. Have students tighten and then loosen parts of their bodies to feel relaxation.
  - Discuss how this can be adapted to be used "in the moment" in class.
- Closing Round: Think back over the past 4 weeks. What have you learned about how stress affects you? What have you learned to do to manage stress that has been particularly helpful?
- Handout: What I Learned . . . (explain purpose of this to students)

Materials:

- Book:[*] The Relaxation and Stress Reduction Workbook (in Counseling office)
- What I Learned . . . Questionnaire (attached)

---

[*]Davis, M., Eshelman, E. R., & McKay, M. (2008). *The relaxation and stress reduction workbook*. Oakland, CA: New Harbinger Publications.

What I Learned . . .

How do you know when you are stressed out?

Besides the deadlines and events that happen in our lives, what else causes stress?

How does the way that you think affect stress (positively and negatively)?

What have you learned in terms of managing stress? What can you do to manage stress?

How was this group for you? What was and wasn't helpful?

APPENDIX D

Basic Skills for Counseling and Classroom Group Work in Schools

This list encompasses a selection of skills utilized in both counseling and classroom groups.[1] Although skills are most easily thought of as "something that the leader does," this list includes skills that the leader strives to use to build member capacity. Each skill, when artfully applied, has utility in small and large counseling and classroom groups. Skillful group leadership draws from sets of skills only as they will assist counseling and classroom members forward toward session and lesson objectives and group goals. The skills are listed alphabetically so readers do not misinterpret those early on the list as easiest or most basic and those late more difficult or advanced.

Leadership Skill	Function in Counseling Groups and Classroom Groups—*Examples*
Active Listening	Active listening is attending to verbal and nonverbal communication. It is often demonstrated by nonverbal resonating with what is being said and by the use of minimal encouragers.
Blocking	Blocking is metaphorically stepping in between or standing in the way of the group heading off course or in a direction that is not conducive to achieving individual and group goals. *"Maybe, I could get in the way here—it seems like you have veered way off course and may have lost sight of what you were working on."*
Clarifying	Clarifying is restating and ensuring what the speaker intended for others to understand. *"I wonder if I heard that completely." "Could you help me understand what you meant when you said . . . ?"*
Closing	Closure is ensuring that adequate time is allocated to the process of ending each session. Closing often asks for personal meaning to be shared, for final comments and reflections, and for next steps to be proposed.
Conflict Resolution, Mediation	Conflict resolution or mediation has to do with building skills between and among members to deal effectively with conflict. The aim, usually, is to reach resolution by consensus rather than exerting force or relying on power or privilege.
Confronting	Confrontation has to do with pointing out discrepancy, incongruence, and/or confusing contributions. Confronting does not imply waging battle, rather it has to do with attending to and respectful illumination of discrepancies.

(continued)

---

[1]Skills presented on this list are quite indistinguishable from similar lists found in many other group texts. Superb definitions and vivid examples can be found elsewhere. We wish to make clear that these skills are not uniquely of our making—we have selected only those from the larger body of group leadership skills that we believe are fundamental and crossover completely between classroom and counseling groups.

Cutting-Off	Limiting how much time someone "takes up in group" and on occasion what content a member seeks to share is the intent of cutting off. Careful cutting-off skills lead one member to stop and another member to begin. *"Eliza, you have offered us a lot today, I wonder if we might check in with Tasha who seems to want to say something to us too?"* Or, *"Wow, the right-hand side of the room seems to be getting all the air time today— let's now shift our attention to my left-hand side of the class—so they don't feel neglected."*
Drawing-Out	Drawing out encourages less verbal members' participation by creating openings for them to engage in conversation and in sharing. The skills of drawing-out members go well beyond "calling on a quiet member" and must consider forces that might reflect privilege or power that permit some to engage actively and others to remain in the shadows.
Empathizing	Empathizing has to do with imagining what another is experiencing or has experienced and the willingness to communicate honestly what it is like to resonate with another person in this way.
Goal-Setting	What the group agrees they will attempt to accomplish, as well as what individuals within the group strive to reach, is the result of goal-setting. Typically fewer goals are more achievable than many.
Interpreting	Interpretation is when possible explanations are offered to something that has been stated or implied regarding member behavior or feelings. Interpreting need not be filled with psychobabble—rather simple hypotheses that might aid in making meaning of experiences. *"I wonder if repeating this behavior over and over—as you have described it, might have a deeper purpose? What if you are . . . ?"* Interpretations should be offered with appropriate tentativeness and followed by a check in to assess accuracy or for client input.
Linking, Joining, Connecting	Linking has to do with connecting members who otherwise might remain distant. Asking members to speak directly to other members rather than speaking to "everyone" or no one in particular. *"Javier, I wonder if you would turn to Adam and speak directly to him?"*
Meaning-Making	Meaning-making refers to creating the possibility for members to make sense of what they are experiencing in the group. This is accomplished by encouraging members to share with other members their "take" on a session or an event or by providing time for members to sift through what they are in the midst of—and see what they will carry away. *"Kids, let's take a few silent moments to see what we will take away from group this morning. What personal meaning does this activity have for you?"*
Modeling	Modeling is purposely demonstrating behaviors and ways of being in the group with the intent of helping group members see new ways or possibilities of ways to achieve their goals. Modeling is often implicit, but can also be brought to the foreground explicitly. *"Let me try to show you what this might look like."*
Offering Feedback	Feedback can be thought of as valuing or appreciating what has been offered and honestly sharing how one responds to what they have heard. Feedback is conveyed verbally and nonverbally. Intended feedback can be deformed by poor delivery, so the group leader must be astute in giving feedback and in facilitating feedback exchange among group members.
Offering Information	Offering information includes teaching, as well as locating resources and helping students learn from one another. This group leader function must be used with caution to ensure that leaders are imparting information and not their values.

Probing	Probing is the skill of poking around gently, shining a beam of light into those hidden places where communication might not otherwise go. Probing, when properly done, rarely requires a question mark.
Protecting	Protecting requires being ever watchful to ensure that all members of all groups are safe. Providing strategies and direction in the group keeps all members psychologically as well as physically safe.
Questioning	Asking questions provides a way for members to uncover additional depth, a new direction, and a means of offering others detail and clarity. Questions provide a means of deepening and extending what someone offers. Remember to ask one question at a time, as piles of questions baffle rather than benefit.
Reflecting Content	Naming what is presented—the "what" of group—should be communicated in words and terms that are understood by all members.
Reflecting Feelings	Reflection of feelings is naming feelings and/or selecting words that capture affect and mood—it brings implicit expression of feelings forth explicitly. Feeling reflections vary in intensity from simply reflecting a feeling word to providing an emotional space for someone to feel. Feeling reflections sometimes are used to increase the client's feeling vocabulary, but typically this action serves to focus attention on the client's or the group's affective state.
Reframing	Reframing asks members to view a wide variety of things (such as an old behavior, a typical way of responding, rigid beliefs about someone or something) in a new and different way. To reframe something usually thought of as "the way it is" allows for new possibilities. *"The rules you seem angry about seem oppressive and unfair to several of you. But, I'm also seeing them as a way to keep you safe. What happens when you look at them in that way?"*
Restatement	Restating is to provide a paraphrase or substitute language to ensure what has been said is what was heard or understood.
Self-Disclosure	Self-disclosure entails purposeful sharing with members about the leader's experiences relevant to what is currently transpiring within the group. Sharing with group members such carefully selected stories or in-the-moment experience is a skill that requires much introspection and self-monitoring. Use with caution.
Shifting Focus	Shifting the focus increases or decreases attention on "where we are" and can nudge (or push) the group in another direction. This can be related to content or process in a group and can also apply to membership (shifting from one member to another). It serves the purpose of narrowing the focus or broadening the client's or group experience. *"Seems to me that we've been aiming many of our comments about this issue at Carmen. I'm curious who might also feel this applies really directly to you?"*
Sub-grouping	Sub-grouping is dividing the larger group into smaller parts it is an action with specific outcomes in mind. Sub-grouping creates smaller groups, which may increase active participation of all members. Also, conversations in dyads may build one-to-one communication among members.
Suggesting	Suggesting refers to offering possibilities for direction, possibilities for exploration and asks members to consider something new.
Summarizing	Summarizing can also be thought of as repackaging content or process that was just explored. Sentence stems that signal summary may include: *"Let's see if I got all of that?" "Here's what I think you're offering us . . ." "May I attempt to summarize all this?"*

(continued)

Supporting

Supporting is helping members to participate fully in group, sometimes encouraging risky steps. Support includes offering numerous ways for a member to accomplish his or her personal goals in group and for the group as a whole to reach their objectives.

Terminating

Terminating is known as a stage as well as a set of skills. Building towards termination may take several sessions and lots of attention and is aimed at helping members make meaning of their experiences in the group and to transfer their learning in the group to "life outside the group."

Time-Keeping

Time-keeping is a crucial function that announces the time left in each session—keeping the group aware of their progress. Also, in a time-limited group, time-keeping ensures that members know how many sessions remain for the group. *"This is a powerful exchange, we are in the middle of, but allow me to keep an eye on the clock. We only have 9 minutes remaining in or time together today."* Or, *"Today we begin the sixth of our eight sessions this quarter on responsibility."*

APPENDIX E

Ethical Standards for School Counselors

PREAMBLE

The American School Counselor Association (ASCA) is a professional organization whose members are certified/licensed in school counseling with unique qualifications and skills to address the academic, personal/social and career development needs of all students. Professional school counselors are advocates, leaders, collaborators and consultants who create opportunities for equity in access and success in educational opportunities by connecting their programs to the mission of schools and subscribing to the following tenets of professional responsibility:

- Each person has the right to be respected, be treated with dignity and have access to a comprehensive school counseling program that advocates for and affirms all students from diverse populations regardless of ethnic/racial status, age, economic status, special needs, English as a second language or other language group, immigration status, sexual orientation, gender, gender identity/expression, family type, religious/spiritual identity and appearance.
- Each person has the right to receive the information and support needed to move toward self-direction and self-development and affirmation within one's group identities, with special care being given to students who have historically not received adequate educational services: students of color, low socioeconomic students, students with disabilities, and students with nondominant language backgrounds.
- Each person has the right to understand the full magnitude and meaning of his/her educational choices and how those choices will affect future opportunities.
- Each person has the right to privacy and thereby the right to expect the counselor-student relationship to comply with all laws, policies and ethical standards pertaining to confidentiality in the school setting.

In this document, ASCA specifies the principles of ethical behavior necessary to maintain the high standards of integrity, leadership and professionalism among its members. The Ethical Standards for School Counselors were developed to clarify the nature of ethical responsibilities held in common by school counseling professionals. The purposes of this document are to:

- Serve as a guide for the ethical practices of all professional school counselors regardless of level, area, population served or membership in this professional association;

Source: ASCA's Ethical Standards for School Counselors were adopted by the ASCA Delegate Assembly, March 19, 1984, revised March 27, 1992, June 25, 1998 and June 26, 2004. Retrieved from http://www .schoolcounselor.org/files/ethical%20standards.pdf

- Provide self-appraisal and peer evaluations regarding counselor responsibilities to students, parents/guardians, colleagues and professional associates, schools, communities and the counseling profession; and
- Inform those served by the school counselor of acceptable counselor practices and expected professional behavior.

A.1. Responsibilities to Students

The professional school counselor:

a. Has a primary obligation to the student, who is to be treated with respect as a unique individual.

b. Is concerned with the educational, academic, career, personal and social needs and encourages the maximum development of every student.

c. Respects the student's values and beliefs and does not impose the counselor's personal values.

d. Is knowledgeable of laws, regulations and policies relating to students and strives to protect and inform students regarding their rights.

A.2. Confidentiality

The professional school counselor:

a. Informs students of the purposes, goals, techniques and rules of procedure under which they may receive counseling at or before the time when the counseling relationship is entered. Disclosure notice includes the limits of confidentiality such as the possible necessity for consulting with other professionals, privileged communication, and legal or authoritative restraints. The meaning and limits of confidentiality are defined in developmentally appropriate terms to students.

b. Keeps information confidential unless disclosure is required to prevent clear and imminent danger to the student or others or when legal requirements demand that confidential information be revealed. Counselors will consult with appropriate professionals when in doubt as to the validity of an exception.

c. In absence of state legislation expressly forbidding disclosure, considers the ethical responsibility to provide information to an identified third party who, by his/her relationship with the student, is at a high risk of contracting a disease that is commonly known to be communicable and fatal. Disclosure requires satisfaction of all of the following conditions:
  - Student identifies partner or the partner is highly identifiable
  - Counselor recommends the student notify partner and refrain from further high-risk behavior
  - Student refuses
  - Counselor informs the student of the intent to notify the partner
  - Counselor seeks legal consultation as to the legalities of informing the partner

d. Requests of the court that disclosure not be required when the release of confidential information may potentially harm a student or the counseling relationship.

e. Protects the confidentiality of students' records and releases personal data in accordance with prescribed laws and school policies. Student information stored and transmitted electronically is treated with the same care as traditional student records.

f. Protects the confidentiality of information received in the counseling relationship as specified by federal and state laws, written policies and applicable ethical standards. Such information is only to be revealed to others with the informed consent of the student, consistent with the counselor's ethical obligation.

g. Recognizes his/her primary obligation for confidentiality is to the student but balances that obligation with an understanding of the legal and inherent rights of parents/guardians to be the guiding voice in their children's lives.

A.3. Counseling Plans

The professional school counselor:

a. Provides students with a comprehensive school counseling program that includes a strong emphasis on working jointly with all students to develop academic and career goals.

b. Advocates for counseling plans supporting students right to choose from the wide array of options when they leave secondary education. Such plans will be regularly reviewed to update students regarding critical information they need to make informed decisions.

A.4. Dual Relationships

The professional school counselor:

a. Avoids dual relationships that might impair his/her objectivity and increase the risk of harm to the student (e.g., counseling one's family members, close friends or associates). If a dual relationship is unavoidable, the counselor is responsible for taking action to eliminate or reduce the potential for harm. Such safeguards might include informed consent, consultation, supervision and documentation.

b. Avoids dual relationships with school personnel that might infringe on the integrity of the counselor/student relationship.

A.5. Appropriate Referrals

The professional school counselor:

a. Makes referrals when necessary or appropriate to outside resources. Appropriate referrals may necessitate informing both parents/guardians and students of applicable resources and making proper plans for transitions with minimal interruption of services. Students retain the right to discontinue the counseling relationship at any time.

A.6. Group Work

The professional school counselor:

a. Screens prospective group members and maintains an awareness of participants' needs and goals in relation to the goals of the group. The counselor takes reasonable precautions to protect members from physical and psychological harm resulting from interaction within the group.

b. Notifies parents/guardians and staff of group participation if the counselor deems it appropriate and if consistent with school board policy or practice.

   c. Establishes clear expectations in the group setting and clearly states that confidentiality in group counseling cannot be guaranteed. Given the developmental and chronological ages of minors in schools, the counselor recognizes the tenuous nature of confidentiality for minors renders some topics inappropriate for group work in a school setting.

   d. Follows up with group members and documents proceedings as appropriate.

A.7. Danger to Self or Others

The professional school counselor:

   a. Informs parents/guardians or appropriate authorities when the student's condition indicates a clear and imminent danger to the student or others. This is to be done after careful deliberation and, where possible, after consultation with other counseling professionals.

   b. Will attempt to minimize threat to a student and may choose to 1) inform the student of actions to be taken, 2) involve the student in a three-way communication with parents/guardians when breaching confidentiality or 3) allow the student to have input as to how and to whom the breach will be made.

A.8. Student Records

The professional school counselor:

   a. Maintains and secures records necessary for rendering professional services to the student as required by laws, regulations, institutional procedures and confidentiality guidelines.

   b. Keeps sole-possession records separate from students' educational records in keeping with state laws.

   c. Recognizes the limits of sole-possession records and understands these records are a memory aid for the creator and in absence of privilege communication may be subpoenaed and may become educational records when they 1) are shared with others in verbal or written form, 2) include information other than professional opinion or personal observations, and/or 3) are made accessible to others.

   d. Establishes a reasonable timeline for purging sole-possession records or case notes. Suggested guidelines include shredding sole possession records when the student transitions to the next level, transfers to another school or graduates. Careful discretion and deliberation should be applied before destroying sole-possession records that may be needed by a court of law such as notes on child abuse, suicide, sexual harassment or violence.

A.9. Evaluation, Assessment, and Interpretation

The professional school counselor:

   a. Adheres to all professional standards regarding selecting, administering and interpreting assessment measures and only utilizes assessment measures that are within the scope of practice for school counselors.

   b. Seeks specialized training regarding the use of electronically based testing programs in administering, scoring and interpreting that may differ from that required in more traditional assessments.

   c. Considers confidentiality issues when utilizing evaluative or assessment instruments and electronically based programs.
   d. Provides interpretation of the nature, purposes, results and potential impact of assessment/evaluation measures in language the student(s) can understand.
   e. Monitors the use of assessment results and interpretations, and takes reasonable steps to prevent others from misusing the information.
   f. Uses caution when utilizing assessment techniques, making evaluations, and interpreting the performance of populations not represented in the norm group on which an instrument is standardized.
   g. Assesses the effectiveness of his/her program in having an impact on students' academic, career and personal/social development through accountability measures especially examining efforts to close achievement, opportunity, and attainment gaps.

A.10. Technology

The professional school counselor:

   a. Promotes the benefits of and clarifies the limitations of various appropriate technological applications. The counselor promotes technological applications (1) that are appropriate for the student's individual needs, (2) that the student understands how to use, and (3) for which follow-up counseling assistance is provided.
   b. Advocates for equal access to technology for all students, especially those historically underserved.
   c. Takes appropriate and reasonable measures for maintaining confidentiality of student information and educational records stored or transmitted over electronic media including although not limited to fax, electronic mail, and instant messaging.
   d. While working with students on a computer or similar technology, takes reasonable and appropriate measures to protect students from objectionable and/or harmful online material.
   e. Who is engaged in the delivery of services involving technologies such as the telephone, videoconferencing, and the Internet takes responsible steps to protect students and others from harm.

A.11. Student Peer Support Program

The professional school counselor has unique responsibilities when working with student-assistance programs. The school counselor is responsible for the welfare of students participating in peer-to-peer programs under his/her direction.

B. RESPONSIBILITIES TO PARENTS/GUARDIANS

B.1. Parent Rights and Responsibilities

The professional school counselor:

   a. Respects the rights and responsibilities of parents/guardians for their children and endeavors to establish, as appropriate, a collaborative relationship with parents/guardians to facilitate the student's maximum development.

   b. Adheres to laws, local guidelines and ethical standards of practice when assisting parents/guardians experiencing family difficulties that interfere with the student's effectiveness and welfare.
   c. Respects the confidentiality of parents/guardians.
   d. Is sensitive to diversity among families and recognizes that all parents/guardians, custodial and noncustodial, are vested with certain rights and responsibilities for the welfare of their children by virtue of their role and according to law.

B.2. Parents/Guardians and Confidentiality

The professional school counselor:

   a. Informs parents/guardians of the counselor's role with emphasis on the confidential nature of the counseling relationship between the counselor and student.
   b. Recognizes that working with minors in a school setting may require counselors to collaborate with students' parents/guardians.
   c. Provides parents/guardians with accurate, comprehensive and relevant information in an objective and caring manner, as is appropriate and consistent with ethical responsibilities to the student.
   d. Makes reasonable efforts to honor the wishes of parents/guardians concerning information regarding the student, and in cases of divorce or separation, exercises a good-faith effort to keep both parents informed with regard to critical information with the exception of a court order.

C. RESPONSIBILITIES TO COLLEAGUES AND PROFESSIONAL ASSOCIATES

C.1. Professional Relationships

The professional school counselor:

   a. Establishes and maintains professional relationships with faculty, staff and administration to facilitate an optimum counseling program.
   b. Treats colleagues with professional respect, courtesy and fairness. The qualifications, views, and findings of colleagues are represented to accurately reflect the image of competent professionals.
   c. Is aware of and utilizes related professionals, organizations, and other resources to whom the student may be referred.

C.2. Sharing Information with Other Professionals

The professional school counselor:

   a. Promotes awareness and adherence to appropriate guidelines regarding confidentiality, the distinction between public and private information, and staff consultation.
   b. Provides professional personnel with accurate, objective, concise, and meaningful data necessary to adequately evaluate, counsel, and assist the student.
   c. If a student is receiving services from another counselor or other mental health professional, the counselor, with student and/or parent/guardian consent, will inform the other professional and develop clear agreements to avoid confusion and conflict for the student.
   d. Is knowledgeable about release of information and parental rights in sharing information.

D. RESPONSIBILITIES TO THE SCHOOL AND COMMUNITY

D.1. Responsibilities to the School

The professional school counselor:

a. Supports and protects the educational program against any infringement not in students' best interest.

b. Informs appropriate officials in accordance with school policy of conditions that may be potentially disruptive or damaging to the school's mission, personnel, and property while honoring the confidentiality between the student and counselor.

c. Is knowledgeable and supportive of the school's mission and connects his/her program to the school's mission.

d. Delineates and promotes the counselor's role and function in meeting the needs of those served. Counselors will notify appropriate officials of conditions that may limit or curtail their effectiveness in providing programs and services.

e. Accepts employment only for positions for which he/she is qualified by education, training, supervised experience, state and national professional credentials, and appropriate professional experience.

f. Advocates that administrators hire only qualified and competent individuals for professional counseling positions.

g. Assists in developing: (1) curricular and environmental conditions appropriate for the school and community, (2) educational procedures and programs to meet students' developmental needs, and (3) a systematic evaluation process for comprehensive, developmental, standards-based school counseling programs, services, and personnel. The counselor is guided by the findings of the evaluation data in planning programs and services.

D.2. Responsibility to the Community

The professional school counselor:

a. Collaborates with agencies, organizations and individuals in the community in the best interest of students and without regard to personal reward or remuneration.

b. Extends his/her influence and opportunity to deliver a comprehensive school counseling program to all students by collaborating with community resources for student success.

E. RESPONSIBILITIES TO SELF

E.1. Professional Competence

The professional school counselor:

a. Functions within the boundaries of individual professional competence and accepts responsibility for the consequences of his/her actions.

b. Monitors personal well-being and effectiveness and does not participate in any activity that may lead to inadequate professional services or harm to a student.

c. Strives through personal initiative to maintain professional competence including technological literacy and to keep abreast of professional information. Professional and personal growth are ongoing throughout the counselor's career.

E.2. Diversity

The professional school counselor:

a. Affirms the diversity of students, staff, and families.

b. Expands and develops awareness of his/her own attitudes and beliefs affecting cultural values and biases and strives to attain cultural competence.

c. Possesses knowledge and understanding about how oppression, racism, discrimination, and stereotyping affects him/her personally and professionally.

d. Acquires educational, consultation, and training experiences to improve awareness, knowledge, skills and effectiveness in working with diverse populations: ethnic/racial status, age, economic status, special needs, ESL or ELL, immigration status, sexual orientation, gender, gender identity/expression, family type, religious/spiritual identity, and appearance.

F. RESPONSIBILITIES TO THE PROFESSION

F.1. Professionalism

The professional school counselor:

a. Accepts the policies and procedures for handling ethical violations as a result of maintaining membership in the American School Counselor Association.

b. Conducts herself/himself in such a manner as to advance individual ethical practice and the profession.

c. Conducts appropriate research and report findings in a manner consistent with acceptable educational and psychological research practices. The counselor advocates for the protection of the individual student's identity when using data for research or program planning.

d. Adheres to ethical standards of the profession, other official policy statements, such as ASCA's position statements, role statement and the ASCA National Model, and relevant statutes established by federal, state and local governments, and when these are in conflict works responsibly for change.

e. Clearly distinguishes between statements and actions made as a private individual and those made as a representative of the school counseling profession.

f. Does not use his/her professional position to recruit or gain clients, consultees for his/her private practice or to seek and receive unjustified personal gains, unfair advantage, inappropriate relationships or unearned goods or services.

F.2. Contribution to the Profession

The professional school counselor:

a. Actively participates in local, state, and national associations fostering the development and improvement of school counseling.

b. Contributes to the development of the profession through the sharing of skills, ideas, and expertise with colleagues.

c. Provides support and mentoring to novice professionals.

G. MAINTENANCE OF STANDARDS

Ethical behavior among professional school counselors, association members and non-members, is expected at all times. When there exists serious doubt as to the ethical behavior of colleagues or if counselors are forced to work in situations or abide by policies that do not reflect the standards as outlined in these Ethical Standards for School Counselors, the counselor is obligated to take appropriate action to rectify the condition. The following procedure may serve as a guide:

1. The counselor should consult confidentially with a professional colleague to discuss the nature of a complaint to see if the professional colleague views the situation as an ethical violation.
2. When feasible, the counselor should directly approach the colleague whose behavior is in question to discuss the complaint and seek resolution.
3. If resolution is not forthcoming at the personal level, the counselor shall utilize the channels established within the school, school district, the state school counseling association and ASCA's Ethics Committee.
4. If the matter still remains unresolved, referral for review and appropriate action should be made to the Ethics Committees in the following sequence:
   • state school counselor association
   • American School Counselor Association
5. The ASCA Ethics Committee is responsible for:
   • educating and consulting with the membership regarding ethical standards
   • periodically reviewing and recommending changes in code
   • receiving and processing questions to clarify the application of such standards; Questions must be submitted in writing to the ASCA Ethics chair.
   • handling complaints of alleged violations of the ethical standards. At the national level, complaints should be submitted in writing to the ASCA Ethics Committee, c/o the Executive Director, American School Counselor Association, 1101 King St., Suite 625, Alexandria, VA 22314.

APPENDIX F

Best Practice Guidelines and Diversity Standards (ASGW)

Association for Specialists in Group Work

BEST PRACTICE GUIDELINES

Approved by the ASGW Executive Board, March 29, 1998
Prepared by: Lynn Rapin and Linda Keel ASGW Ethics Committee Co-Chairs
Revised by: R. Valorie Thomas and Deborah A. Pender ASGW Ethics Committee
  Co-Chairs
Revisions Approved by the ASGW Executive Board, March 23, 2007

The Association for Specialists in Group Work (ASGW) is a division of the American Counseling Association whose members are interested in and specialize in group work. Group Workers are defined as mental health professionals who use a group modality as an intervention when working with diverse populations. We value the creation of community while recognizing diverse perspectives; service to our members, clients, and the profession; and value leadership as a process to facilitate the growth and development of individuals and groups within their social and cultural contexts.

PREAMBLE

The Association for Specialists in Group Work recognizes the commitment of its members to the Code of Ethics (as revised in 2005) of its parent organization, the American Counseling Association, and nothing in this document shall be construed to supplant that code. These Best Practice Guidelines are intended to clarify the application of the ACA Code of Ethics to the field of group work by defining Group Workers' responsibility and scope of practice involving those activities, strategies and interventions that are consistent and current with effective and appropriate professional, ethical, and community standards. ASGW views ethical process as being integral to group work and views Group Workers as ethical agents. Group Workers, by their very nature in being responsible and responsive to their group members, necessarily embrace a certain potential for ethical vulnerability. It is incumbent upon Group Workers to give considerable attention to the intent and context of their actions because the attempts of Group Workers to influence human behavior through group work always have ethical implications. These Best Practice Guidelines address Group Workers' responsibilities in planning, performing, and processing groups.

SECTION A: BEST PRACTICE IN PLANNING

A.1. Professional Context and Regulatory Requirements

Group Workers actively know, understand and, apply the ACA Code of Ethics (2005), the ASGW Professional Standards for the Training of Group Workers, these ASGW Best Practice Guidelines, the ASGW diversity competencies, and the AMCD

Multicultural Counseling Competencies and Standards, relevant state laws, accreditation requirements, relevant National Board for Certified Counselors Codes and Standards, their organization's standards, and insurance requirements impacting the practice of group work.

A.2. Scope of Practice and Conceptual Framework

Group Workers define the scope of practice related to the core and specialization competencies defined in the ASGW Training Standards. Group Workers are aware of personal strengths and weaknesses in leading groups. Group Workers develop and are able to articulate a general conceptual framework to guide practice and a rationale for use of techniques that are to be used. Group Workers limit their practice to those areas for which they meet the training criteria established by the ASGW Training Standards.

A.3. Assessment

  a. Assessment of self. Group Workers actively assess their knowledge and skills related to the specific group(s) offered. Group Workers assess their values, beliefs and theoretical orientation and how these impact upon the group, particularly when working with a diverse and multicultural population.
  b. Ecological assessment. Group Workers assess community needs, agency or organization resources, sponsoring organization mission, staff competency, attitudes regarding group work, professional training levels of potential group leaders regarding group work, client attitudes regarding group work, and multicultural and diversity considerations. Group Workers use this information as the basis for making decisions related to their group practice, or to the implementation of groups for which they have supervisory, evaluation, or oversight responsibilities.

A.4. Program Development and Evaluation

  a. Group Workers identify the type(s) of group(s) to be offered and how they relate to community needs.
  b. Group Workers concisely state in writing the purpose and goals of the group. Group Workers also identify the role of the group members in influencing or determining the group goals.
  c. Group Workers set fees consistent with the organization's fee schedule, taking into consideration the financial status and locality of prospective group members.
  d. Group Workers choose techniques and a leadership style appropriate to the type(s) of group(s) being offered.
  e. Group Workers have an evaluation plan consistent with regulatory, organization, and insurance requirements, where appropriate.
  f. Group Workers take into consideration current professional guidelines when using technology, including but not limited to Internet communication.

A.5. Resources

Group Workers coordinate resources related to the kind of group(s) and group activities to be provided, such as: adequate funding; the appropriateness and availability of a trained co-leader; space and privacy requirements for the type(s) of group(s) being offered; marketing and recruiting; and appropriate collaboration with other community agencies and organizations.

A.6. Professional Disclosure Statement

Group Workers maintain awareness and sensitivity regarding cultural meaning of confidentiality and privacy. Group Workers respect differing views towards disclosure of information. They have a professional disclosure statement, which includes information on confidentiality and exceptions to confidentiality, theoretical orientation, information on the nature, purpose(s) and goals of the group, the group services that can be provided, the role and responsibility of group members and leaders, Group Workers qualifications to conduct the specific group(s), specific licenses, certifications and professional affiliations, and address of licensing/credentialing body.

A.7. Group and Member Preparation

a. Group Workers screen prospective group members, if appropriate, to the type of group being offered. When selection of group members is appropriate, Group Workers identify group members whose needs and goals are compatible with the goals of the group.

b. Group Workers facilitate informed consent. They communicate information in ways that are both developmentally and culturally appropriate. Group Workers provide in oral and written form to prospective members (when appropriate to group type): the professional disclosure statement; group purpose and goals; group participation expectations including voluntary and involuntary membership; role expectations of members and leader(s); policies related to entering and exiting the group; policies governing substance use; policies and procedures governing mandated groups (where relevant); documentation requirements; disclosure of information to others; implications of out-of-group contact or involvement among members; procedures for consultation between group leader(s) and group member(s); fees and time parameters; and potential impacts of group participation.

c. Group Workers obtain the appropriate consent/assent forms for work with minors and other dependent group members.

d. Group Workers define confidentiality and its limits (for example, legal and ethical exceptions and expectations; waivers implicit with treatment plans, documentation and insurance usage). Group Workers have the responsibility to inform all group participants of the need for confidentiality, potential consequences of breaching confidentiality and that legal privilege does not apply to group discussions (unless provided by state statute).

A.8. Professional Development

Group Workers recognize that professional growth is a continuous, ongoing, developmental process throughout their career.

a. Group Workers remain current and increase knowledge and skill competencies through activities such as continuing education, professional supervision, and participation in personal and professional development activities.

b. Group Workers seek consultation and/or supervision regarding ethical concerns that interfere with effective functioning as a group leader. Supervisors have the responsibility to keep abreast of consultation, group theory, process, and adhere to related ethical guidelines.

c. Group Workers seek appropriate professional assistance for their own personal problems or conflicts that are likely to impair their professional judgement or work performance.

d. Group Workers seek consultation and supervision to ensure appropriate practice whenever working with a group for which all knowledge and skill competencies have not been achieved.

e. Group Workers keep abreast of group research and development.

A.9. Trends and Technological Changes

Group Workers are aware of and responsive to technological changes as they affect society and the profession. These include but are not limited to changes in mental health delivery systems; legislative and insurance industry reforms; shifting population demographics and client needs; and technological advances in Internet and other communication devices and delivery systems. Group Workers adhere to ethical guidelines related to the use of developing technologies.

SECTION B: BEST PRACTICE IN PERFORMING

B.1. Self Knowledge

Group Workers are aware of and monitor their strengths and weaknesses and the effects these have on group members. They explore their own cultural identities and how these affect their values and beliefs about group work.

B.2. Group Competencies

Group Workers have a basic knowledge of groups and the principles of group dynamics, and are able to perform the core group competencies, as described in the ASGW Professional Standards for the Training of Group Workers. They gain knowledge, personal, personal awareness, sensitivity, and skills pertinent to working with a diverse client population. Additionally, Group Workers have adequate understanding and skill in any group specialty area chosen for practice (psychotherapy, counseling, task, psychoeducation, as described in the ASGW Training Standards).

B.3. Group Plan Adaptation

a. Group Workers apply and modify knowledge, skills and techniques appropriate to group type and stage, and to the unique needs of various cultural and ethnic groups.

b. Group Workers monitor the group's progress toward the group goals and plan.

c. Group Workers clearly define and maintain ethical, professional, and social relationship boundaries with group members as appropriate to their role in the organization and the type of group being offered.

B.4. Therapeutic Conditions and Dynamics

Group Workers understand and are able to implement appropriate models of group development, process observation, and therapeutic conditions.

Group Workers manage the flow of communication, addressing safely and pacing of disclosures as to protect group members from physical, emotional, or psychological trauma.

B.5. Meaning

Group Workers assist members in generating meaning from the group experience.

B.6. Collaboration

Group Workers assist members in developing individual goals and respect group members as co-equal partners in the group experience.

B.7. Evaluation

Group Workers include evaluation (both formal and informal) between sessions and at the conclusion of the group.

B.8. Diversity

Group Workers practice with broad sensitivity to client differences including but not limited to ethnic, gender, religious, sexual, psychological maturity, economic class, family history, physical characteristics or limitations, and geographic location. Group Workers continuously seek information regarding the cultural issues of the diverse population with whom they are working both by interaction with participants and from using outside resources.

B.9. Ethical Surveillance

Group Workers employ an appropriate ethical decision making model in responding to ethical challenges and issues and in determining courses of action and behavior for self and group members. In addition, Group Workers employ applicable standards as promulgated by ACA, ASGW, or other appropriate professional organizations.

SECTION C: BEST PRACTICE IN GROUP PROCESSING

C.1. Processing Schedule

Group Workers process the workings of the group with themselves, group members, supervisors or other colleagues, as appropriate. This may include assessing progress on group and member goals, leader behaviors and techniques, group dynamics and interventions; developing understanding and acceptance of meaning. Processing may occur both within sessions and before and after each session, at time of termination, and later follow up, as appropriate.

C.2. Reflective Practice

Group Workers attend to opportunities to synthesize theory and practice and to incorporate learning outcomes into ongoing groups.

Group Workers attend to session dynamics of members and their interactions and also attend to the relationship between session dynamics and leader values, cognition and affect.

C.3. Evaluation and Follow-Up

a. Group Workers evaluate process and outcomes. Results are used for ongoing program planning, improvement and revisions of current group and/or to contribute to professional research literature.

Group Workers follow all applicable policies and standards in using group material for research and reports.

b. Group Workers conduct follow-up contact with group members, as appropriate, to assess outcomes or when requested by a group member(s).

C.4. Consultation and Training with Other Organizations

Group Workers provide consultation and training to organizations in and out of their setting, when appropriate. Group Workers seek out consultation as needed with competent professional persons knowledgeable about group work.

Association for Specialists in Group Work

Principles for Diversity-Competent Group Workers
Approved by the Executive Board, August 1, 1998
Prepared by Lynn Haley-Bañez, Sherlon Brown, and Bogusia Molina
Consultants: Michael D'Andrea, Patricia Arrendondo, Niloufer Merchant, and
Sandra Wathen

PREAMBLE

The Association for Specialists in Group Work (ASGW) is committed to understanding how issues of diversity affect all aspects of group work. This includes but is not limited to: training diversity competent group workers; conducting research that will add to the literature on group work with diverse populations; understanding how diversity affects group process and dynamics; and assisting group facilitators in various settings to increase their awareness, knowledge, and skills as they relate to facilitating groups with diverse memberships.

As an organization, ASGW has endorsed this document with the recognition that issues of diversity affect group process and dynamics, group facilitation, training, and research. As an organization, we recognize that racism, classism, sexism, heterosexism, ableism, and so forth, affect everyone.

As individual members of this organization, it is our personal responsibility to address these issues through awareness, knowledge, and skills. As members of ASGW, we need to increase our awareness of our own biases, values, and beliefs and how they impact the groups we run. We need to increase our awareness of our group members' biases, values, and beliefs and how they also impact and influence group process and dynamics. Finally, we need to increase our knowledge in facilitating, with confidence, competence, and integrity, groups that are diverse on many dimensions.

DEFINITIONS

For the purposes of this document, it is important that the language used is understood. Terms such as "dominant," "nondominant," and "target" persons and/or populations are used to define a person or groups of persons who historically, in the United States, do not have equal access to power, money, certain privileges (such as access to mental health services because of financial constraints, or the legal right to marry, in the case of a gay or lesbian couple), and/or the ability to influence or initiate social policy because of unequal representation in government and politics.

These terms are not used to denote a lack of numbers in terms of representation in the overall U.S. population. Nor are these terms used to continue to perpetuate the very biases and forms of oppression, both overt and covert, that this document attempts to address.

For the purposes of this document, the term "disabilities" refers to differences in physical, mental, emotional, and learning abilities and styles among people. It is not meant as a term to define a person, such as a learning disabled person, but rather in the context of a person with a learning disability.

Given the history and current cultural, social, and political context in which this document is written, the authors of this document are limited to the language of this era. With this in mind, we have attempted to construct a "living document" that can and will change as the sociopolitical and attempted to construct a "living document" that can and will change as the sociopolitical and cultural context changes.

THE PRINCIPLES

I. Awareness of Self

A. Attitudes and Beliefs

Diversity-competent group workers demonstrate movement from being unaware to being increasingly aware and sensitive to their own race, ethnic and cultural heritage, gender, socioeconomic status (SES), sexual orientation, abilities, and religion and spiritual beliefs, and to valuing and respecting differences.

Diversity-competent group workers demonstrate increased awareness of how their own race, ethnicity, culture, gender, SES, sexual orientation, abilities, and religion and spiritual beliefs are impacted by their own experiences and histories, which in turn influence group process and dynamics.

Diversity-competent group workers can recognize the limits of their competencies and expertise with regard to working with group members who are different from them in terms of race, ethnicity, culture (including language), SES, gender, sexual orientation, abilities, religion, and spirituality and their beliefs, values, and biases. (For further clarification on limitations, expertise, and type of group work, refer to the training standards and best practice guidelines, Association for Specialists in Group Work, 1998; and the ethical guidelines, American Counseling Association, 1995.)

Diversity-competent group workers demonstrate comfort, tolerance, and sensitivity with differences that exist between themselves and group members in terms of race, ethnicity, culture, SES, gender, sexual orientation, abilities, religion, and spirituality and their beliefs, values, and biases.

B. Knowledge

Diversity-competent group workers can identify specific knowledge about their own race, ethnicity, SES, gender, sexual orientation, abilities, religion, and spirituality, and how they personally and professionally affect their definitions of "normality" and the group process.

Diversity-skilled group workers demonstrate knowledge and understanding regarding how oppression in any form—such as, racism, classism, sexism, heterosexism, ableism, discrimination, and stereotyping—affects them personally and professionally.

Diversity-skilled group workers demonstrate knowledge about their social impact on others. They are knowledgeable about communication style differences, how their style may inhibit or foster the group process with members who are different from themselves along the different dimensions of diversity, and how to anticipate the impact they may have on others.

C. Skills

Diversity-competent group workers seek out educational, consultative, and training experiences to improve their understanding and effectiveness in working with group members who self-identify as Indigenous Peoples, African Americans, Asian Americans, Hispanics, Latinos/Latinas, gays, lesbians, bisexuals, or transgendered persons and persons with physical, mental/emotional, and/or learning disabilities, particularly with regard to race and ethnicity. Within this context, group workers are able to recognize the limits of their competencies and: (a) seek consultation, (b) seek further training or education, (c) refer members to more qualified group workers, or (d) engage in a combination of these.

Group workers who exhibit diversity competence are constantly seeking to understand themselves within their multiple identities (apparent and unapparent differences), for example, gay, Latina, Christian, working-class and female, and are constantly and actively striving to unlearn the various behaviors and processes they covertly and overtly communicate that perpetuate oppression, particularly racism.

II. GROUP WORKER'S AWARENESS OF GROUP MEMBER'S WORLDVIEW

A. Attitudes and Beliefs

Diversity-skilled group workers exhibit awareness of any possible negative emotional reactions toward Indigenous Peoples, African Americans, Asian Americans, Hispanics, Latinos/Latinas, gays, lesbians, bisexuals, or transgendered persons and persons with physical, mental/emotional, and/or learning disabilities that they may hold. They are willing to contrast in a nonjudgmental manner their own beliefs and attitudes with those of Indigenous Peoples, African Americans, Asian Americans, Hispanics, Latinos/Latinas, gays, lesbians, bisexuals, or transgendered persons and persons with physical, mental/emotional, and/or learning disabilities who are group members.

Diversity-competent group workers demonstrate awareness of their stereotypes and preconceived notions that they may hold toward Indigenous Peoples, African Americans, Asian Americans, Hispanics, Latinos/Latinas, gays, lesbians, bisexuals, or transgendered persons and persons with physical, mental/emotional, and/or learning disabilities.

B. Knowledge

Diversity-skilled group workers possess specific knowledge and information about Indigenous Peoples, African Americans, Asian Americans, Hispanics, Latinos/Latinas, gays, lesbians, bisexuals, and transgendered people and group members who have mental/emotional, physical, and/or learning disabilities with whom they are working. They are aware of the life experiences, cultural heritage, and sociopolitical background of Indigenous Peoples, African Americans, Asian Americans, Hispanics, Latinos/Latinas, gays, lesbians, bisexuals, or transgendered persons and group members with physical, mental/emotional, and/or learning disabilities. This particular knowledge-based competency is strongly linked to the various racial/minority and sexual identity development models available in the literature (Atkinson, Morten, & Sue, 1993; Cass, 1979; Cross, 1995; D'Augelli & Patterson, 1995; Helms, 1992).

Diversity-competent group workers exhibit an understanding of how race, ethnicity, culture, gender, sexual identity, different abilities, SES, and other immutable personal characteristics may affect personality formation, vocational choices, manifestation of characteristics may affect personality formation, vocational choices, manifestation of psychological disorders, physical "dis-ease" or somatic symptoms, help-seeking behavior(s), and the appropriateness or inappropriateness of the various types of and theoretical approaches to group work.

Group workers who demonstrate competency in diversity in groups understand and have the knowledge about sociopolitical influences that impinge upon the lives of Indigenous Peoples, African Americans, Asian Americans, Hispanics, Latinos/Latinas, gays, lesbians, bisexuals, or transgendered persons and persons with physical, mental/emotional, and/or learning disabilities. Immigration issues, poverty, racism, oppression, stereotyping, and/or powerlessness adversely impacts many of these individuals and therefore impacts group process or dynamics.

C. Skills

Diversity-skilled group workers familiarize themselves with relevant research and the latest findings regarding mental health issues of Indigenous Peoples, African Americans, Asian Americans, Hispanics, Latinos/Latinas, gays, lesbians, bisexuals, or transgendered persons and persons with physical, mental/emotional, and/or learning disabilities. They actively seek out educational experiences that foster their knowledge and understanding of skills for facilitating groups across differences.

Diversity-competent group workers become actively involved with Indigenous Peoples, African Americans, Asian Americans, Hispanics, Latinos/Latinas, gays, lesbians, bisexuals, or transgendered persons and persons with physical, mental/emotional, and/or learning disabilities outside of their group work/counseling setting (community events, social and political functions, celebrations, friendships, neighborhood groups, etc.) so that their perspective of minorities is more than academic or experienced through a third party.

III. DIVERSITY-APPROPRIATE INTERVENTION STRATEGIES

A. Attitudes and Beliefs

Diversity-competent group workers respect clients' religious and/or spiritual beliefs and values, because they affect worldview, psychosocial functioning, and expressions of distress.

Diversity-competent group workers respect indigenous helping practices and respect Indigenous Peoples, African Americans, Asian Americans, Hispanics, Latinos/Latinas, gays, lesbians, bisexuals, or transgendered persons and persons with physical, mental/emotional, and/or learning disabilities and can identify and utilize community intrinsic help-giving networks.

Diversity-competent group workers value bilingualism and sign language and do not view another language as an impediment to group work.

B. Knowledge

Diversity-competent group workers demonstrate a clear and explicit knowledge and understanding of generic characteristics of group work and theory and how they may clash with the beliefs, values, and traditions of Indigenous Peoples, African Americans, Asian Americans, Hispanics, Latinos/Latinas, gays, lesbians, bisexuals, or transgendered persons and persons with physical, mental/emotional, and/or learning disabilities.

Diversity-competent group workers exhibit an awareness of institutional barriers that prevent Indigenous Peoples, African Americans, Asian Americans, Hispanics, Latinos/Latinas, gays, lesbians, bisexuals, or transgendered members and members with physical, mental/emotional, and/or learning disabilities from actively participating in or using various types of groups, that is, task groups, psychoeducational groups, counseling groups, and psychotherapy groups or the settings in which the services are offered.

Diversity-competent group workers demonstrate knowledge of the potential bias in assessment instruments and use procedures and interpret findings, or actively participate in various types of evaluations of group outcome or success, keeping in mind the linguistic, cultural, and other self-identified characteristics of the group member.

Diversity-competent group workers exhibit knowledge of the family structures, hierarchies, values, and beliefs of Indigenous Peoples, African Americans, Asian Americans, Hispanics, Latinos/Latinas, gays, lesbians, bisexuals, or transgendered persons and persons with physical, mental/emotional, and/or learning disabilities. They are knowledgeable about the community characteristics and the resources in the community as well as about the family.

Diversity-competent group workers demonstrate an awareness of relevant discriminatory practices at the social and community level that may be affecting the psychological welfare of persons and access to services of the population being served.

C. Skills

Diversity-competent group workers are able to engage in a variety of verbal and nonverbal group-facilitating functions, dependent upon the type of group (task, counseling, psychoeducational, psychotherapy), and the multiple, self-identified status of various group members (such as Indigenous Peoples, African Americans, Asian Americans, Hispanics, Latinos/Latinas, gays, lesbians, bisexuals, or transgendered persons and persons with physical, mental/emotional, and/or learning disabilities). They demonstrate the ability to send and receive both verbal and nonverbal messages accurately, appropriately, and across/between the differences represented in the group.

They are not tied down to one method or approach to group facilitation and recognize that helping styles and approaches may be culture-bound. When they sense that their group facilitation style is limited and potentially inappropriate, they can anticipate and ameliorate its negative impact by drawing upon other culturally relevant skill sets.

Diversity-competent group workers have the ability to exercise institutional intervention skills on behalf of their group members. They can help a member determine whether a "problem" with the institution stems from the oppression of Indigenous Peoples, African Americans, Asian Americans, Hispanics, Latinos/Latinas, gays, lesbians, bisexuals, or transgendered persons and persons with physical, mental/emotional, and/or learning disabilities, such as in the case of developing or having a "healthy" paranoia, so that group members do not inappropriately personalize problems.

Diversity-competent group workers do not exhibit a reluctance to seek consultation with traditional healers, religious and spiritual healers, and practitioners in the treatment of members who are self-identified Indigenous Peoples, African Americans, Asian Americans, Hispanics, Latinos/Latinas, gays, lesbians, bisexuals, and transgendered persons and/or group members with mental/emotional, physical, and/or learning disabilities, when appropriate.

Diversity-competent group workers take responsibility for interacting in the language requested by the group member(s) and, if not feasible, make an appropriate referral. A serious problem arises when the linguistic skills of a group worker and a group member or members, including sign language, do not match. The same problem occurs when the linguistic skills of one member or several members do not match. This being the case, the group worker, should (a) seek a translator with cultural knowledge and appropriate professional background, and (b) refer to a knowledgeable, competent bilingual group worker or a group worker competent or certified in sign language. In some cases, it may be necessary to have a group for group members of similar languages or to refer the group member for individual counseling.

Diversity-competent group workers are trained and have expertise in the use of traditional assessment and testing instruments related to group work, such as in screening potential members, and they also are aware of the cultural bias/limitations of these tools and processes. This allows them to use the tools for the welfare of diverse group members following culturally appropriate procedures.

Diversity-competent group workers attend to as well as work to eliminate biases, prejudices, oppression, and discriminatory practices. They are cognizant of how sociopolitical contexts may affect evaluation and provision of group work and should develop sensitivity to issues of oppression, racism, sexism, heterosexism, classism, and so forth.

Diversity-competent group workers take responsibility in educating their group members to the processes of group work, such as goals, expectations, legal rights, sound ethical practice, and the group worker's theoretical orientation with regard to facilitating groups with diverse membership.

CONCLUSION

This document is the "starting point" for group workers as we become increasingly aware, knowledgeable, and skillful in facilitating groups whose memberships represent the diversity of our society. It is not intended to be a "how to" document. It is written as a call to action and/or a guideline and represents ASGW's commitment to moving forward with an agenda for addressing and understanding the needs of the populations we serve. As a "living document," the Association for Specialists in Group Work acknowledges the changing world in which we live and work and therefore recognizes that this is the first step in working with diverse group members with competence, compassion, respect, and integrity. As our awareness, knowledge, and skills develop, so too will this document evolve. As our knowledge as a profession grows in this area and as the sociopolitical context in which this document was written, changes, new editions of these Principles for Diversity-Competent Group Workers will arise. The operationalization of this document (article in process) will begin to define appropriate group leadership skills and interventions as well as in process) will begin to define appropriate group leadership skills and interventions as well as make recommendations for research in understanding how diversity in group membership affects group process and dynamics.

REFERENCES

American Counseling Association (1995). *Code of ethics and standards*. Alexandria, VA: Author.

Association for Multicultural Counseling and Development (1996). *Multicultural competencies*. Alexandria, VA: American Counseling Association.

Association for Specialists in Group Work (1991). Professional standards for training of group workers. *Together*, 20, 9–14.

Association for Specialists in Group Work (1998). Best practice guidelines. *Journal for Specialists in Group Work*, 23, 237–244.

Atkinson, D. R., Morten, G., & Sue, D. W. (Eds.). (1993). *Counseling American minorities* (4th ed.). Madison, WI: Brown & Benchmark.

Cass, V. C. (1979). Homosexual identity formation: A theoretical model. *Journal of Homosexuality*, 4, 219–236.

Cross, W. E. (1995). The psychology of Nigrescence: Revising the Cross model. In J.G. Ponterotto, J. M. Casas, L.A. Suzuki, & C. M. Alexander (Eds.), *Handbook of multicultural counseling* (pp. 93–122). Thousand Oaks, CA: Sage.

D'Augelli, A. R., & Patterson, C. J. (Eds.). (1995). *Lesbian, gay and bisexual identities over the lifespan*. New York: Oxford University Press.

Helms, J. E. (1992). *A race is a nice thing to have*. Topeka, KS: Context Communications.

REFERENCES

Albert, L. (1996). *Cooperative discipline*. Circle Pines, MN: American Guidance Service, Inc.

American Counseling Association. (2005). *Code of ethics and standards of practice*. Alexandria, VA: Author.

American School Counseling Association (ASCA). (2004). *Ethical standards for school counselors*. Alexandria, VA: Author.

American School Counselor Association (ASCA). (2005). *The ASCA national model: A framework for school counseling programs* (2nd ed.). Alexandria, VA: Author.

Association for Specialists in Group Work (ASGW). (1998, approved). *ASGW principles for diversity-competent group workers*. Retrieved February 5, 2009, from http://www.asgw.org/.html

Association for Specialists in Group Work (ASGW). (2007, revisions approved). *ASGW best practice guidelines*. Retrieved February 5, 2009, from http://www.asgw.org/.html

Authoritarian leadership. (n.d.). Retrieved January 13, 2009, from http://www.businessdictionary.com/definition/authoritarian-leadership.html

Bateson, C. (1994). *Peripheral visions. Learning along the way*. NY: HarperCollins.

Beals, M. P. (1994). *Warriors don't cry*. NY: Washington Square Press.

Backler, A., Eakin, S., & Harris, P. (1994). *Managing the disruptive classroom: Strategies for educators* [video recording]. Bloomington, IN: Agency for Instructional Technology.

Bemak, F., & Chung, R. C. (2005). Advocacy as a critical role for urban school counselors: Working towards equity and social justice. *Professional School Counseling, 8*(3), 196–202.

Bloom, B. (Ed.). (1956). *Taxonomy of educational objectives, handbook 1: Cognitive domain*. NY: David McKay.

Brenner, M. H., Curbow, B., & Legro, M. W. (1995). The proximal-distal continuum of multiple health outcome measures: The case of cataract surgery. *Medical Care 33*(4), AS236–AS244. Supplement. Retrieved from http://www.jstor.org/pss/3766632

Burr, V. (1995). *An introduction to social constructionism*. London: Routledge.

Brophy, J. (1999). Perspectives of classroom management: Yesterday, today, and tomorrow. In H. J. Freiberg, *Beyond behaviorism; Changing the classroom management paradigm* (pp. 43–56). Boston: Allyn & Bacon.

Bruner, J. (1990). *Acts of meaning*. Cambridge, MA: Harvard University Press.

Carroll, M. R., & Kraus, K. L. (2007). *Elements of group counseling: Back to the basics* (4th ed.). Denver, CO: Love.

Cavaiola, A. A., & Colford, J. E. (2006). *A practical guide to crisis intervention*. Boston: Lahaska/Houghton Mifflin.

Charles, C. M. (2005). *Building classroom discipline* (8th ed.). Boston: Pearson Education.

Charles, C. M., & Senter, G. W. (2002). *Elementary classroom management* (3rd ed.). Boston: Allyn & Bacon.

Charney, R. S. (1991). *Teaching children to care. Management in the responsive classroom*. Greenfield, MA: Northeast Foundation for Children.

Cobia, D. C., & Henderson, D. A. (2007). *Developing an effective and accountable school counseling program* (2nd ed.). Upper Saddle River, NJ: Pearson Education.

Cohen, E. G. (1994). *Designing group work. Strategies for the heterogeneous classroom* (2nd ed.). NY: Teachers College Press.

Cohen, H. S. (Exec. Producer). (2002). *That's a family. A film for kids about family diversity* [video recording]. (Available from Women's Educational Media, 2180 Bryant St., Suite #203. San Francisco, CA 94110).

Cohen, A. M., & Smith, R. D. (1976). *The critical incident in growth groups: Theory and technique*. La Jolla, CA: University Associates.

Corey, M. S., & Corey, G. (2006). *Process and practice groups* (7th ed.). Belmont, CA: Thompson Brooks/Cole.

Corey, G. (2007). *Theory & practice of group counseling* (7th ed.). Belmont, CA: Brooks/Cole Wadsworth.

Derman-Sparks, L. (1993). Revisiting multicultural education. What children need to live in a diverse society. *Dimensions of Early Childhood, 22*(1), 6–10.

DeLucia-Waack, J. L. (2006). *Leading psychoeducational groups for children and adolescents.* Thousand Oaks, CA: Sage.

Douthit, K. (2008). Cognition, culture and society: Understanding cognitive development in the tradition of Vygotski. In K. L. Kraus, *Lenses: Applying lifespan development theories in counseling* (pp. 83–118). Boston: Lahaska Press.

Emmer, E. T., & Evertson, C. M. (2009). *Classroom management for middle and high school teachers* (8th ed.). Upper Sadle River, NJ: Pearson Education.

Gazda, G. (1989). *Group counseling: A developmental approach* (4th ed.). Boston: Allyn & Bacon.

Geroski, A., & Kraus, K. (2002). Process and content in school psychoeducational groups: Either, both or none? *Journal for Specialists in Group Work, 27*(2), 233–245.

Gladding, S. T. (2003). *Group work. A counseling specialty* (4th ed.). Upper Saddle River, NJ: Pearson Education.

Gladding, S. T. (2008). *Groups: A Counseling Specialty* (5th ed.). Upper Saddle River, NJ: Pearson Education.

Glasser, W. (1998a.). *Choice theory in the classroom* (revised edition). NY: HarperCollins.

Glasser, W. (1998b.). *Choice Theory. A new psychology of personal freedom.* NY: HarperCollins.

Goodnough, G., Perusse, R., & Erford, B. T. (2003). Developmental classroom guidance. In B. T. Erford (Ed.), *Transforming the school counseling profession* (pp. 121–152). Upper Saddle River, NJ: Merrill Prentice Hall.

Grant, C. A. (1998). Challenging the myths about multicultural education. In C. L. Nelson, & K. A. Wilson (Eds.), *Seeding the process of multicultural education* (pp. 189–201). Plymouth, MN: Minnesota Inclusiveness Program.

Gronlund, N. E. (2000). *How to write and use instructional objectives* (6th ed.). Upper Saddle River, NJ: Merrill Prentice Hall.

Hardin, C. J. (2008). *Effective classroom management* (2nd ed.). Upper Saddle River, NJ: Pearson Education.

Henderson, J. G. (1996). Two stories of caring. In S. Gordon, P. Benner, & N. Noddings (Eds.), *Caregiving. Readings in knowledge, practice, ethics, and politics* (pp. 189–202). Philadelphia: University of Pennsylvania Press.

Holcomb-McCoy, C. (2004). Assessing the multicultural competence of school counselors: A checklist. *Professional School Counseling, 7*(3), 178–186.

Hoover, R. L., & Kindsvatter, R. (1997). *Democratic discipline: Foundation and practice.* Columbus, OH: Merrill.

Hughes, J. N. (2002). Authoritative teaching: Tipping the balance in favor of school versus peer effects. *Journal of School Counseling, 40*(6), 485–492.

Hulse-Killacky, D., Killacky, J., & Donigian, J. (2001). *Making task groups work in your world.* Upper Saddle River, NJ: Prentice Hall.

Ingersoll, G. M. (1996). What is your classroom management profile? *Teacher Talk, 1*(2). Retrieved from http://education.indiana.edu/cas/tt/v1i2/authoritative.html

Ivey, A. E., Pedersen, P. B., & Ivey, M. B. (2001). *Intentional group counseling. A microskills approach.* Belmont, CA: Wadsworth/Thomson Learning.

Jacobs, E. E., Masson, R. L., & Harvill, R. L. (2005). *Group counseling. Strategies and skills.* Pacific Grove, CA: Brooks/Cole.

James, R. K., & Gilliland, B. E. (2001). *Crisis intervention strategies* (4th ed.). Belmont, CA: Wadsworth/Thomson.

Johnson, R., & Johnson, D. (2004). *Assessing students in groups.* Thousand Oaks, CA: Corwin Press.

Johnson, S., Johnson, C., & Downs, L. (2006). *Building a results-based student support program.* Boston: Lahaska Press.

Johnson, D. W., Johnson, R. T., & Holubec, E. J. (1994). *Cooperative learning in the classroom.* Alexandria, VA: Association for Supervision and Curriculum Development.

Jones, V. F., & Jones, L. S. (2001). *Comprehensive classroom management* (6th ed.). Needham Heights, MA: Allyn & Bacon.

Kauffman, J. M., Mostert, M. P., Trent, S. C., & Hallahan, D. P. (2002). *Managing classroom behavior. A reflective case-based approach* (3rd ed.). Boston: Allyn & Bacon.

Kees, N. L., & Jacobs, E. (1990). Conducting more effective groups: How to select and process group exercises. *The Journal for Specialists in Group Work, 15*(1), 21–29.

Kerr, M. M., & Nelson, C. M. (1998). *Strategies for managing behavior problems in the classroom* (3rd ed.). Upper Saddle River, NJ: Merrill Prentice Hall.

Kline, W. B. (2003). *Interactive group counseling and therapy.* Upper Saddle River, NJ: Merrill Prentice Hall.

Larrivee, B. (2005). *Authentic classroom management. Creating a learning community and building reflective practice* (2nd ed.). Boston: Allyn & Bacon.

Lewis, J., Arnold, M., House, R., & Torporek, R. (n.d.) *Advocacy Competencies.* Retrieved Oct 26, 2008 from http://www.counseling.org/Publications/

Lieberman, M. A., Yalom, I. D., & Miles, M. B. (1973) *Encounter groups: First facts.* NY: Basic Books.

Linde, L. (2007). Ethical, legal, and professional issues in school counseling. In B.C. Erford, *Transforming the school counseling profession* (2nd ed.) (pp. 51–72). Upper Saddle River, NJ: Pearson Education.

Lindwall, J. J., & Coleman, K. (2008). The elementary school counselor's role in fostering caring in school communities. *Professional School Counseling, 12*(2), 144–148.

Logan, J., Chasnoff, D., & Cohen, H. S. (2002). *That's a family. Discussion and teaching guide.* San Francisco: Women's Educational Media.

Luckner, J. L., & Nadler, R. S. (1997). *Processing the experience. Strategies to enhance and generalize learning* (2nd ed.). Montecito, CA: Kendall/Hunt.

McIntosh, P. (1998). Interactive phases of curricular and personal re-vision with regard to race. In L. C. Nelson & K. A. Wilson (Eds.), *Seeding the process of multicultural education* (pp. 166–188). Plymouth, MN: Minnesota Inclusiveness Press.

Meier, D. (2002) *The power of their ideas.* Boston: Beacon Press.

Mendler, A. N. (1992). *What do I do when . . . ? How to achieve discipline with dignity in the classroom.* Bloomington, IN: National Educational Service.

Mendler, A. N. (2005). *Just in time.* Bloomington, IN: National Education Service.

Noddings, N. (1992). *The challenge to care in schools.* NY: Teachers College Press.

Noddings, N. (1996). The caring professional. In S. Gordon, P. Benner, & N. Noddings (Eds.), *Caregiving. Readings in knowledge, practice, ethics, and politics* (pp. 160–172). Philadelphia: University of Pennsylvania Press.

Pang, L. (1998). Humor as armor. In L. C. Nelson & K. A. Wilson (Eds.), *Seeding the process of multicultural education* (pp. 57–63). Plymouth, MN: Minnesota Inclusiveness Press.

Piaget, J. (1966). *Psychology of intelligence.* Totowa, NJ: Littlefield, Adams & Co.

Piaget, J. (1972). *To understand is to invent.* NY: Viking Press.

Popkin, M. H. (1994). *Active teaching. Teacher's handbook grades K–6.* Atlanta, GA: Active Parenting Pub.

Price, K. M., & Nelson, K. L. (1999). *Daily planning for today's classrooms. A guide for writing lesson and activity plans.* Belmont, CA: Wadsworth.

Queen, J. A., Blackwelder, B. B., & Mallen, L. P. (1997). *Responsible classroom management for teachers and students.* Upper Saddle River, NJ: Merrill Prentice Hall.

Richardson, J., & Parnell, P. (2005). *And tango makes three*. NY: Simon & Schuster.

Roberts, A. R. (2005). Bridging the past and present to the future of crisis intervention and crisis management. In A. R. Roberts (Ed.), *Crisis intervention handbook* (3rd ed.) (pp. 3–35). NY: Oxford University Press.

Schmidt, J. J. (2007). *Counseling in schools* (5th ed.). Boston: Allyn & Bacon.

Sciarra, D. T. (2004). *School counseling. Foundations and contemporary issues*. Belmont, CA: Brooks/Cole-Thomson Learning.

Sexton, T. L., Whiston, S. C., Bleuer, J. C., & Walz, G. R. (1997). *Integrating outcome research into counseling practice and training*. Alexandria, VA: ACA Press.

Sink, C. A. (2005). The contemporary school counselor. In C. A. Sink (Ed.), *Contemporary school counseling. Theory, research, and practice* (pp. 1–42). Boston: Lahaska Press.

Smead, R. (1995). *Skills and techniques for group work with children and adolescents*. Champaign, IL: Research Press.

Sprick, R. S. (2006). *Discipline in the secondary classroom* (2nd ed.). San Francisco: Jossey-Bass.

Sternberg, R. J. (2007). Culture, instruction, and assessment. *Comparative Education, 43*(1), 5–22.

Stone, C. B., & Dahir, C. A. (2006). *The transformed school counselor*. Boston: Lahaska.

Style, E. (1998). Curriculum as Window and Mirror. In L. C. Nelson & K. A. Wilson (Eds.), *Seeding the process of multicultural education* (pp. 149–156). Plymouth, MN: Minnesota Inclusiveness Press.

Tatum, B. D. (1997). *Why are all the black kids sitting together in the cafeteria?* NY: Basic Books.

Tileston, D. W. (2004). *What every teacher should know about instructional planning*. Thousand Oaks, CA: Corwin Press.

Trotzer, J. P. (1999). *The counselor and the group: Integrating theory, training, and practice* (3rd ed.). Philadelphia: Brunner-Routledge.

Trusty, J., & Brown, D. (2005). Advocacy competencies for professional school counselors. *Professional School Counseling, 8*(3), 259–265.

Tuckman, B. (1965). Developmental sequence in small groups. *Psychological Bulletin, 63,* 384–399.

Vygotsky, L. S. (1978). *Mind and society: The development of higher mental processes*. Cambridge, MA: Harvard University Press. (Original works published 1930, 1933, and 1935.)

Wheelan, S. A. (1990). *Facilitating training groups: A guide to leadership and verbal intervention skills*. Westport, CT: Greenwood Publishing Group.

Whiston, S. C. (2007). Outcomes research on school counseling interventions and programs. In B. T. Erford (Ed.), *Transforming the school counseling profession* (pp. 38–50). Upper Saddle River, NJ: Pearson Education.

Whiston, S. C., & Sexton, T. L. (1998). A review of school counseling outcome research: Implications for practice. *Journal of Counseling and Development, 76,* 412–426.

White, M. (2004). Folk psychology and narrative practice. In L. E. Ahgus & J. McLeod (Eds.), *The handbook of narrative and psychotherapy practice, theory, and research* (pp. 15–51). Thousand Oaks, CA: Sage.

Williams, M., Nielsen, M., & Bystrom, J. (1998). Targets of oppression: GLBT students. In L. C. Nelson & K. A. Wilson (Eds.), *Seeding the process of multicultural education* (pp. 64–72). Plymouth, MN: Minnesota Inclusiveness Press.

Wubbolding, R. E. (1988). *Using reality therapy*. NY: Harper Perennial.

Wubbolding, R. E., & Brickell, J. (1999). *Counseling with reality therapy*. Oxon, UK: Winslow Press.

Yalom, I. D. (2005). *Theory and practice of group psychotherapy* (5th ed.). NY: Basic Books.

Zirpoli, T. J., & Melloy, K. J. (1997). *Behavior management. Applications for teachers and parents* (2nd ed.). Upper Saddle River, NJ: Merrill Prentice Hall.

INDEX